I0800969

IMAGES
of America

OAKMONT

IMAGES
of America

OAKMONT

Vince Gagetta with Paula A. Calabrese,
Cheryl Zentgraf, and Gary Rogers

ARCADIA
PUBLISHING

Copyright © 2003 by Vince Gagetta
ISBN 978-0-7385-1235-8

Published by Arcadia Publishing
Charleston, South Carolina

Printed in the United States of America

Library of Congress Catalog Card Number: 2003105091

For all general information contact Arcadia Publishing at:
Telephone 843-853-2070
Fax 843-853-0044
E-mail sales@arcadiapublishing.com
For customer service and orders:
Toll-Free 1-888-313-2665

Visit us on the Internet at www.arcadiapublishing.com

Contents

ACKNOWLEDGMENTS

The authors wish to acknowledge with thanks those who made significant contributions to the compilation and completion of this book.

Our thanks go to the following individuals who offered and supplied personal pictures and allowed their publication: Vince Provenza, Gary Rogers, Cheryl Provenza Zentgraf, Marjorie King, Caroline Cooper Carroll, Bob Finlay, the Kokales family, Frank James Furko, Stella Marangoni, Sue Harbison, Mrs. Walter L. Curran, Bill Cosnotti, Louise and Gladys Ferrante, Suzanne Roach, Patti Dehus, Jane Vollbrecht, and Harriet Blaine Miller. These individuals helped identify photographs or provided other valuable information that helped put photographs into historical context: Patricia Aubele, John M. Kaus, Bob Flowers, and Earl Fentzel.

The following organizations provided photographs or supplied historical information: the borough of Oakmont, the Riverview School District, the Oakmont post office, the Riverview Community Action Corporation, the Catholic Diocese of Pittsburgh, the Oakmont-Verona Memorial Day Planning Committee, and the Dr. Thomas R. Kerr Memorial Museum.

Many individuals and organizations have donated photograph collections to the Oakmont Carnegie Library. Photographs in the library archives from the collections of these individuals or their estates were selected for inclusion in this book: Joseph Grubbs, Dorothy Grubbs, Lucretia "Lue" Anderson, Rita Young, Earl Fentzel, Katheryn Ebner Wilkie, Clark Manglesdorf, Juliet Bossert, Nelva Pfeffer, Robert McElhose, Keith McAuly, Martha E. Anderson, Bob Fedarko, Jane Pyle, Marty Rowand, Charlie King, Richard Davis, Helen Maryanski, Paul C. Nicholas, Louis Devic, Nancy Hurley, Len Flowers, E. Lewis, Nancy Federici, and two collections identified only as the Moss collection and the Cooper collection. Also furnished were original photographs by Maureen Favo and photographs from the files of the Oakmont Centennial Book Committee.

Our sincere thanks go to all of these individuals and organizations.

INTRODUCTION

The history of Oakmont dates back to April 1, 1889. That is the day the area covered by what had been Verona's second ward was incorporated into a new borough, and Oakmont was born. But the story of Oakmont precedes the date of its incorporation as a borough.

The story of Oakmont had its beginnings on April 2, 1816, when Robert Elliott, a land speculator, sold a 234-acre tract of land bordering the Allegheny River to Michael Bright, a farmer, for $2,808. The tract Bright purchased extended from the foot of what now is Delaware Avenue along the river to about 1,000 feet beyond where Hulton Road is now and eastward to almost Sixth Street.

Bright is credited with being the first true settler of the land that was to become Oakmont. He earned that distinction because his land purchase marked the beginning of the establishment of an organized community here. He and those who followed him—notably Jonathan Hulton, Caleb Lee, and David Grier—interacted with each other, built roads linking their properties, and even had a rudimentary map of the area drawn up. They did not merely occupy the land as renters or squatters, as had some earlier inhabitants. They owned their land, and more importantly, they developed it. They and their children and grandchildren not only cleared the land and farmed it, they also established the area's first businesses, supported the area's first schools, and founded the area's first churches. They were true settlers.

The settlers put down roots, which most others before them had not done. Bright built a home, farmed, and operated a pottery at about where Riverview High School now stands. With his wife and several of his heirs, he is buried here in the small cemetery on Fourth Street next to St. Irenaeus School. Hulton was the area's first postmaster (in fact, the first post office was named the Hulton post office). His son James operated a ferry across the Allegheny River from the family's property near the present Hulton Road and Hulton Bridge. Lee was a prosperous tailor who, when it was feared that the Confederate army might attack Pittsburgh in 1863, was put in charge of erecting fortifications in Highland Park as part of the city's defenses. Grier was a wealthy Pittsburgher who cleared and developed 154 acres of land along Plum Creek. His grandson founded the Dexter Spring Company in town.

Bright, Hulton, Lee, and Grier were the pioneers. Those who followed them built on the foundations they laid by fostering growth, creating employment opportunities, and helping to bring prosperity to the area. The early industrialists and business owners, who moved here because they recognized the opportunities the area afforded them, certainly made their contributions. Among them were J.C. Agnew, Charles Scaife, William Grier, Jacob W. Paul, Harry W. Armstrong, James B.D. Meeds, William A. Tomlinson, William A. Diamond, Richard T. Crain, George Best, M.S. Verner, and James Verner.

There were others who helped smooth the area's rough edges, people like Abraham Greenwood, who operated what was likely the area's first hotel; Stephen Rodnok and a man known only as Mr. Smith, who brought motion pictures to Oakmont; Edward Reinhold, whose company made ice cream here; Harry C. Fownes, who founded the Oakmont Country Club; Leander Morris, who convinced his cousin, Andrew Carnegie, to provide the money to start Oakmont's library; William A. Wade, who conducted a young ladies' finishing school in his Hulton Road home; Rev. J.D. Irons, who instructed the most famous pupil of Wade's school, Helen Keller; and Elizabeth Bradley, whose large house on Hulton Road became the site of the Bradley Children's Home.

Early merchants John Hastings and Obadiah M. Bossert played vital supporting roles in the story of Oakmont, as did B.F. Reynolds, the area's first physician; C.M. Campbell, a physician and Oakmont's first mayor; William H. Cooper, a physician and the Oakmont postmaster for many years; and Thomas R. Kerr, a physician and very influential early resident.

Those mentioned above are among the most recognized and most recognizable names on the list of early Oakmonters who sparked the early growth and development of the town and whose influence is still felt today. They are on the list because they either cleared and settled a wilderness area and laid the earliest foundations for what was to come, or later brought order to the area, helped it blossom into a recognizable municipality, and shaped it into the vibrant community that exists here today. Although they were not alone in doing so (thousands have contributed to the growth and development of the town over the years and hundreds more continue to do so today), they were the ones who over many years shaped this town and brought it stability and a measure of prideful prominence.

They helped write Oakmont's history by becoming the principal characters of the Oakmont story. This book is a pictorial celebration of their strength of character, their work and dedication, their sacrifices and accomplishments, and their visions and dreams.

One

A Town Is Born

In 1768, the Commonwealth of Pennsylvania purchased most of the land east of the Allegheny River as far north as Kittanning from various Native American tribes and, to encourage development, offered it for sale for as little as 13¢ an acre. The offer attracted more land speculators than developers, however, and little in the way of permanent settlement happened in what became Oakmont until April 2, 1816. That is when a speculator named Robert Eliott sold a 234-acre tract bordering the Allegheny River from Plum Creek north to a little beyond where the Hulton Bridge now stands to a 53-year-old farmer named Michael Bright.

Thus began the process that transformed what had been woodlands—which had resisted occasional efforts to clear small patches of it for farming and was inhabited mostly by squatters and trappers—into an area that could legitimately be termed a settlement. The transformation continued until that humble settlement became a town called Oakmont.

It proved to be a slow process. By 1834, 18 years after Michael Bright received his deed, the settlement's population had grown to only 15 people, many of them members of the Bright family. But as others were attracted to the area to join the Brights, the Hultons, the Lees, and other early settlers, the settlement took on the look of permanence. Roads were built, James Hulton started his ferry service, and, probably the most important factor in hastening development, the Allegheny Valley Railroad began operating in 1853.

Such infrastructure development attracted more people and businesses to serve them. The first church, Valley United Presbyterian, was organized. The first school was built on College Avenue in 1863. Following his discharge from the Union Army after the Civil War, B.F. Reynolds set up practice as the area's first physician. Travelers to the area could find lodging at the first hotel, the Greenwood, after it opened in 1867.

The area's population had grown to about 1,550 by 1870, when, as an early example of manufacturers expanding by moving from crowded cities to the suburbs, the Agnew Glass Company plant moved here from Pittsburgh. Three years later, William D. Houghtelin opened a wagon-making shop here. Perhaps because wagons need springs, the Dexter Spring Company opened shop at Sixth and Plum Streets a year after that.

John Hastings opened the area's first grocery store in 1875, the same year the first drugstore opened at Oakmont and Woodland Avenues. In 1884, Obadiah M. Bossert opened a tin shop on Fourth Street, and a year later, moved it to Maryland Avenue, where it soon evolved into the area's first hardware store.

William B. Scaife and Sons relocated its Pittsburgh factory here in 1889, just in time to help the more than 1,600 people living here celebrate the birth of Oakmont borough and the election of C.M. Campbell as the first burgess, as the mayor was then called.

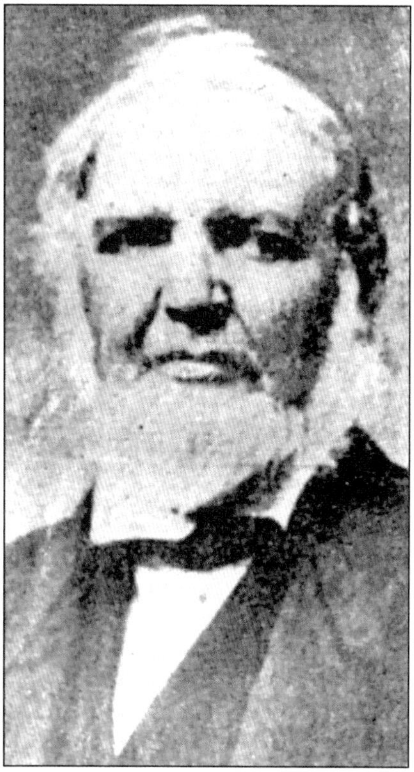

The name of Jonathan Hulton, one of the area's earliest settlers, certainly is well known in Oakmont since it graces both Hulton Road and the Hulton Bridge. The area north of Hulton Road once was called Hulton, as was a post office—Hulton was the area's first postmaster—and a railroad station. When Oakmont became a borough in 1889, there was considerable support for naming the town Hulton.

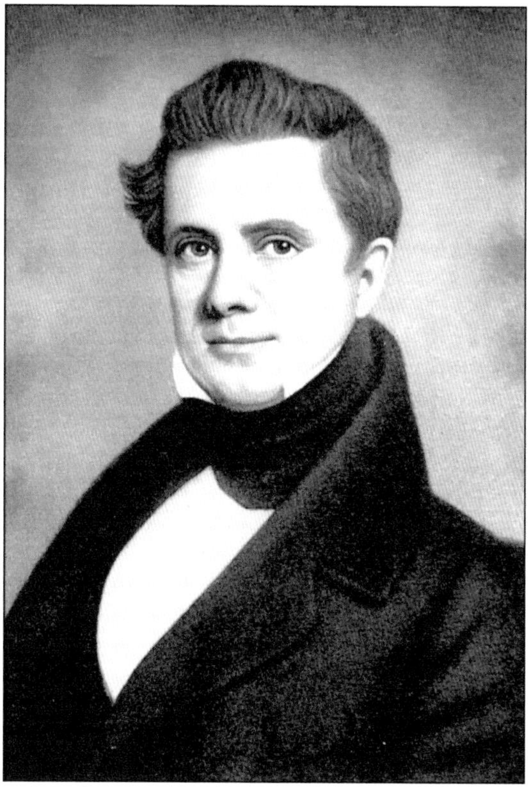

Caleb Lee, a prosperous tailor who settled in what now is Oakmont before 1842, had extensive land holdings in the area. His property was north of what now is Hulton Road adjacent to Jonathan Hulton's tract. During the Civil War, Lee was put in charge of erecting fortifications in Pittsburgh as part of the city's defense against a feared Confederate army invasion.

Peter Bright, son of Michael Bright, the area's first true settler, became a prosperous farmer and had extensive landholdings. In 1858, he gave property adjacent to the Bright Cemetery on Fourth Street to the United Presbyterian Church for a church building. The building's foundation still survives as the foundation of the Oakmont American Legion post's building.

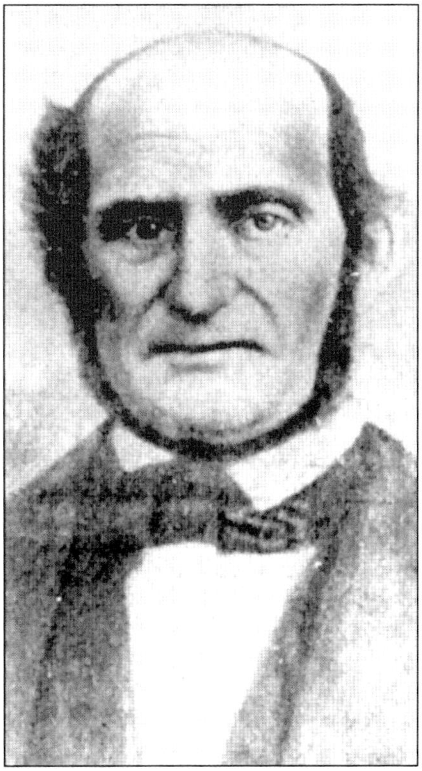

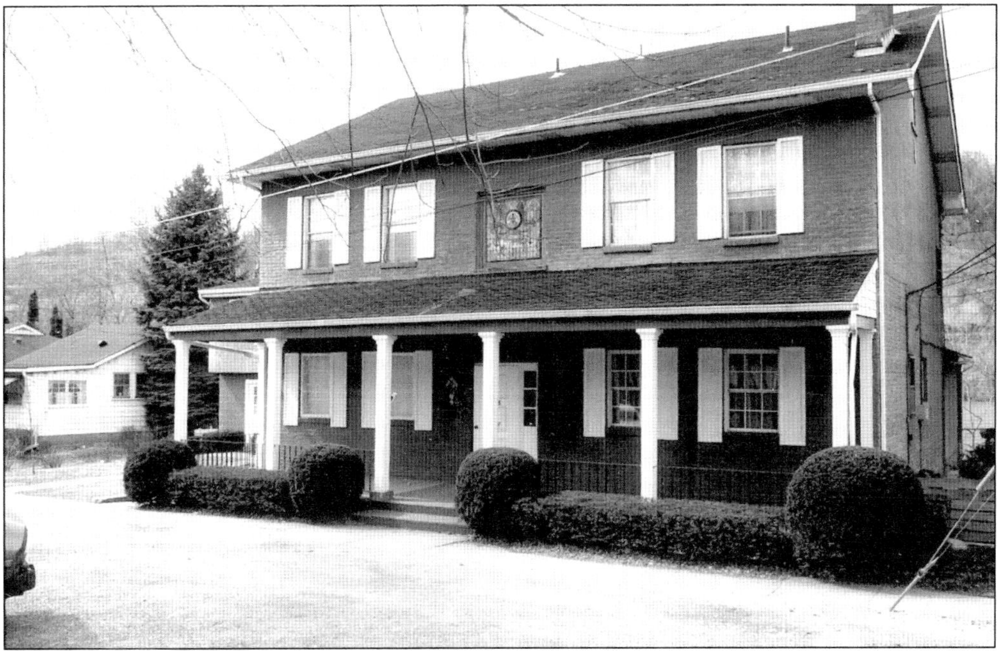

In 1820, Peter Bright built this large house that still stands at 106 Pennsylvania Avenue and lived there with his wife, Mary, and their 11 children. The bricks used in the construction were made on site. The house, which originally was near Second Street, was moved closer to the river in 1949.

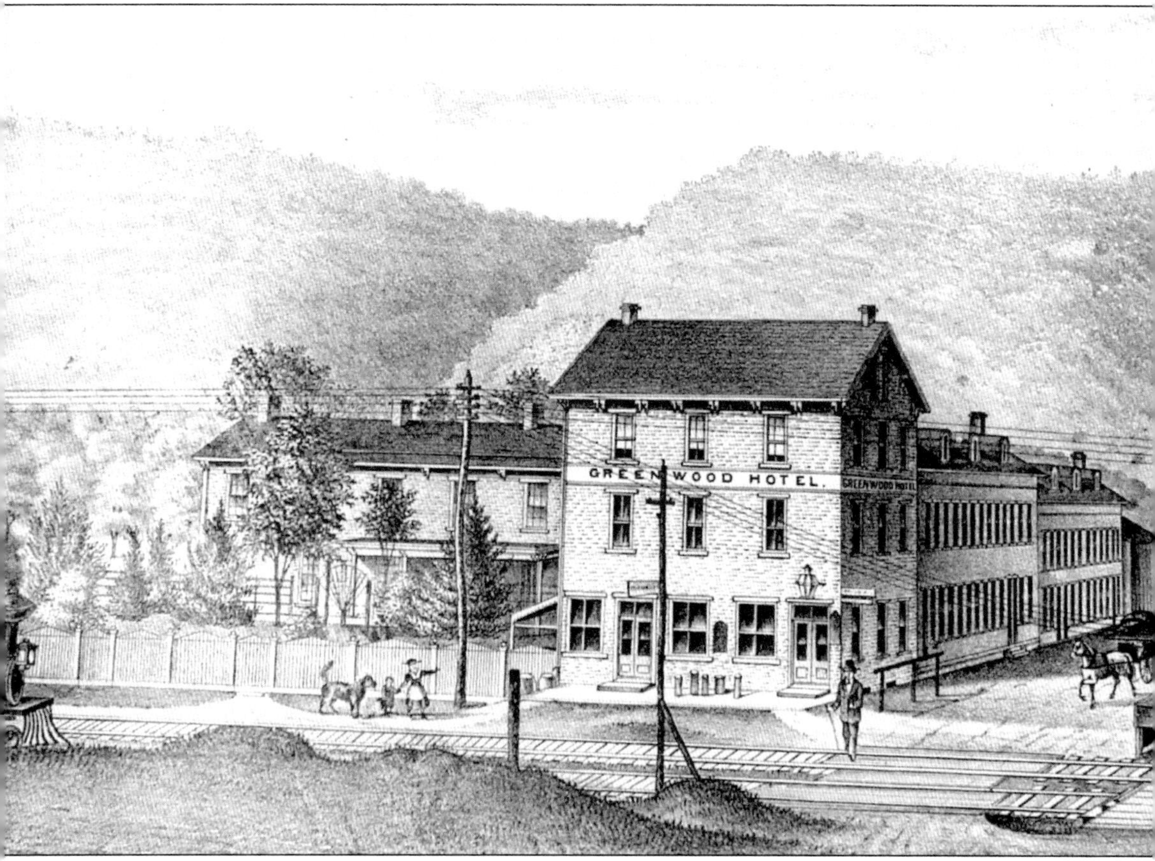

In 1867, Abraham Greenwood bought the building that stood at the corner of Hulton Road and Allegheny Avenue, then West Railroad Avenue, to house his Greenwood Hotel. The building, shown with its convenient hitching post along the Hulton Road side of the building, was built in 1864 by James Dalzell.

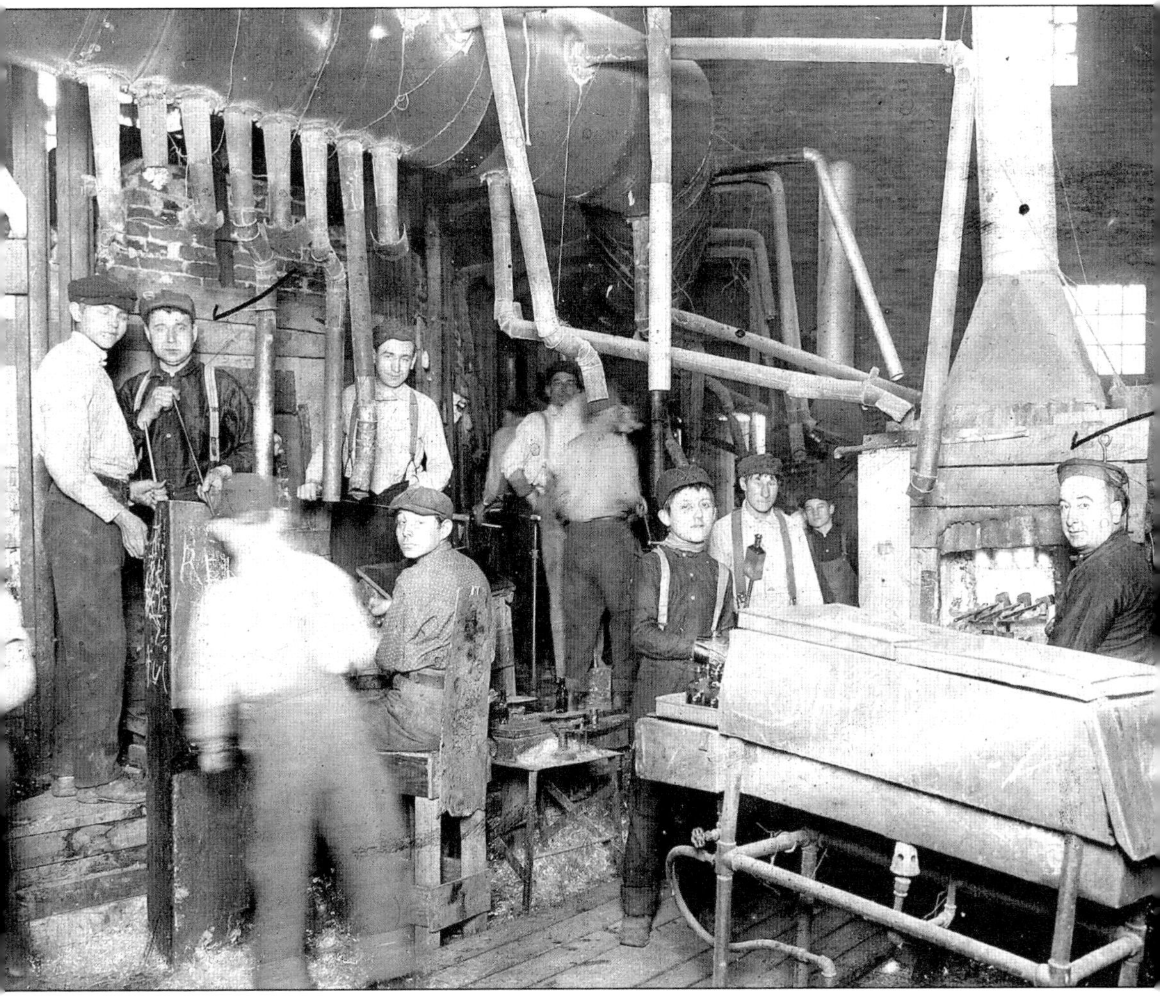

The industrialization of the area that was to become Oakmont began in 1870, when the Agnew Glass Company relocated its Pittsburgh plant to a riverside tract of land near Oakmont Avenue. Most of the workers shown in this undated photograph of Agnew's old glass house appear to be teenaged boys. Two adults identified are "Pop" Grubbs, second from the left, and Abe Grubbs, on the right.

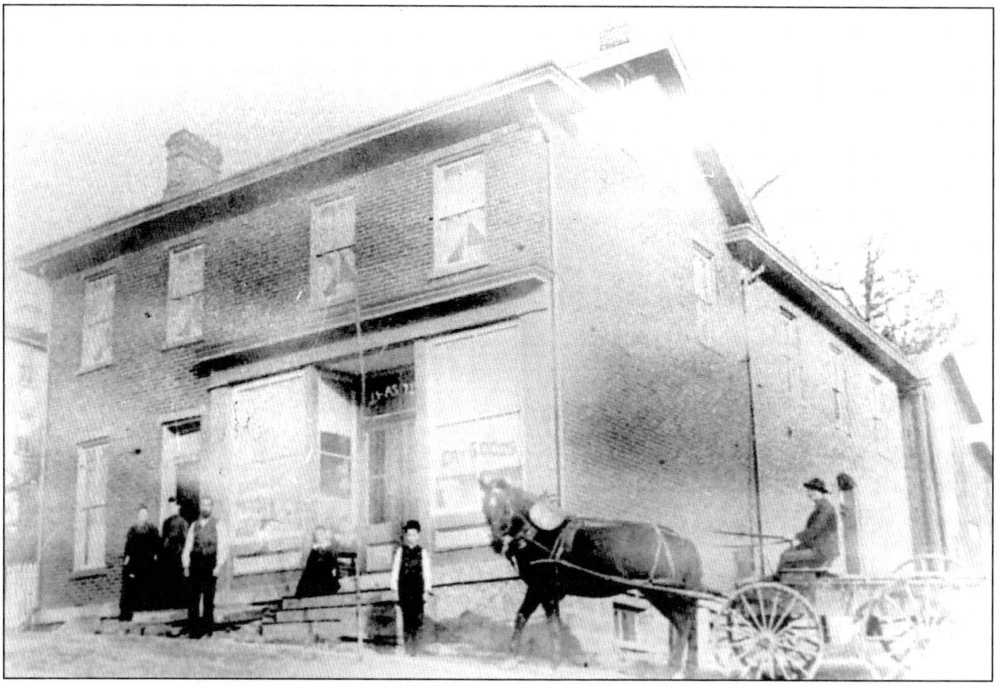

John Hastings opened his grocery and dry goods store at the corner of Sixth Street and Maple Way in 1875, a few years after moving here to work for the Dexter Spring Company. The store was one of the first of its kind in the area. Mrs. Hastings ran the store until her husband left his job at Dexter Spring to manage the operation.

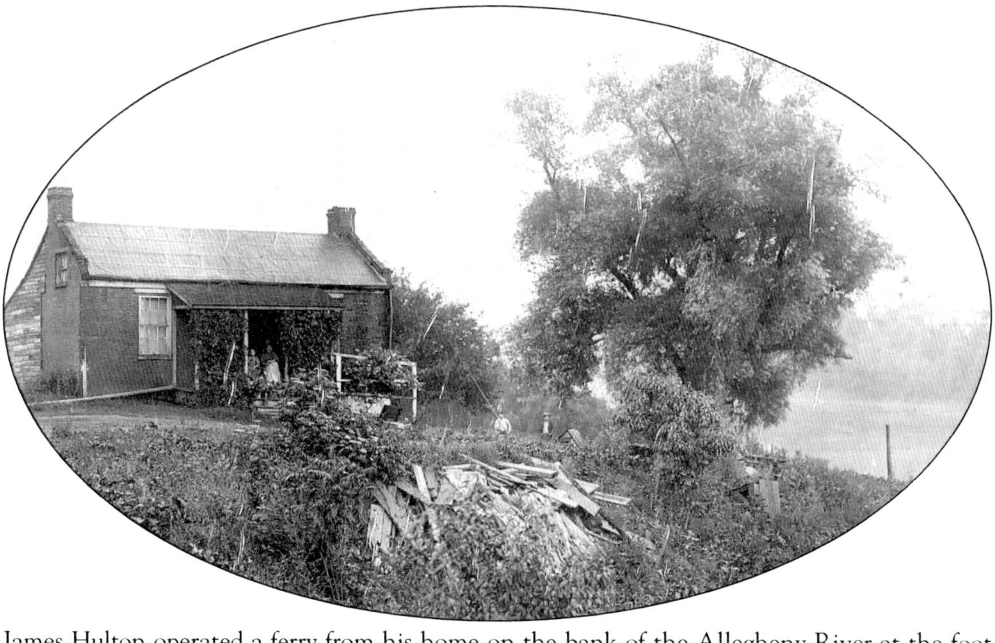

James Hulton operated a ferry from his home on the bank of the Allegheny River at the foot of what now is Hulton Road. Individuals were ferried across the river by rowboat while cargo and wagons were carried on a flatboat. Shown in this 1897 photograph are two female family members sitting on the porch while two men work nearby. The river is seen on the right.

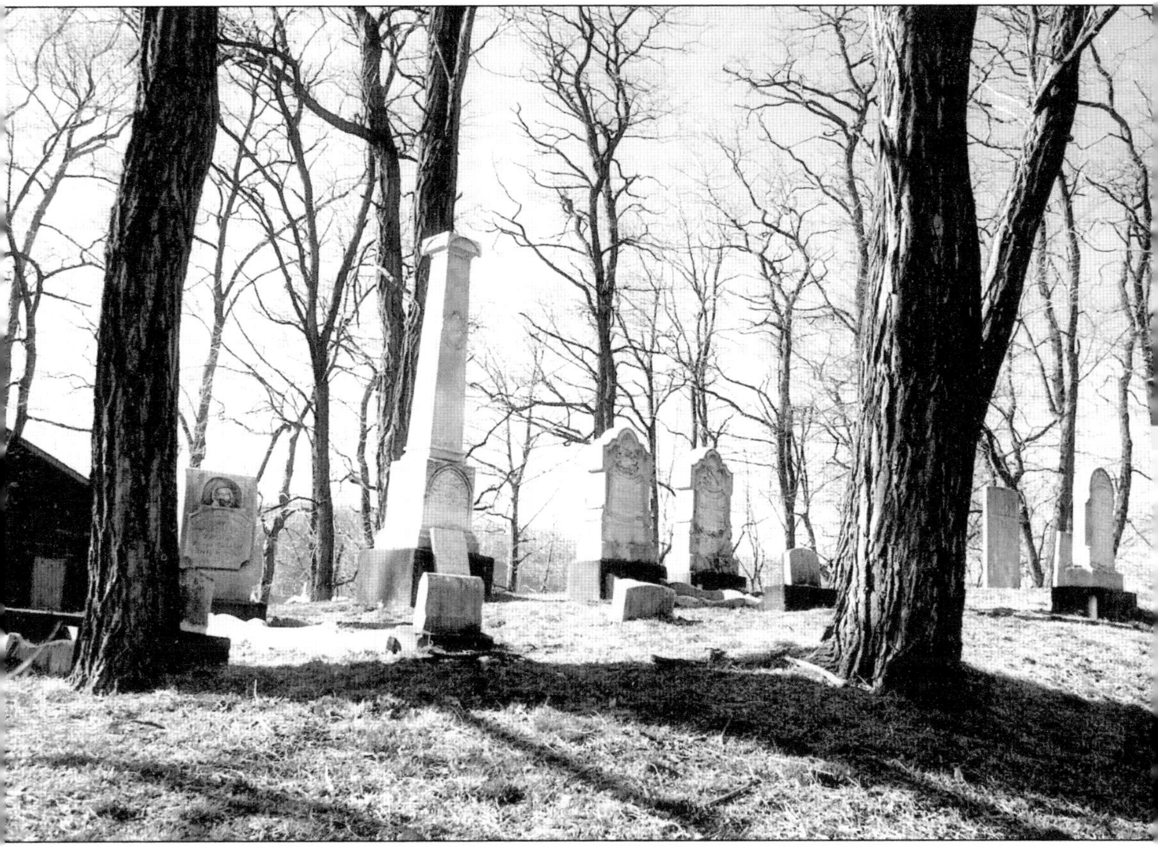

Michael Bright, one of the original settlers of the area that eventually became Oakmont, set aside a section of his 234-acre tract of land in 1823 to establish a family cemetery when his wife Barbara died. Michael Bright, who died in 1847, and most of his direct descendants are buried in the cemetery, which fronts on Fourth Street adjacent to St. Irenaeus School and the American Legion post. In 1883, when Oakmont still was part of Verona, Michael Bright's five granddaughters filed suit in the court of common pleas and won an injunction preventing borough officials from building a road through part of the cemetery. Bright's heirs in 1897 did allow Oakmont borough to open Fourth Street through the upper end of the cemetery. In return, the borough paid the heirs $500, reburied bodies displaced by the road construction in other parts of the cemetery, and built a retaining wall and sidewalk along Fourth Street. Today, the cemetery is maintained by the Oakmont American Legion post.

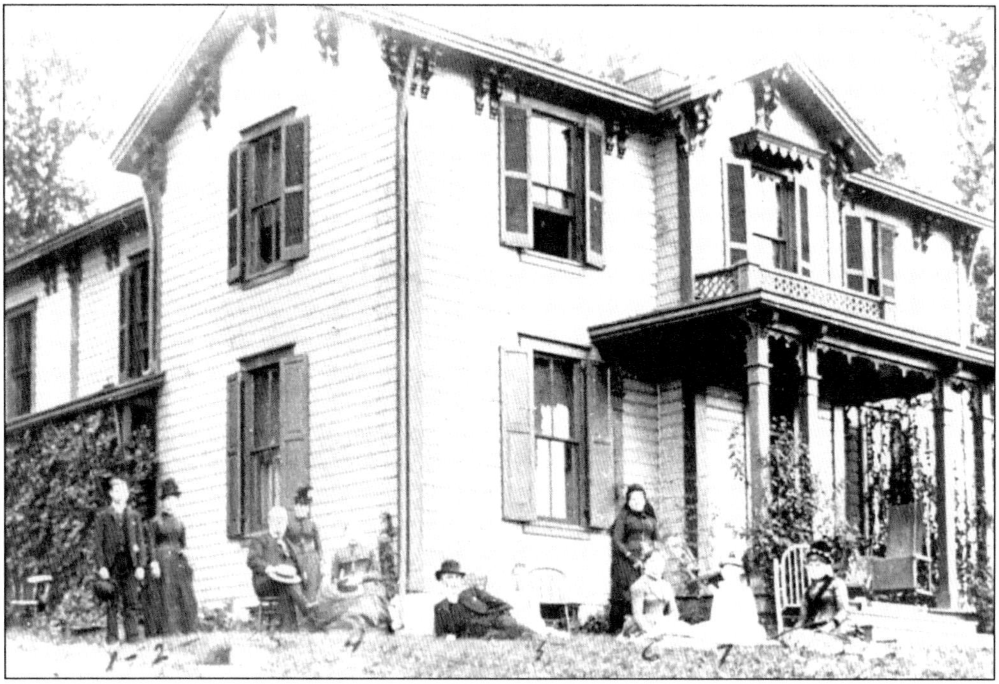

James B.D. Meeds, a wealthy Pittsburgher and a founder of Dollar Savings Bank, built this home on Seventh Street *c.* 1863, and maintained a sizable orchard there. He and his family donned their Sunday best when they posed for this photograph in front of the house they resided in until 1897. The house, still occupied, is at 520 Seventh Street.

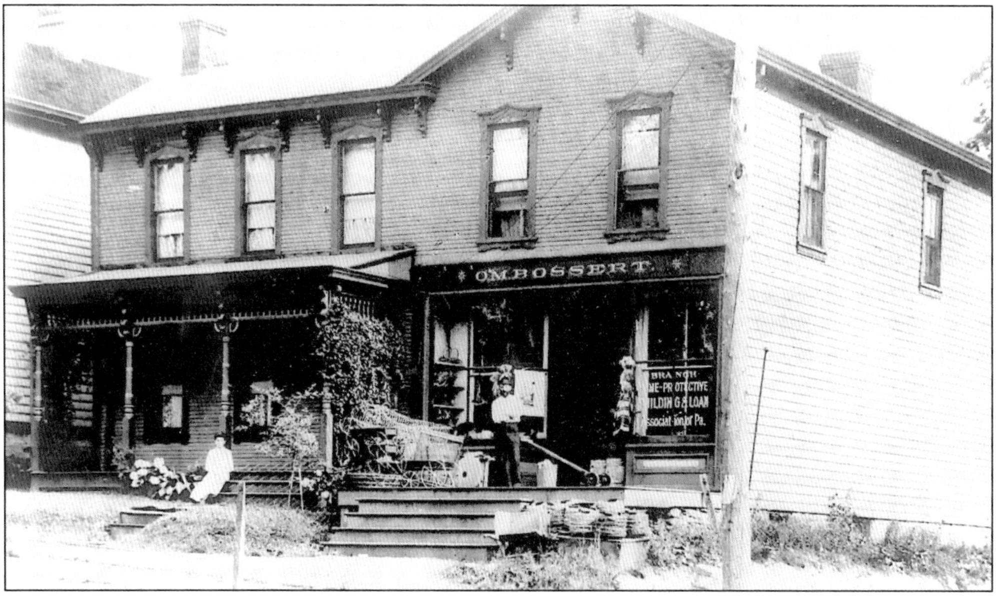

Obadiah M. Bossert's hardware store at Fourth Street and Maryland Avenue was also, his window proclaims, a branch of the Home Protective Building & Loan Association of Pennsylvania. Originally a tin shop, Bossert's was founded in 1884 and located farther down Fourth Street. The shop moved to this location a year later and eventually became a hardware store. It was the first store in Oakmont to sell radios.

This four-room schoolhouse, erected in 1868 at Fifth and E Streets and used until it was replaced in 1893 by a larger school on this site, was the second school building built in what now is Oakmont. Earlier schools were a two-room building on College Avenue, which was named for that school, and a one-room cabin located near the present-day entrance of the Oakmont Country Club.

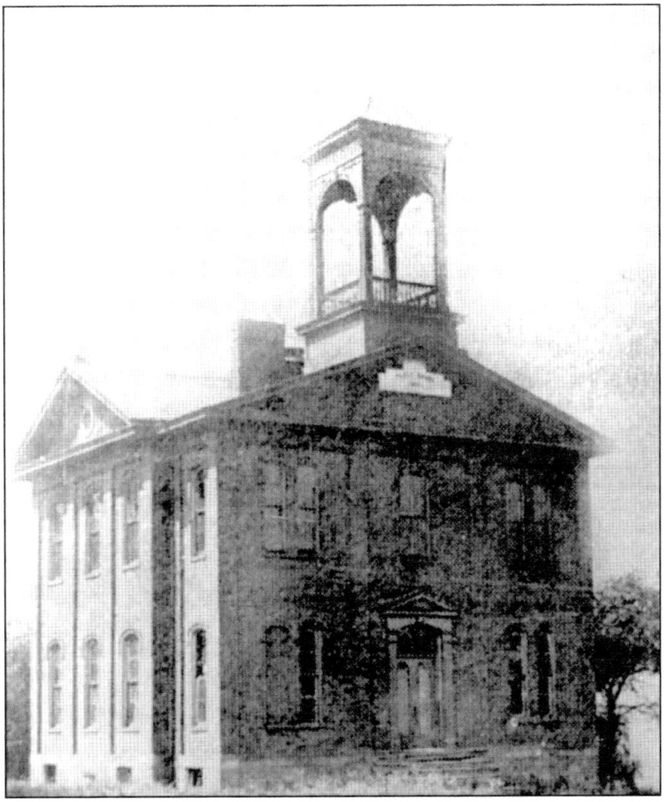

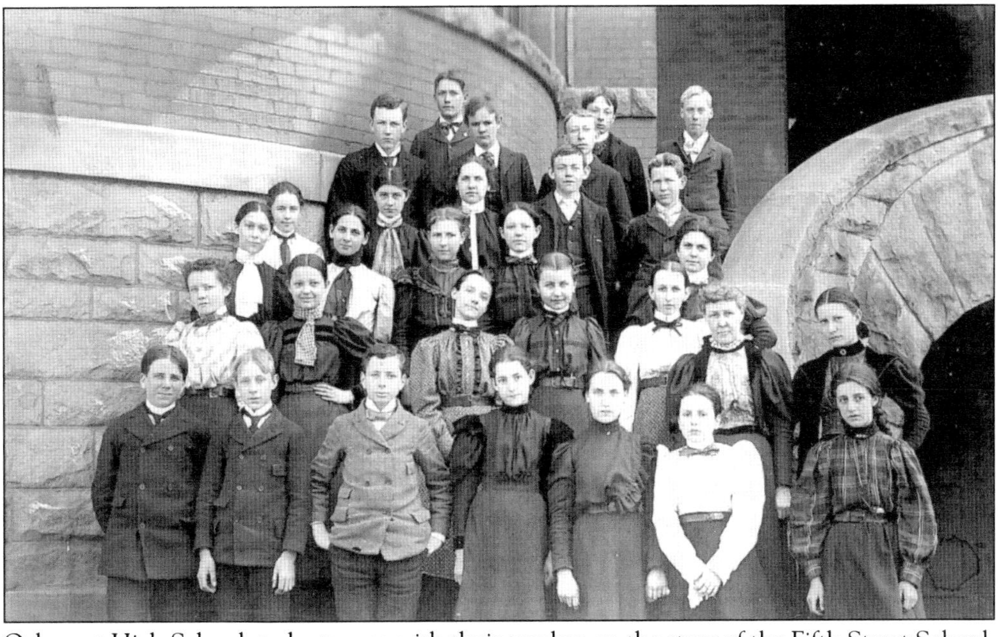

Oakmont High School students pose with their teacher on the steps of the Fifth Street School. In this photograph, which was taken in 1897 or 1898, the young lady fourth from the left in the second row is Lucretia "Lue" Anderson. Anderson, born in 1881, was a great-granddaughter of Peter Bright, one of the first settlers of the area that became Oakmont.

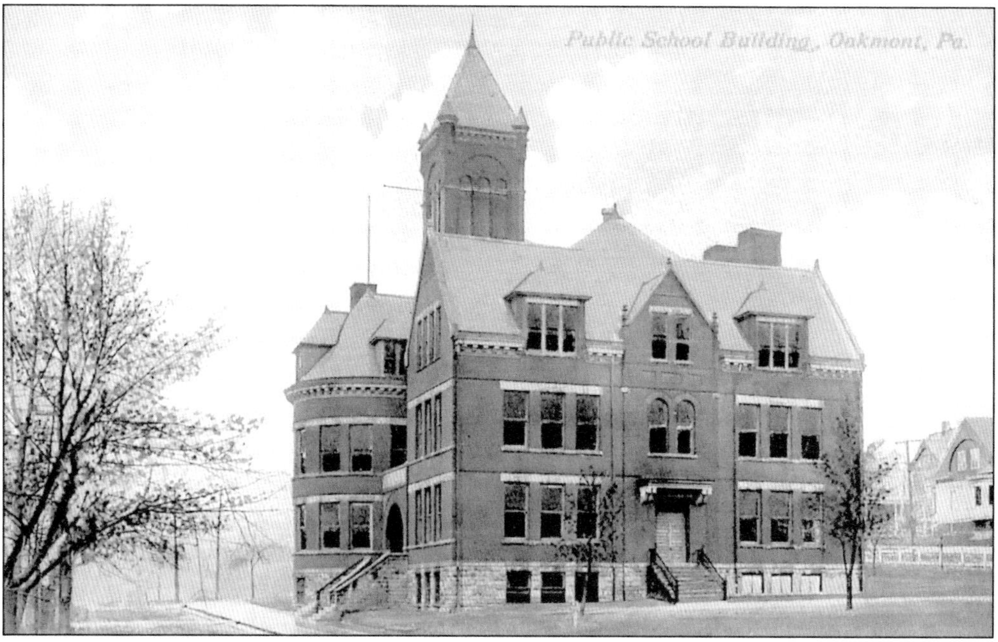

Oakmont Elementary School was located at Fifth and E Streets. It was a beautiful and uniquely designed structure that featured a tall spire and a rotunda, which are seen on the left side of the building. Constructed of red brick and stone and completed in 1893, it replaced a four-room school at the same site and was itself replaced by Memorial School in 1950.

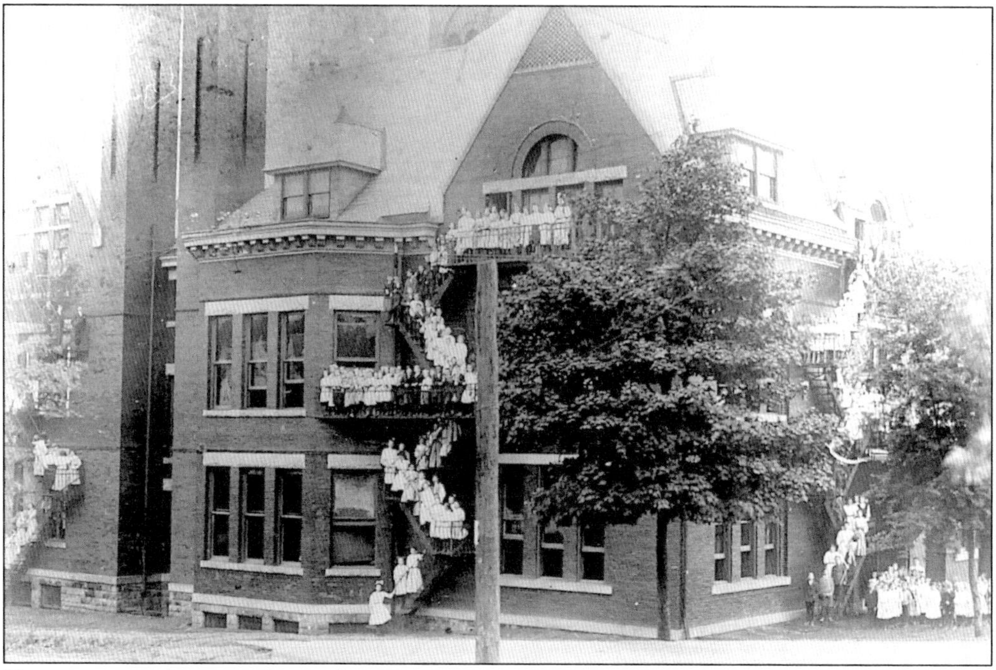

Here is a novel approach to class pictures. Instead of taking the usual stiffly posed group photograph, the photographer lined the students up on the Oakmont Elementary School's fire escapes.

Two

THE FIRST FLUSH OF YOUTH

By the beginning of the new century, Oakmont's population had grown to 2,323 people, and the new town was beginning to define itself culturally and socially. There was talk of building a library to serve the growing population if sufficient funds could be raised. Fortunately for the town and the library proposal, residing here at the time was Leander M. Morris, who happened to be a cousin of the industrialist, philanthropist, and library builder Andrew Carnegie. Morris was able to convince his illustrious cousin to donate money for the cause.

Responding to a letter Morris had written requesting assistance, Carnegie replied, "You can have the $15,000 with my blessing whenever the borough agrees to maintain the library. I will make it $20,000 if they will make the maintenance $2,000." The borough agreed to Carnegie's conditions, and eventually, Carnegie raised the amount of his donation to $25,000. Oakmonters had their library, and in an expression of thanks to their benefactor, named it Oakmont Carnegie Library. It opened on May 18, 1901, with a collection of 2,603 books purchased with the help of a $1,000 donation by Oakmont's school board. Blanche McIlvaine was hired as the first librarian at a salary of $70 a month.

The early 1900s saw many other developments in town, and 1903 was a notably busy year. That is when Elizabeth Bradley bought a large house on Hulton Road and transformed it into the Bradley Children's Home, which operated until 1975. The Oakmont Boat Club, later the Oakmont Yacht Club, was organized in 1903, as was the Oakmont Country Club. The First National Bank of Oakmont opened its first office in the library's basement.

Oakmonters were beginning to be able to travel faster and farther that year. Streetcar service to Wilkinsburg had begun, and Allegheny Valley Railroad expanded its service to East Liberty and Shadyside. The railroad and streetcars made Oakmont a summertime resort. Pittsburghers by the hundreds rode the trains and the streetcars to town on weekends to enjoy boating on the Allegheny River. Many of them set up camps along the river's banks and some built permanent summer cottages here. Many of the cottages still are used as year-round residences. The paving of Oakmont's cinder and mud streets began in 1905. In 1907, the Oakmont Fire Company was organized with Thomas A. Hunter as chief. To put out fires, firefighters used three two-wheeled hose carts housed at different locations around town.

Oakmont's industrial base expanded in 1908, when Richard T. Crane of Chicago bought the land that later would be the Edgewater Steel property and began building a machine shop and an iron and brass foundry for making pipe and fittings. It later merged with the Best Manufacturing Company of Pittsburgh.

To cap off the decade in great style, the Hulton Bridge opened.

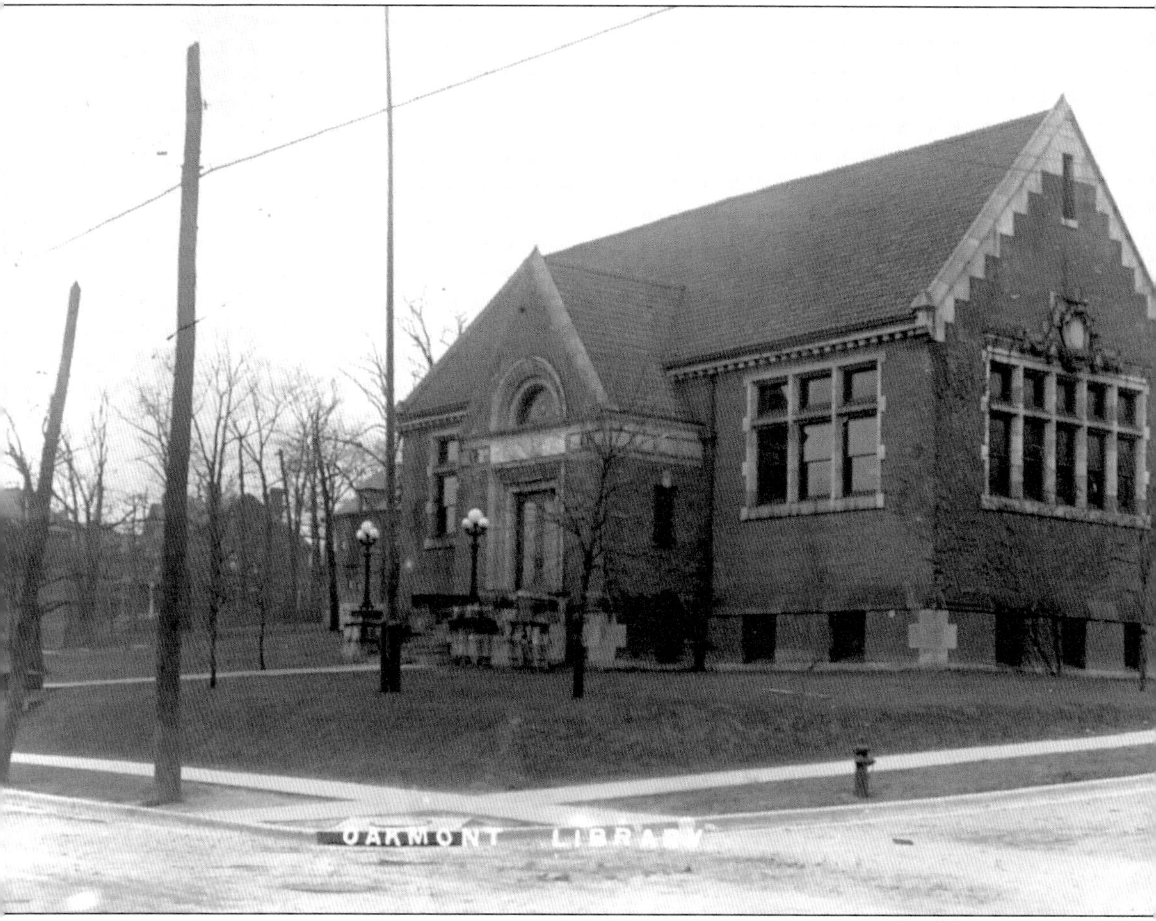

The Oakmont Carnegie Library opened its doors to the public on Saturday, May 18, 1901. Initial funding for construction of the library building, which began in March 1900, was provided by Andrew Carnegie. The philanthropist pledged $25,000 to the project at the request of his cousin, Oakmont resident Leander M. Morris. The building was designed by the architectural firm of Alden and Harlow. William Braithwaite, a local resident, was the building contractor. Until 1966, the library was maintained by Oakmont's school board and served as the library for the borough's schools while also serving the public. The school board levied a one-mill tax on real estate in the borough for upkeep and maintenance of the building. In 1903, a group of local residents founded the borough's first bank, the First National Bank of Oakmont, and started business in the library's basement.

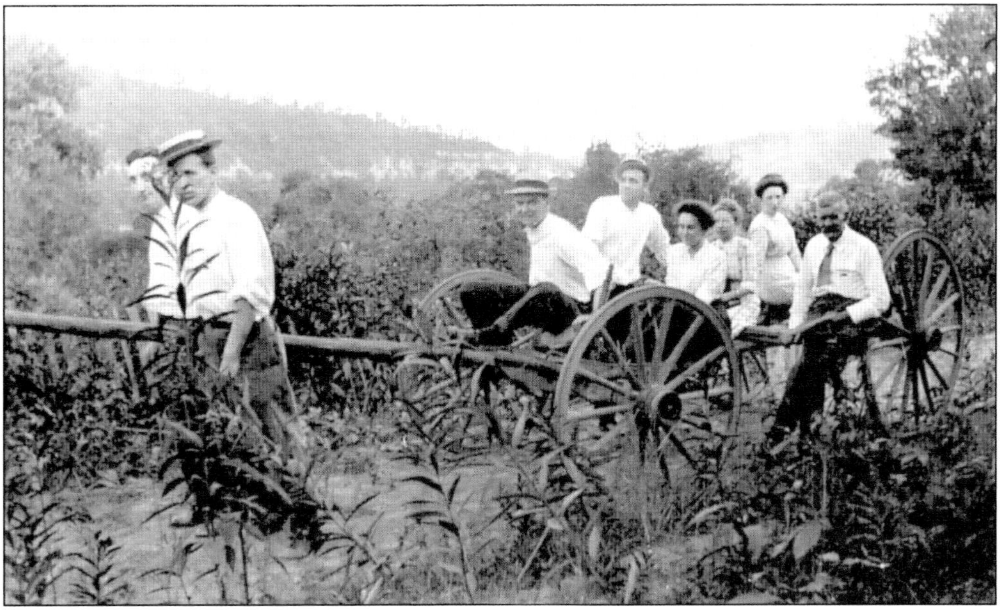

A summertime outing attracted these fun-loving Oakmonters in the early 1900s. The location of these festivities is on what probably was vacant land or farmland identified only as being "between the library and the river." Two of the merrymakers have been identified. Lucretia "Lue" Anderson and her father James Herron Anderson are seated in the back of the wagon.

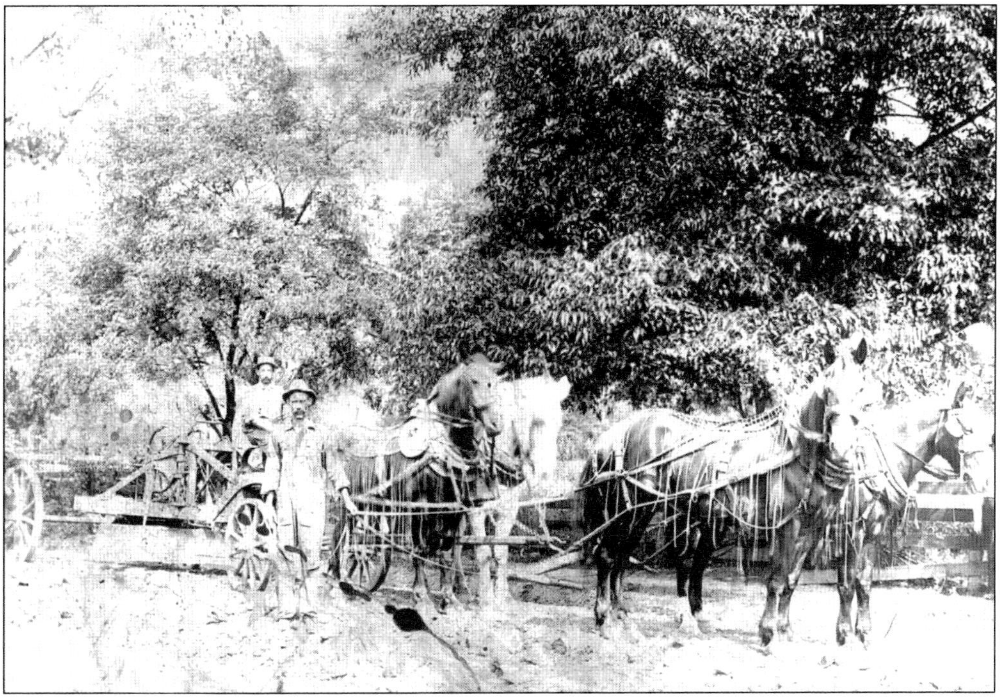

Horsepower was the power of choice when the Oakmont area was principally a farming community. These teams of sturdy, strong Belgian horses were the power providers on the Fentzel farm, located in what was called White Oak Levels just beyond present Fifteenth Street. The farm was owned and operated by John and Martha Gettis Fentzel until the 1930s.

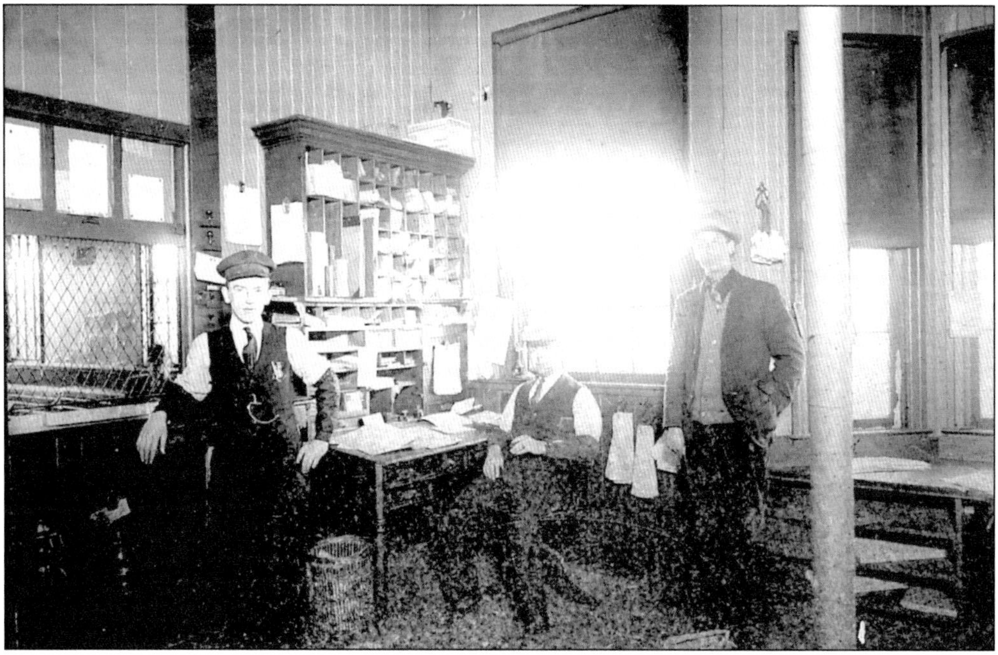

Postal clerks are shown working in one of Oakmont's early post offices. The first post office here opened in 1857 with Jonathan Hulton as postmaster. The office was called the Hulton post office until it became the Oakmont post office in 1894. The local post office was located in several buildings around town, including the Hulton Railroad Station, before moving into its current building on Allegheny River Boulevard.

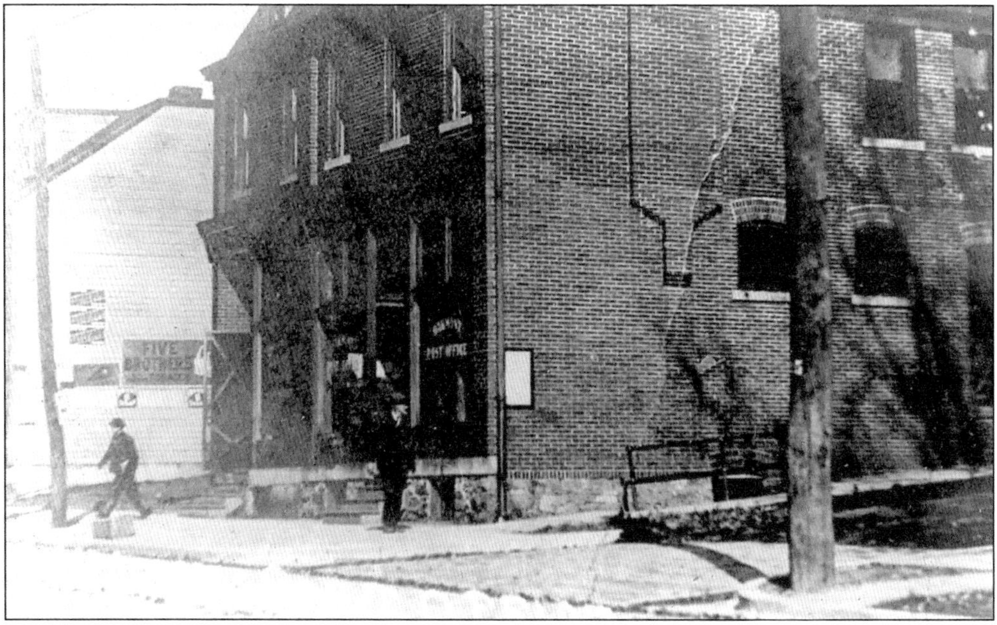

This building at Allegheny River Boulevard and Virginia Avenue was home to the Oakmont post office at one time. Originally housed in the Hulton Railroad Station, the post office moved several times before moving into its present location at Allegheny River Boulevard and Maryland Avenue. Retail stores now occupy the building pictured here.

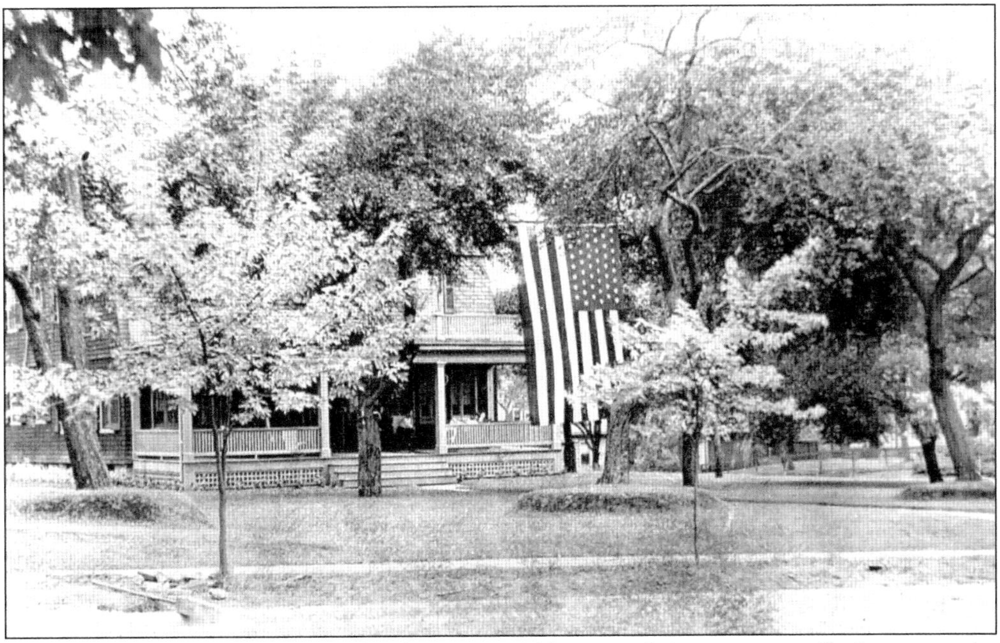

The paving of Oakmont streets that began in 1905 required that many roadbeds in town be lowered. That meant many lawns had to be graded to conform to the new levels of sidewalks and streets. Older trees in those lawns sat higher than the new grade, creating small grassy islands. This photograph is of a home at Fourth Street and California Avenue.

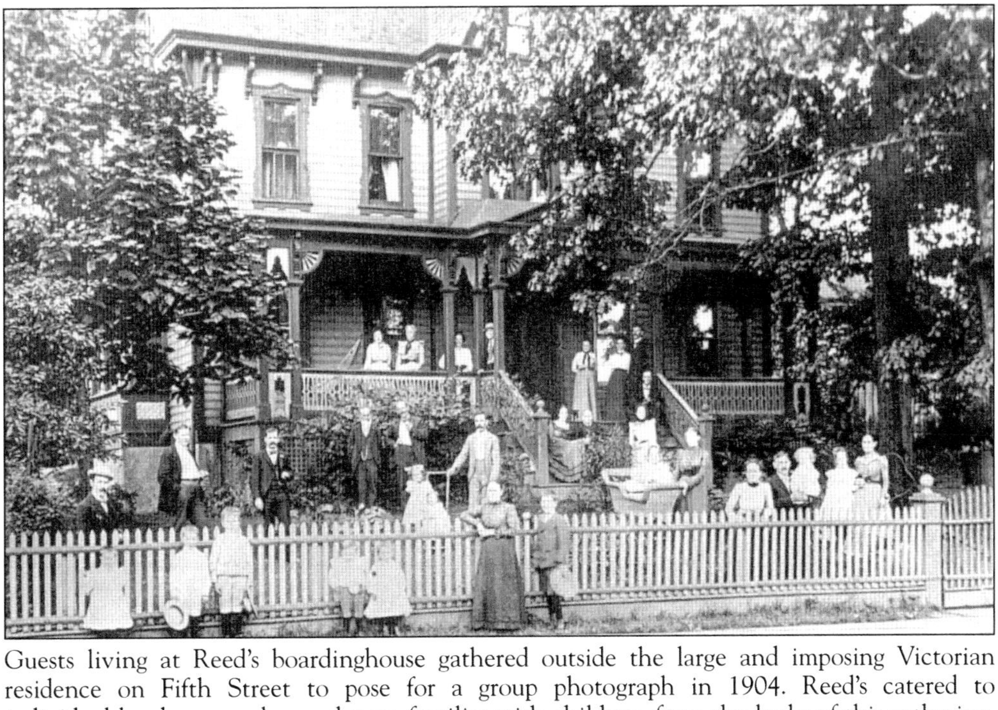

Guests living at Reed's boardinghouse gathered outside the large and imposing Victorian residence on Fifth Street to pose for a group photograph in 1904. Reed's catered to individual borders, couples, and even families with children, from the looks of this gathering. Boardinghouses were popular at the time, especially among people moving into town in search of employment.

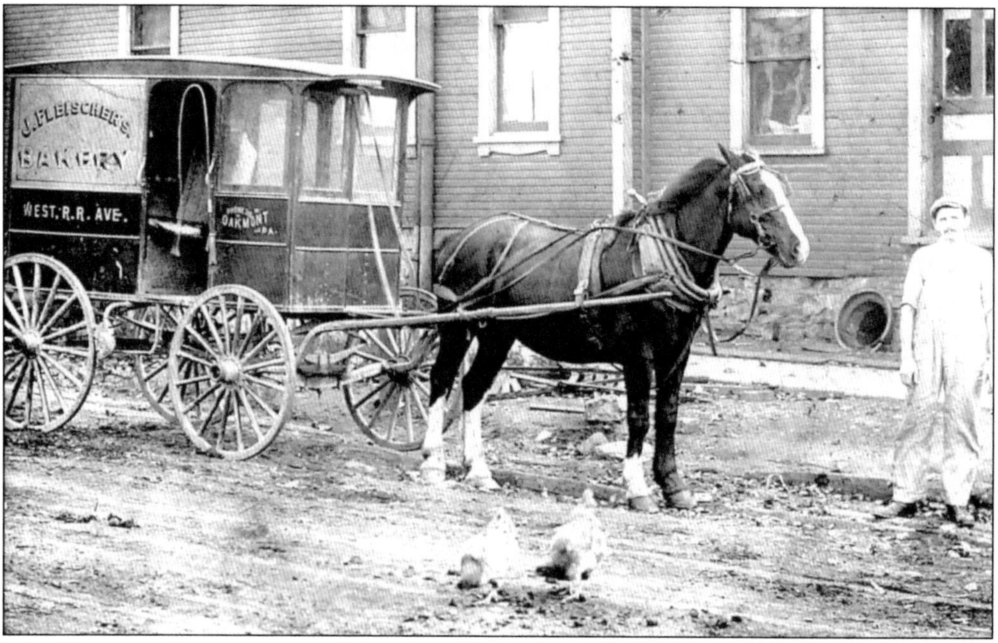

John Fleischer, shown posing with his delivery wagon in this photograph, operated a bakery in town for many years. His original shop was on West Railroad Avenue, and in 1940, he opened a second bake shop at Allegheny and Delaware Avenues. The business closed in the 1950s. Notice the chickens foraging for food in the middle of the unpaved street.

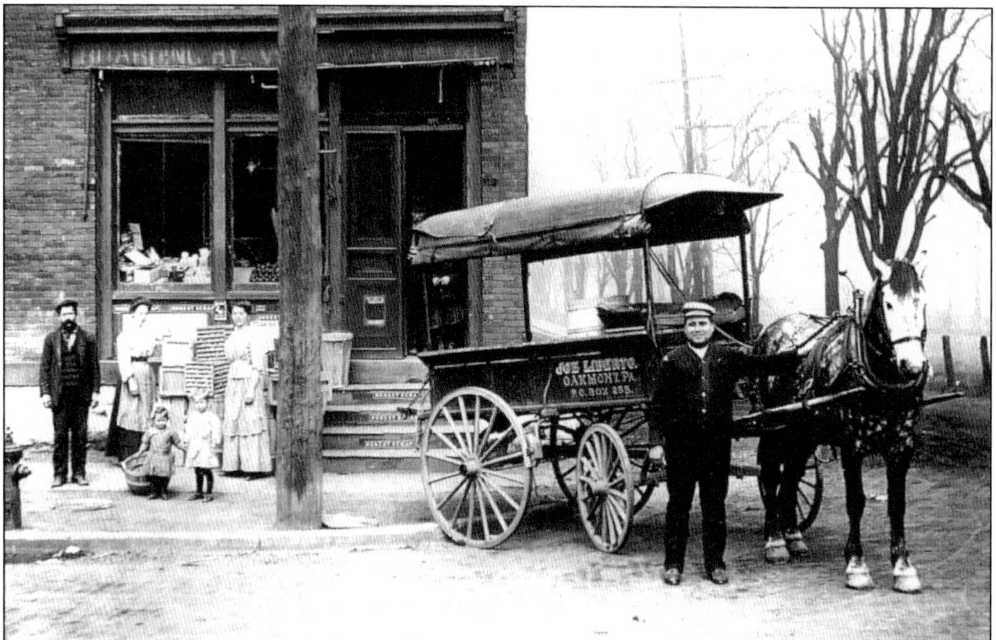

Joe Liberto operated a store at 854 Oakmont Avenue, now Allegheny River Boulevard, for many years. He is shown with his horse and wagon, which carries his post office address, box 255, as he is about to start out on his delivery rounds. On the left is his brother John, who also worked in the store.

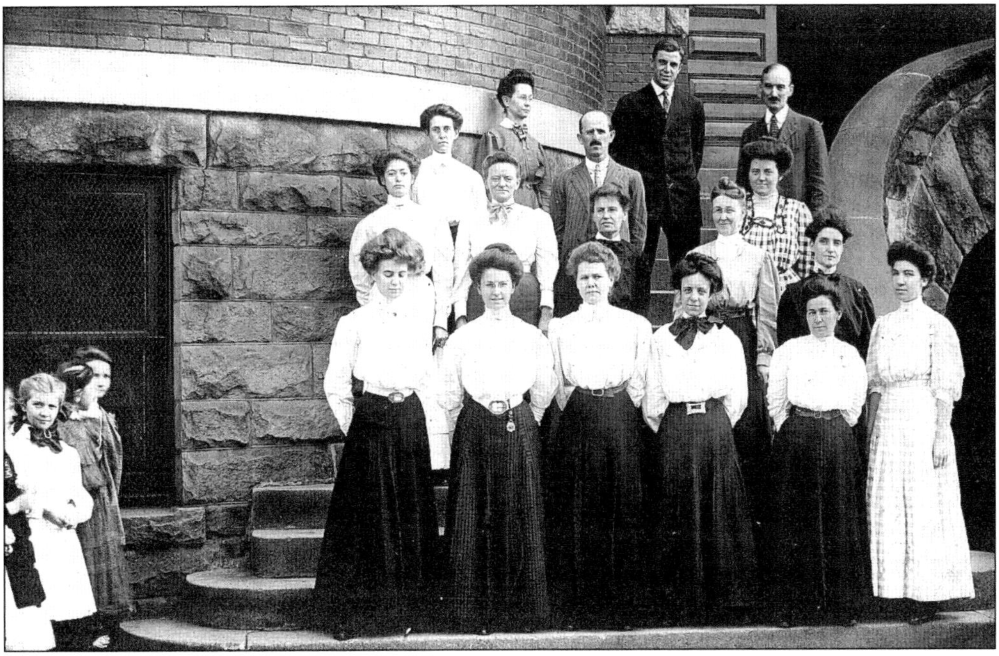

Young students on the left watch the photographer take a picture of their teachers at the Fifth Street School. Note the predominance of women in the teaching ranks. The school's stone staircase, which arched above the basement entrance to the school, was a favorite site for group photographs of students and faculty.

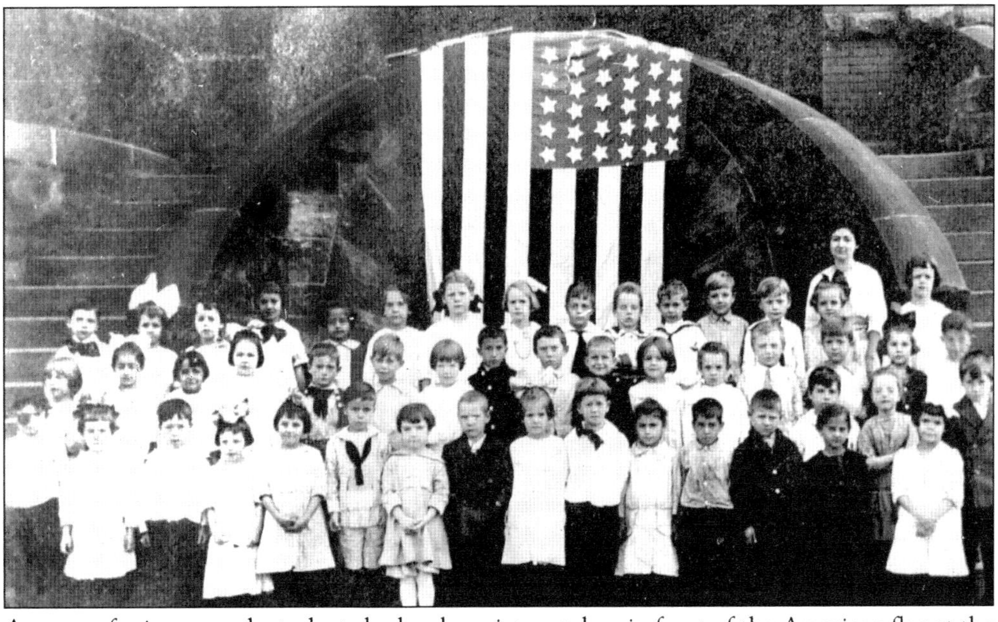

A group of primary grade students had a class picture taken in front of the American flag at the basement entrance of the Fifth Street School. The arched stone staircase was a distinguishing feature of the three-story school, which was built in 1893 at Fifth Street and Pennsylvania Avenue, then E Street.

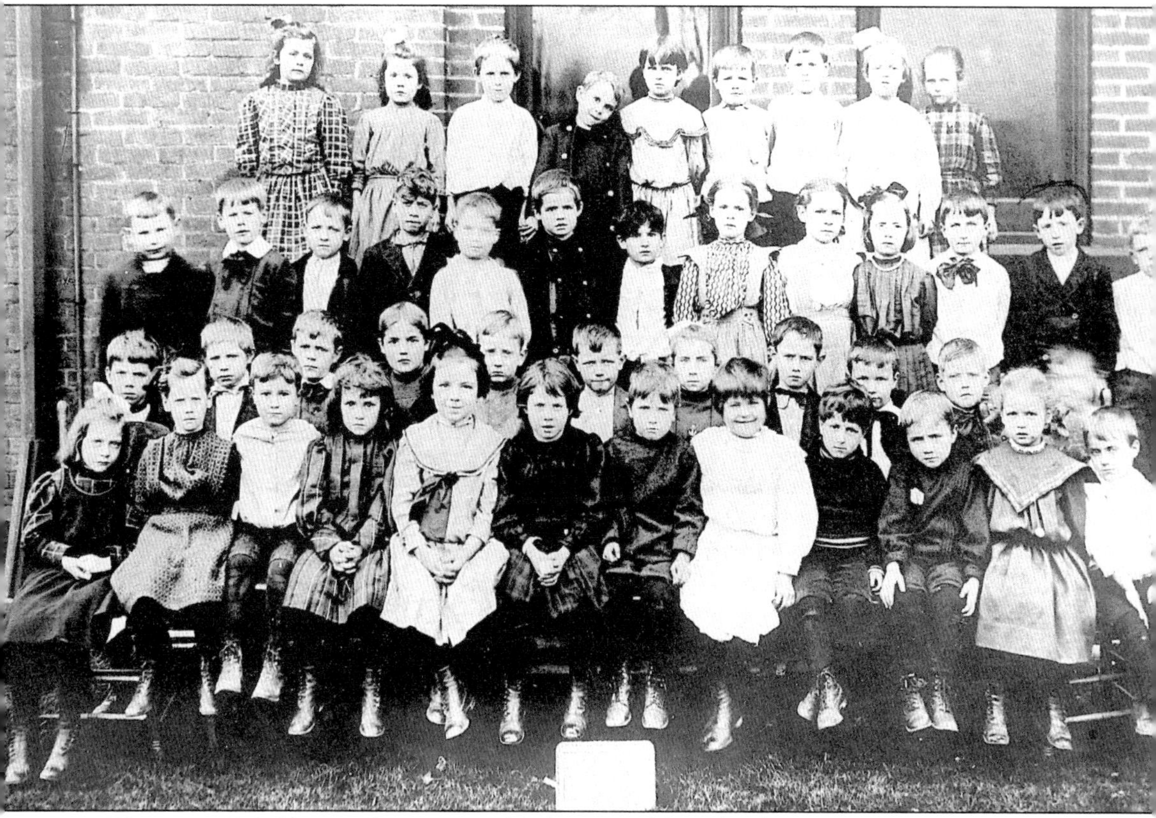

There are 45 children in this picture of Oakmont Public School's 1904 first-grade class, a strong indication of the town's growth rate in the years following its incorporation as a borough in 1889. Improved railroad service to Pittsburgh and the opening and expansion of manufacturing plants in Oakmont contributed significantly to the town's growth.

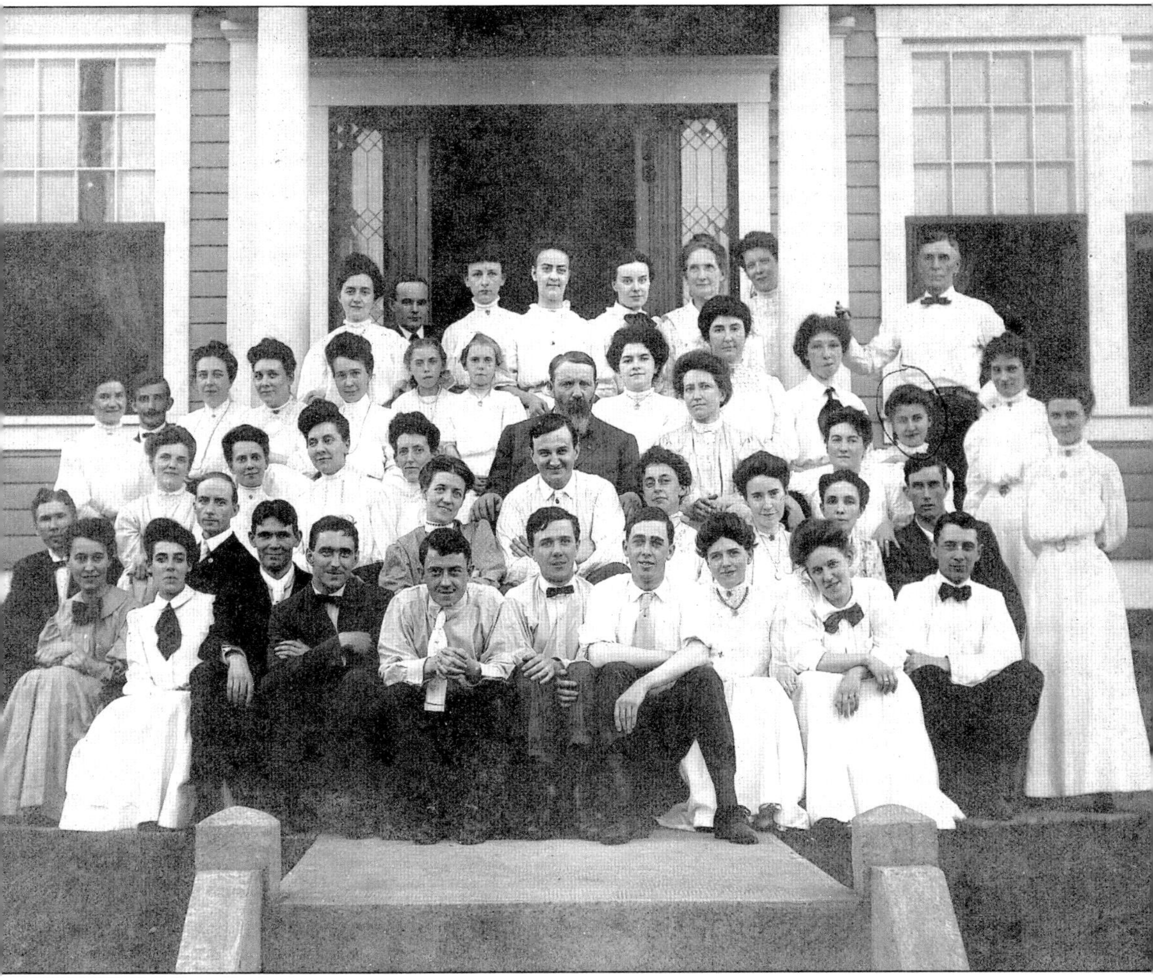

The woman in the third row of this 1900 photograph with her face circled is Lucretia "Lue" Anderson. Those pictured likely are members of a group associated with the United Presbyterian Church. The church, founded in 1856 as the Associated Reformed Church and later known as Valley United Presbyterian Church, was the first church organized in what now is Oakmont.

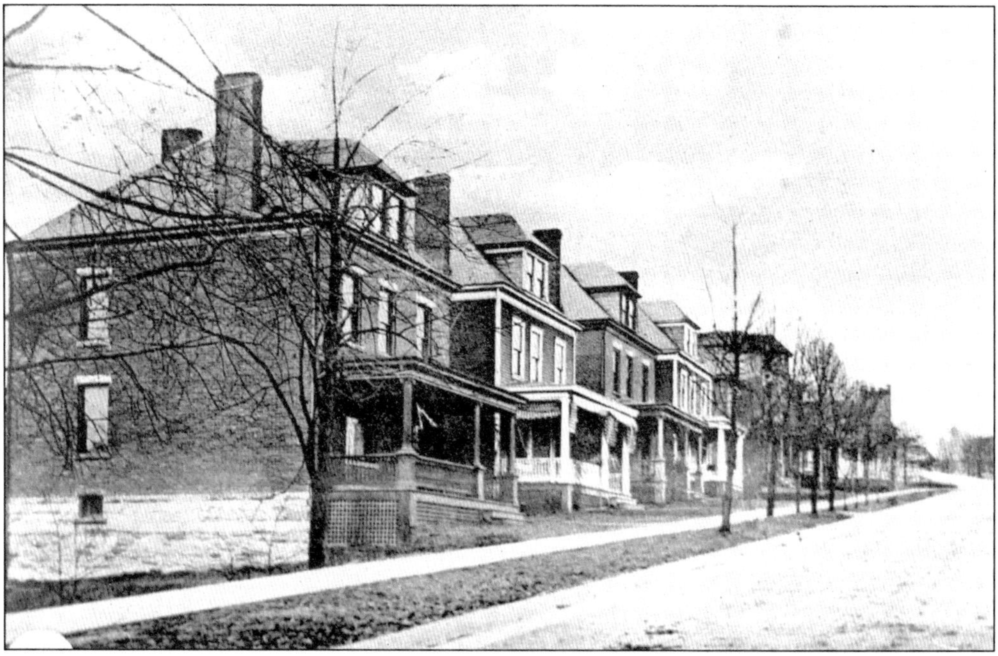

The name of E Street was changed to Pennsylvania Avenue when Oakmont's so-called "up" streets were renamed in 1912. This view up E Street shows a line of lookalike homes along the road before Oakmont's streets were paved. The homes still stand in the 300 block of Pennsylvania Avenue.

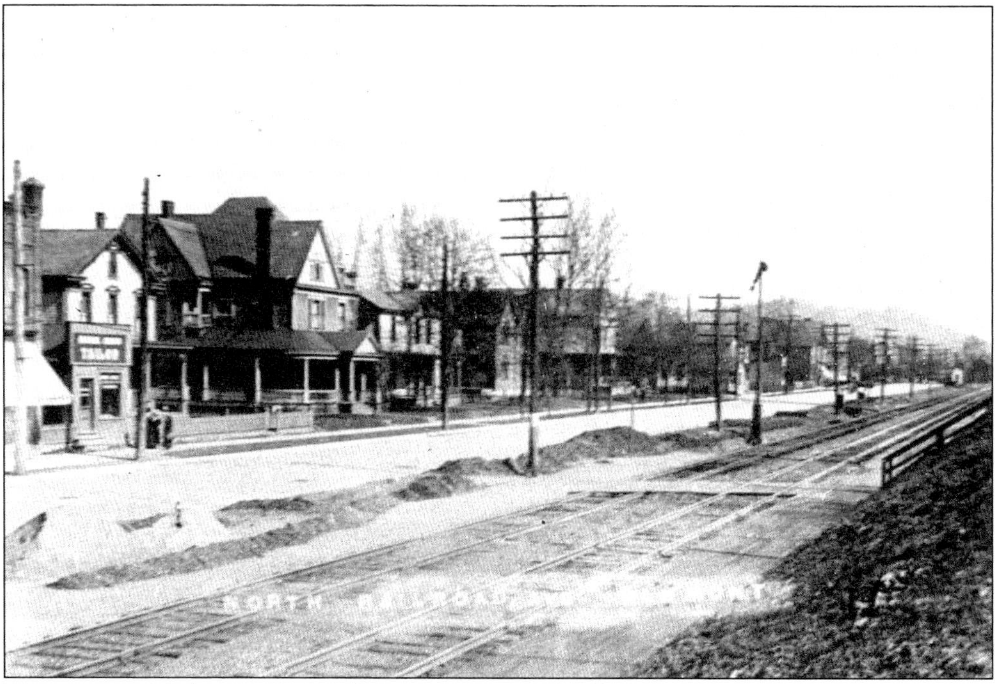

The paving of Oakmont's streets began in 1905, and Allegheny Avenue, then West Railroad Avenue, was among the first streets completed. Note the piles of dirt lining the side of the street near the railroad tracks, evidence that paving crews had only recently completed their work.

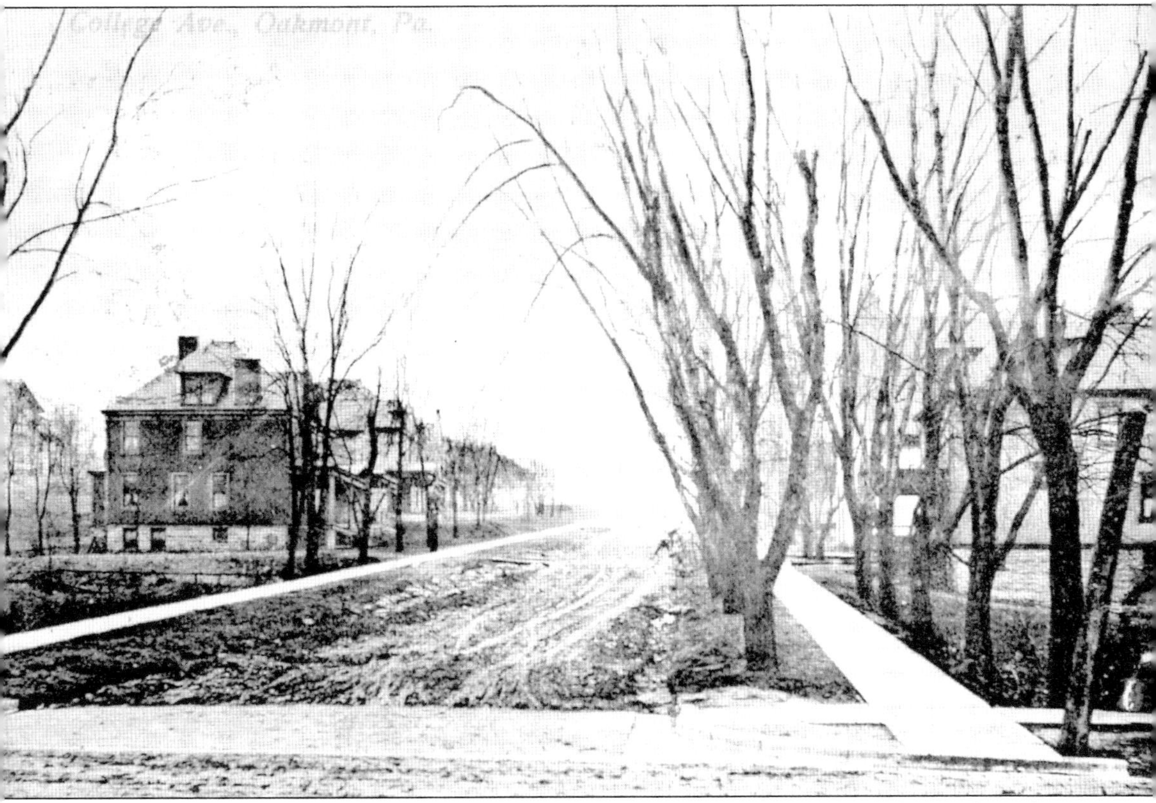

In 1910, five years after Oakmont's street paving had begun, College Avenue still was a heavily rutted mud road. Notice that cement sidewalks had been laid, however. This postcard, from an Oakmont resident named Grace to a friend in Yatesboro, was postmarked August 23, 1910. The card's message read, "This is the street that we live on, but you can't see our house."

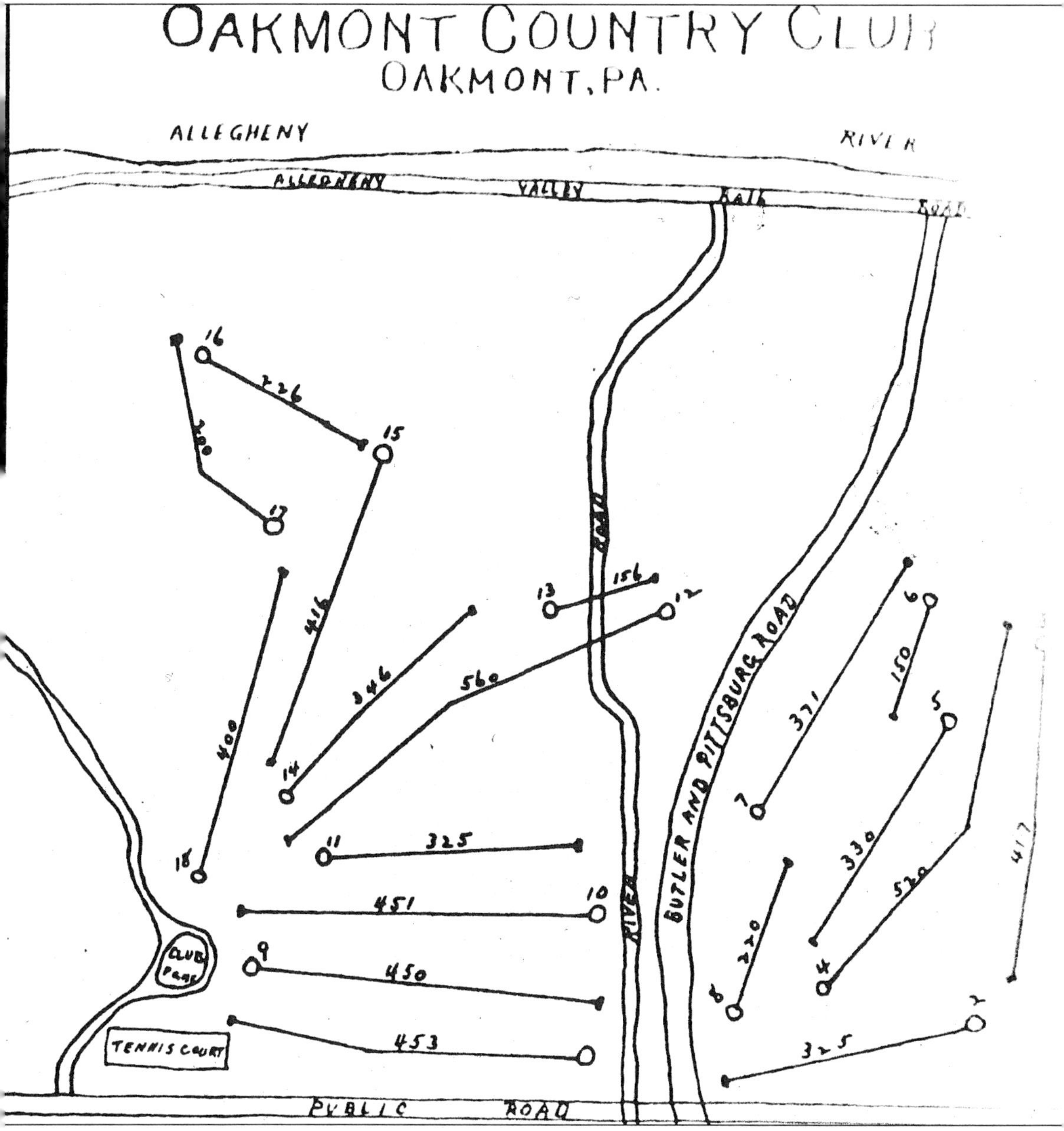

Henry C. Fownes, a Pittsburgh steel manufacturer, along with several friends and relatives organized the Oakmont Country Club in 1903. The club was built over a two-year period on the hilltop in an area then known as White Oak Levels. Although he was not a golf course architect, Fownes designed the course and supervised its construction. Remarkably, the current layout of the golf course's 18 holes is essentially the same as Fownes's original design, shown on this old hand-drawn map, except for changes in yardage brought about by improvements in golf equipment. The Oakmont Country Club has hosted more major championships than any other course in the United States, including seven U.S. Opens, five U.S. Amateurs, three Professional Golf Association championships, and one U.S. Women's Open. In the 1973 U.S. Open, Johnny Miller's final round 63 has been dubbed, "the greatest round of the 20th Century." Incidentally, most of the Oakmont Country Club's golf course is in Plum Borough, not Oakmont.

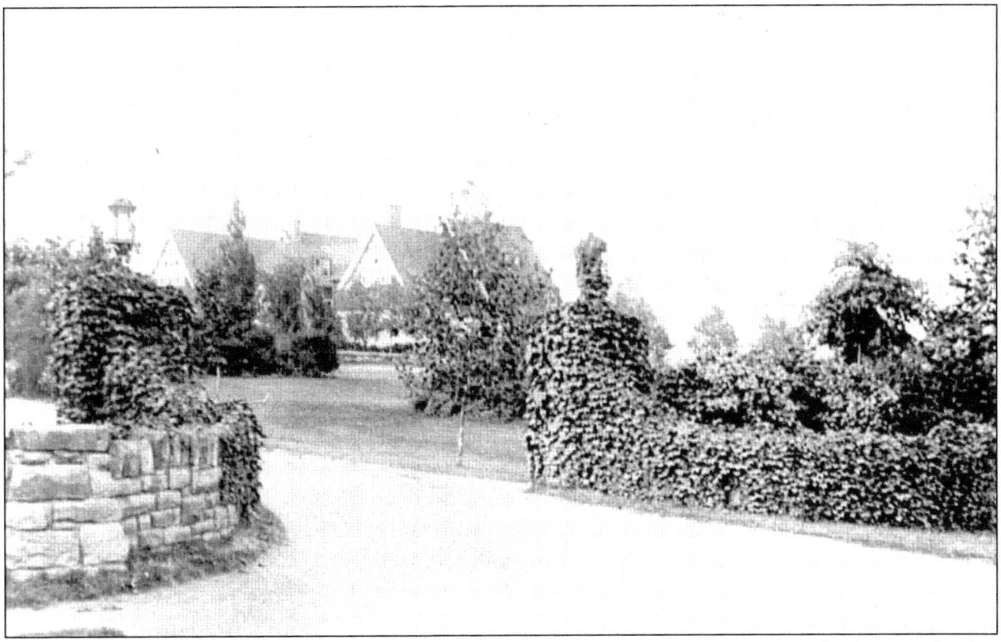

The carriage house that now is located just inside the ivy-covered stone wall that marks the Hulton Road entrance to the Oakmont Country Club had not been built when this photograph was taken shortly after the club began operating in 1905. In 1987, the Oakmont Country Club became the first golf course in the country to be designated a national landmark by the National Register of Historic Places.

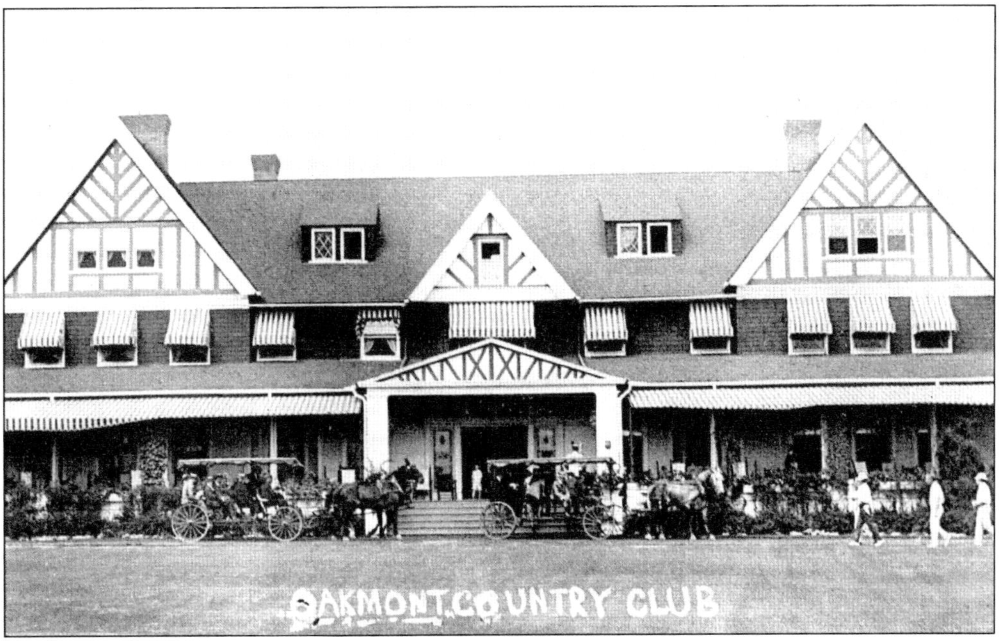

In the early 1900s, many golfers who came to Oakmont to play the country club course traveled by train. They were met at the railroad station and transported to the club atop Hulton Road by horse-drawn wagons. Passengers in the wagons shown here in front of the clubhouse either have just arrived at the club or are waiting to be driven back to the railroad station for the trip home.

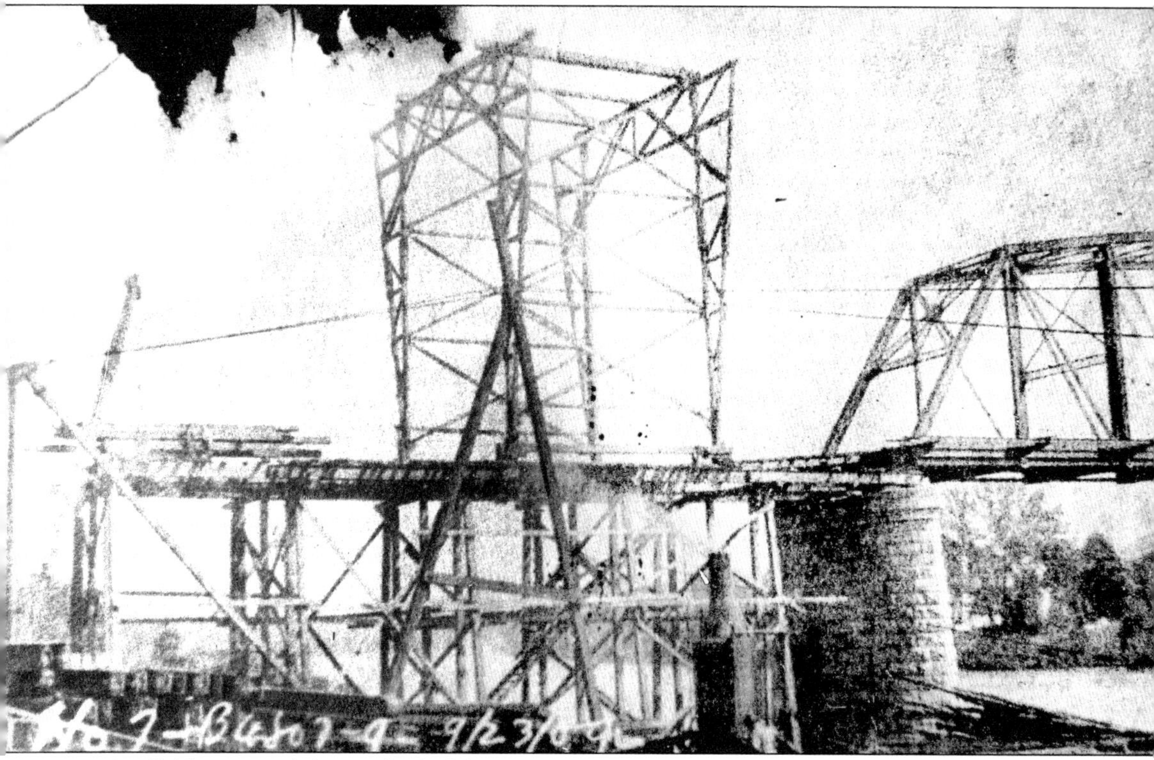

Scaffolds surround the roadbed of the Hulton Bridge in this photograph taken in the final stages of construction in 1909. One of the bridge's five through-truss spans can be seen to the right of the scaffolding. The Hulton was the first bridge built by Allegheny County. It was designed by J.G. Chalfont, a county engineer, and cost $306,000. The bridge, which spans the Allegheny River and links Oakmont and Harmarville, is 1,544 feet long. Its original roadway measured 21 feet 8 inches wide, although the installation of concrete barriers during renovations have narrowed the width. Local motorists and commuters faced traffic headaches when a major repair project closed the bridge, beginning in March 1975 and lasting seven months. The name of the span was changed briefly to the Joseph Bonetto Bridge in 1989 to honor a state legislator from neighboring Plum who had died a few years earlier. A public outcry and a borough-wide petition drive succeeded in getting the Hulton name restored in time for the celebration of Oakmont's centennial that year.

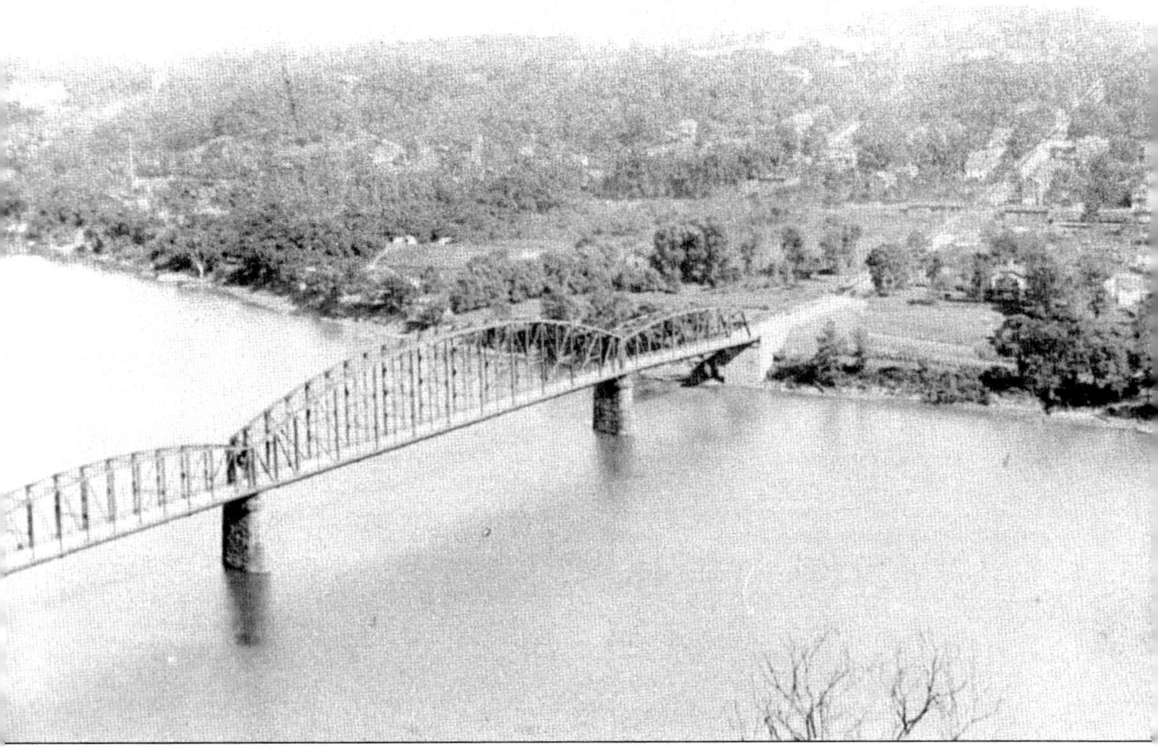

Traffic on the Hulton Bridge was so light as to be practically non-existent when this photograph of the span was taken shortly after it opened in 1909. Note there also were no buildings on the riverbanks on either side of the bridge. Hulton Road looks like a peaceful rural lane as it rises up the hill from the bridge.

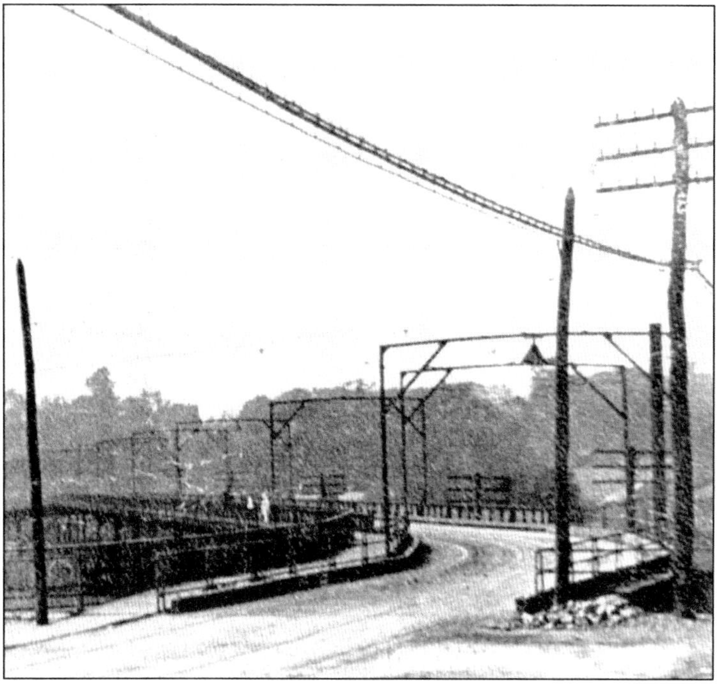

Streetcars that traveled across the wooden bridge linking Oakmont and Verona carried passengers to Wilkinsburg via Rosedale and Sandy Creek. Service began in 1903 by the Wilkinsburg and Verona Street Railway Company. When buses replaced streetcars, the wooden bridge, which sometimes caught fire in the summer when lit cigars were thrown from the cars by passengers, was replaced in 1938 by the cement viaduct.

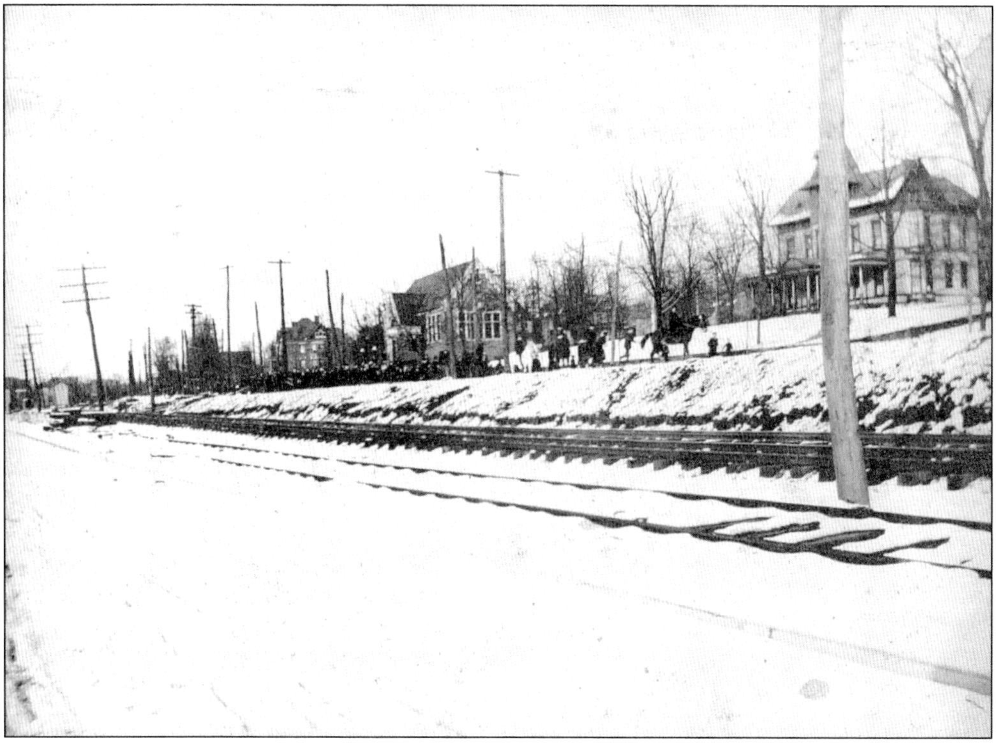

Oakmonters always have loved a parade—even in the snow. This parade along the main street in the early 1900s, led by Mabel Pyle and several others on horseback, attracted few spectators, at least at this juncture in front of the library. On the right is the Paul house, owned by Harry W. Paul, superintendent of Verona Tool Works.

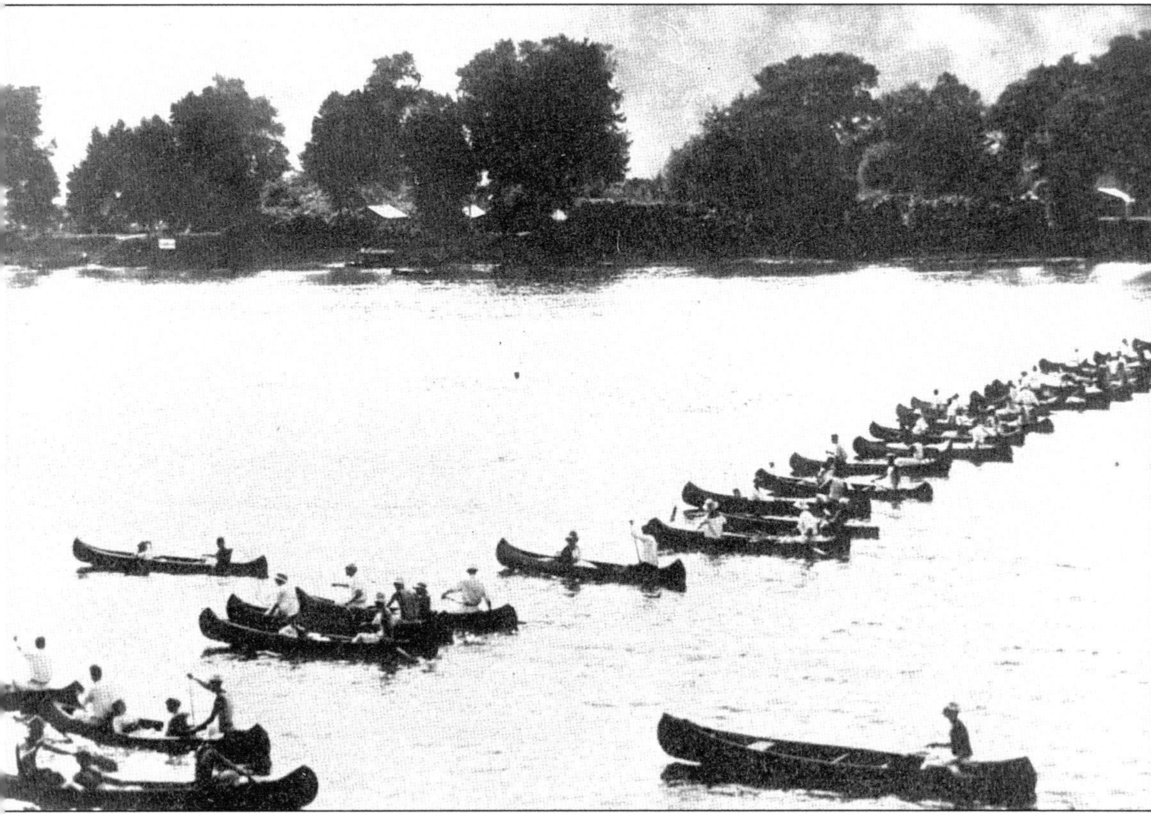

Canoeing and canoe racing were very popular summertime activities on the Allegheny River. Rowers are shown lined up, awaiting the signal to start what likely was a professional canoe race. In the 1880s and 1890s, national and even international professional rowing events were held over what was called the Hulton Course. The course, considered to be one of the best in the country, extended from Twelve Mile Island, just upriver from where the Hulton Bridge now spans the Allegheny, to Verona. During many of the races, a train of flatcars with bleacher seats for spectators followed the racers along the railroad tracks on the Harmarville side of the river. Spectators and the racers themselves were said to have bet heavily on the events. Professional rowing on the Hulton Course was discontinued in the late 1890s amid charges of corruption, boat tampering, and race rigging.

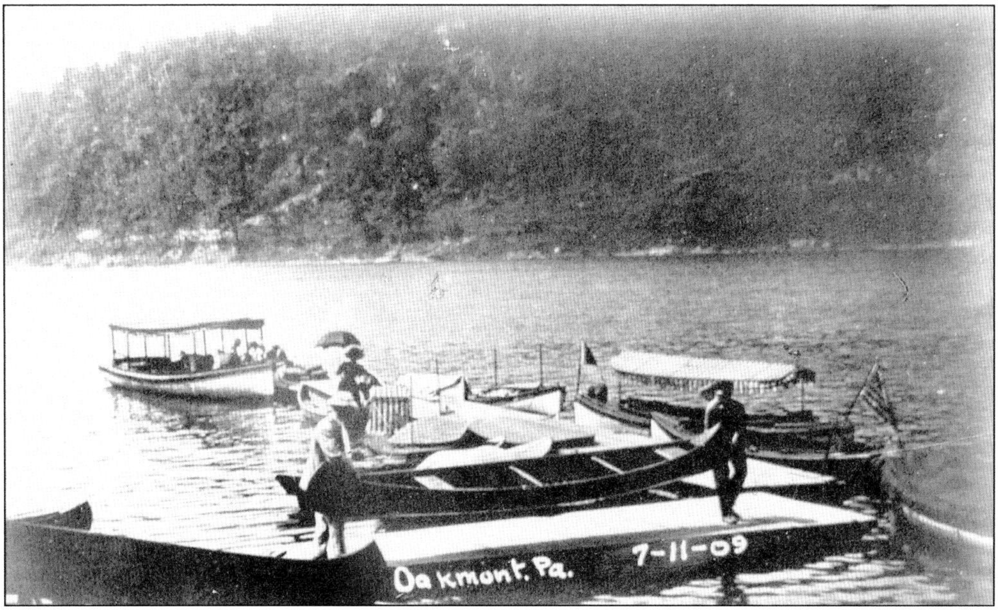

Members of the Oakmont Boat Club put canoes into the river on a July morning in 1909 in preparation for what likely was to be another busy day of summer fun on the Allegheny. Note the woman in the center of the photograph sporting a parasol to ward off the summer sun as she waits to board one of the larger boats.

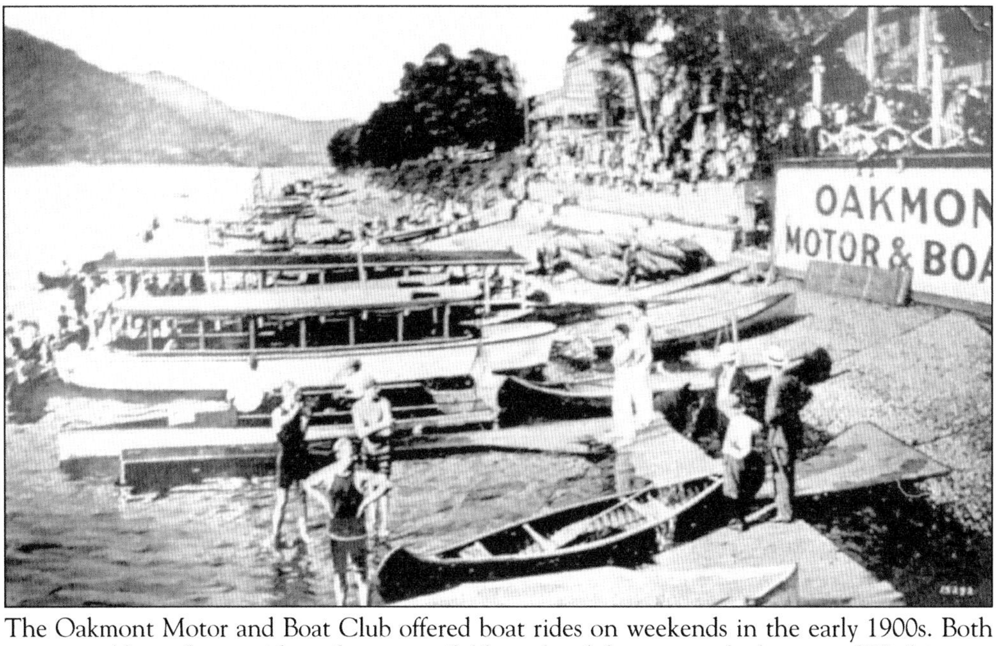

The Oakmont Motor and Boat Club offered boat rides on weekends in the early 1900s. Both canoes and larger boats with roofs were available at the club ramps at the bottom of Washington Avenue. Boaters had a wide range of river to traverse in the days before dams were erected on the Allegheny to protect Pittsburgh and upriver towns like Oakmont from flooding.

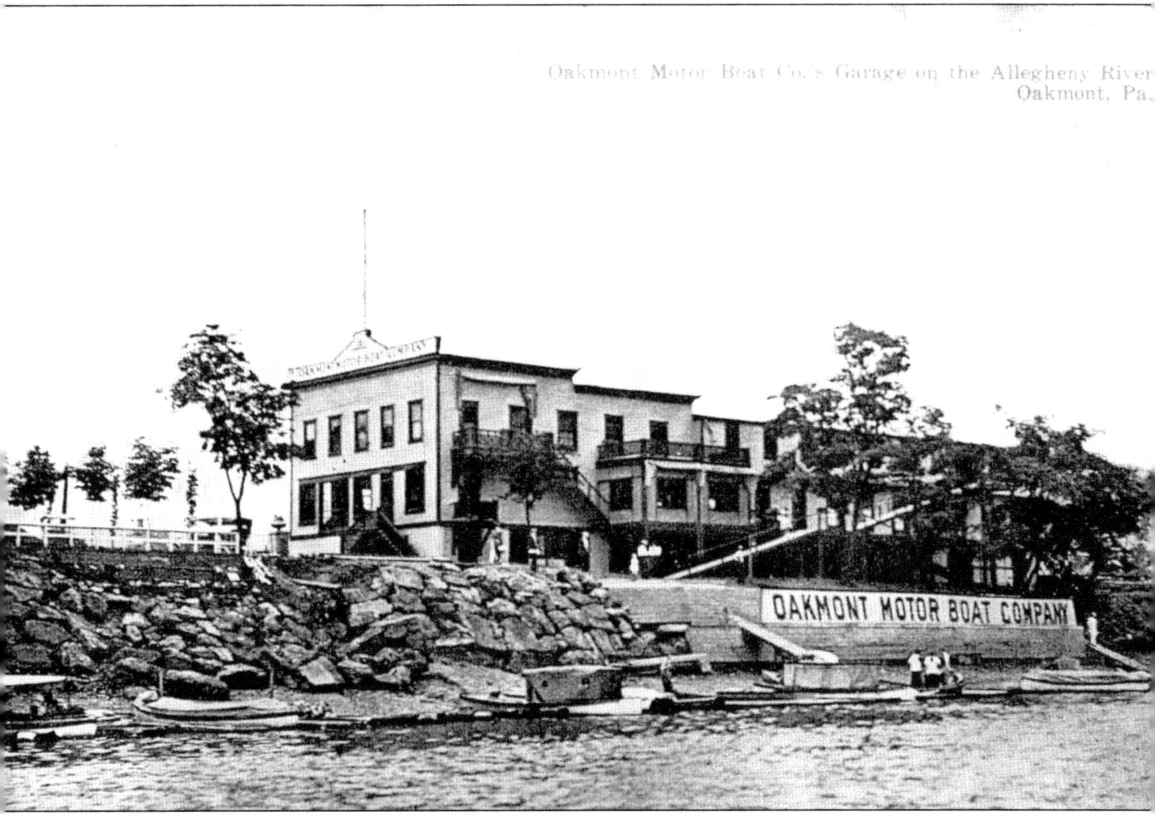

The Oakmont Motor Boat Company did a brisk business among boaters from this facility on the Allegheny Riverbank at the bottom of Washington Avenue. The company, owned by J.T. Anderson, sold, serviced, stored, and rented boats. This building is identified as the company's garage, but its size indicates that it was used for many other purposes as well.

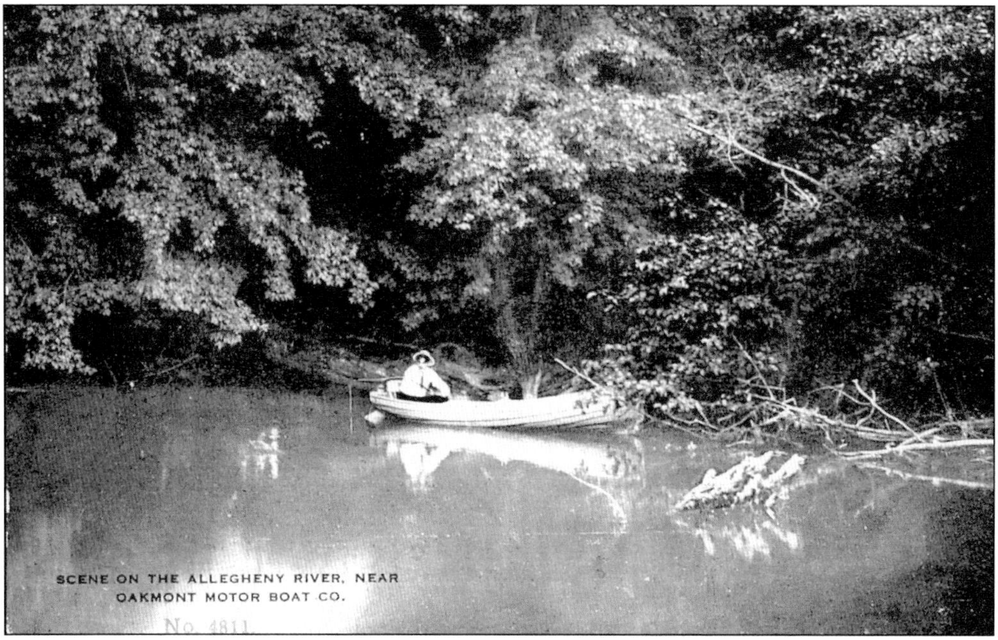

Quiet, secluded fishing holes were numerous all along the Allegheny River's bank in Oakmont before riverside development. Such spots as this one are rare now that homes and commercial buildings line the shore.

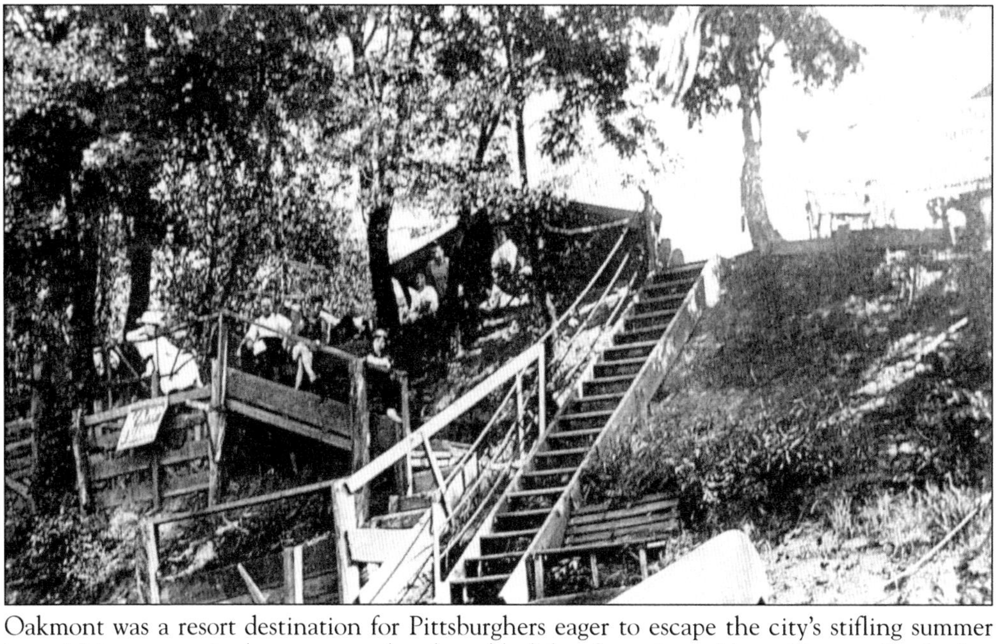

Oakmont was a resort destination for Pittsburghers eager to escape the city's stifling summer heat. Visitors came in droves on weekends and holidays by train and boat. Extra police had to be hired to keep the peace. Many summer cottages built in the Morris Camps section of the borough were converted to permanent residences that are still occupied today. Camps like this one dotted the Allegheny Riverbanks.

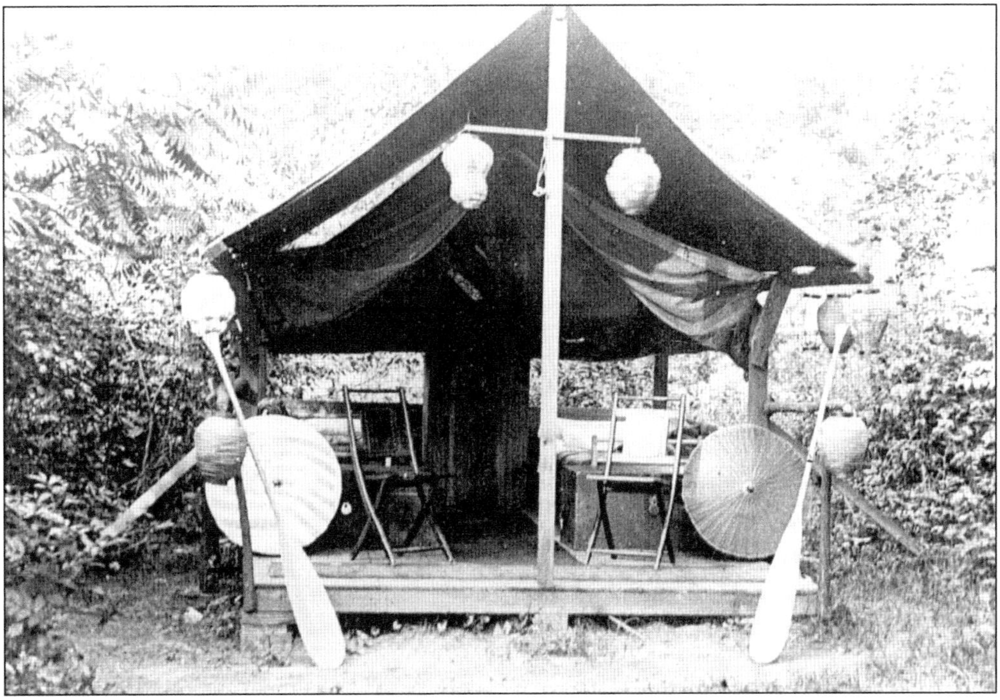

Riverside camps established by summertime visitors to Oakmont ranged from costly and elaborate structures, many of which later were converted into permanent residences, to tents like this one, decidedly less costly to erect and maintain. Furnishings were simple and often selected for their utility and weather resistance rather than comfort or beauty.

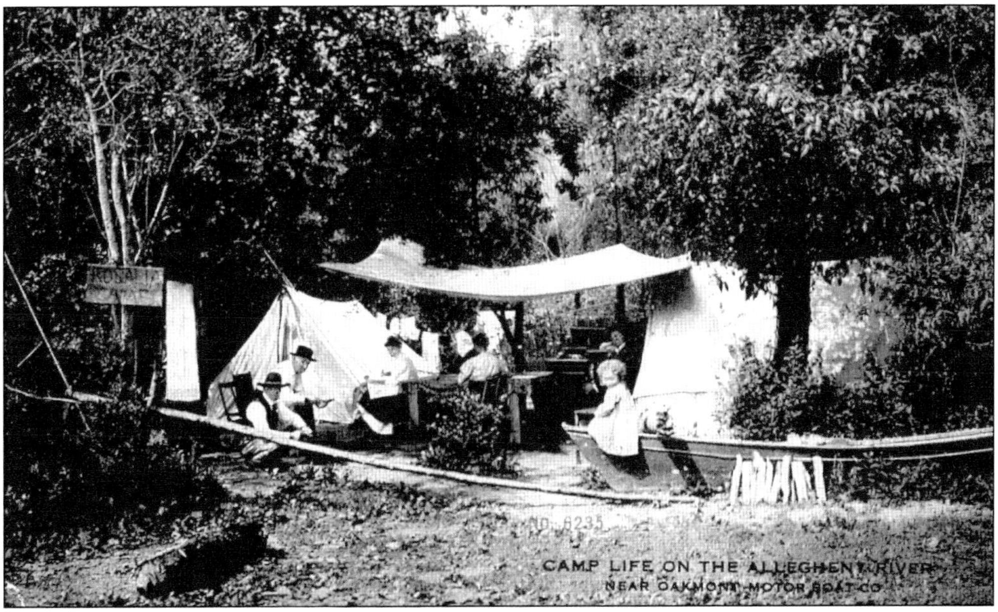

A group of riverside campers enjoyed roughing it on the banks of the Allegheny River in Oakmont. Pittsburghers, accustomed to the citified ways and conveniences of life in the city, made their way to Oakmont by train and trolley to weekend in the country. The wooden plank nailed to the tree on the left declares this to be Rosalia Camp.

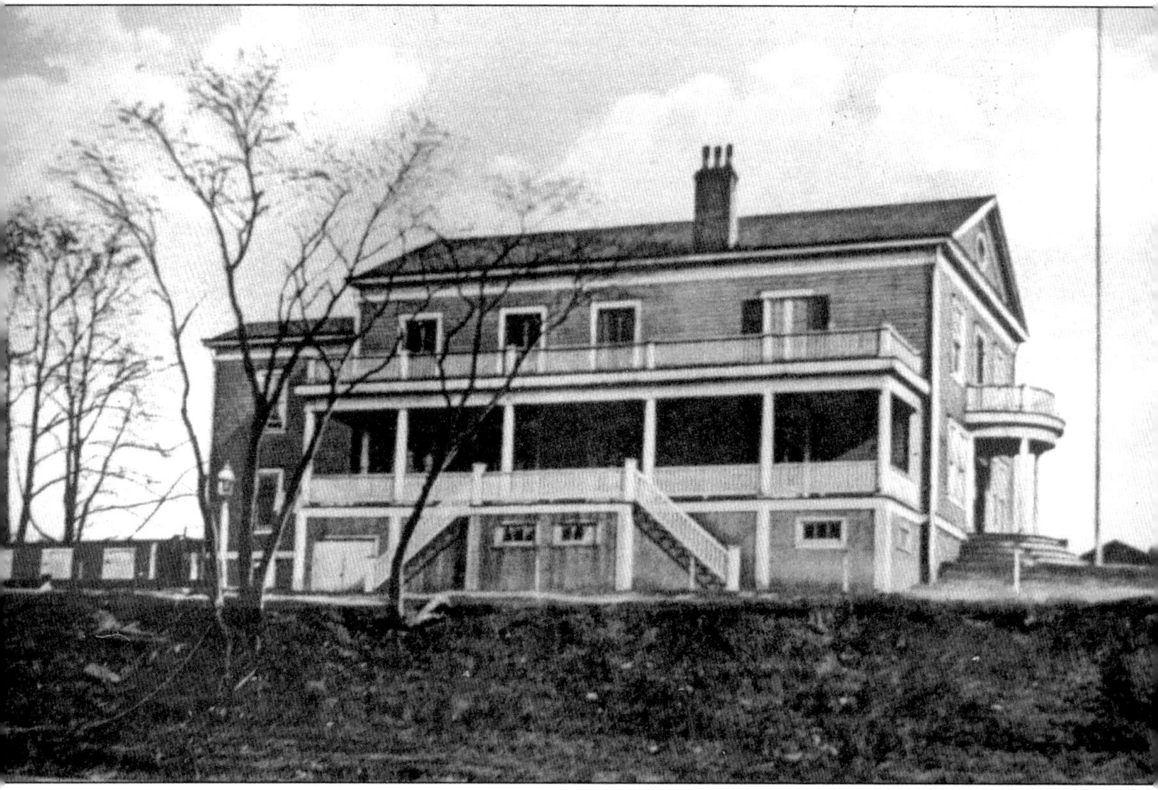

Today's Oakmont Yacht Club was known as the Oakmont Boat Club when this photograph of the clubhouse at the bottom of Washington Avenue was taken in 1909. This riverside view features the clubhouse's long porch, a favorite vantage point from which to watch the regattas the club still sponsors annually. Founded on July 4, 1903, by C.V. Tiers and some of his friends, the Oakmont club is the oldest inland yacht club in the United States. The club's first clubhouse was a rented houseboat of questionable river-worthiness. The earliest members had to agree to take turns sleeping aboard the houseboat so they could adjust the lines to suit the conditions on the Allegheny and man the bilge pumps in the event that the boat took on water, which it did with some regularity. The club's first fleet consisted mostly of rowboats, with canoes and sailboats added in later years. Motor boats were introduced in 1916. The Oakmont Yacht Club's current fleet includes houseboats and cruisers.

Three

Shaping a Community

When the Hulton Bridge was dedicated, a Pittsburgh newspaper rhapsodized, "Surely there is not a community anywhere, and especially one so close to our great city, offering the attractions which glisten from all sides of Oakmont." The start of a new decade brought more such attractions, like the town's first movie house, the Delmont Theater, later renamed the Lehigh, on C Street, and a new high school, which opened in 1912 at Fifth Street and Pennsylvania Avenue.

Several Oakmont streets that had retained the same names since the town was part of Verona were renamed in 1912. A, B, C, D, E, G, and I Streets became California, Washington, Delaware, Maryland, Pennsylvania, Virginia, and Woodland Avenues. H Street became Hulton Road, and West Railroad Avenue became Allegheny Avenue. That same year, the newly named streets began getting newly installed electric streetlights.

The Best Manufacturing Company closed in 1916, but not before the company's owner created the beautiful Best Company Park on Washington Avenue. The Best plant was taken over by Edgewater Steel.

The new borough building, constructed in 1917 at Fifth Street and Virginia Avenue, also included a police station with three jail cells. The station was the first real home for the police department since its founding in 1899.

When the United States entered World War I, a training camp for the 15th Army Engineers was set up on the Pyle farm just outside of town. Residents often visited the soldiers at the camp and even gathered at the railroad station to see them off when they left for overseas duty. After the war, those who fought were not forgotten. In 1923, Oakmont honored them by erecting a veterans memorial monument on the grounds of the library.

To better serve the town's 4,512 residents, the fire department was reorganized as the Oakmont Volunteer Fire Company in 1921 and bought its first fire truck. Four years later, they fought one of the town's biggest fires when the Willows nightclub burned. Oakmont was not without a Willows facility long. The Willows pool debut was in June 1926 and took youngsters' minds off the new school year, which was marked by the opening of two new schools: the Tenth Street School and St. Irenaeus School.

Oakmont's economy got a boost in 1927 with the opening of the Thompson Paint Company plant and Edgewater Steel's purchase of additional property for a planned expansion. The town's morale got a boost the following year, when the Willows reopened.

Throughout the 1920s, poor children from Pittsburgh could escape the city's oppressive heat and spend two weeks in the summer at the Fresh Air Fund home that was between Ninth and Tenth Streets and operated by the Pittsburgh Association for the Improvement of the Poor.

Most of these happenings were chronicled in the Allegheny *Advance* newspaper. Local resident Len Anderson bought the paper and brought it to town in 1929, just in time to report the local impact of that year's market crash.

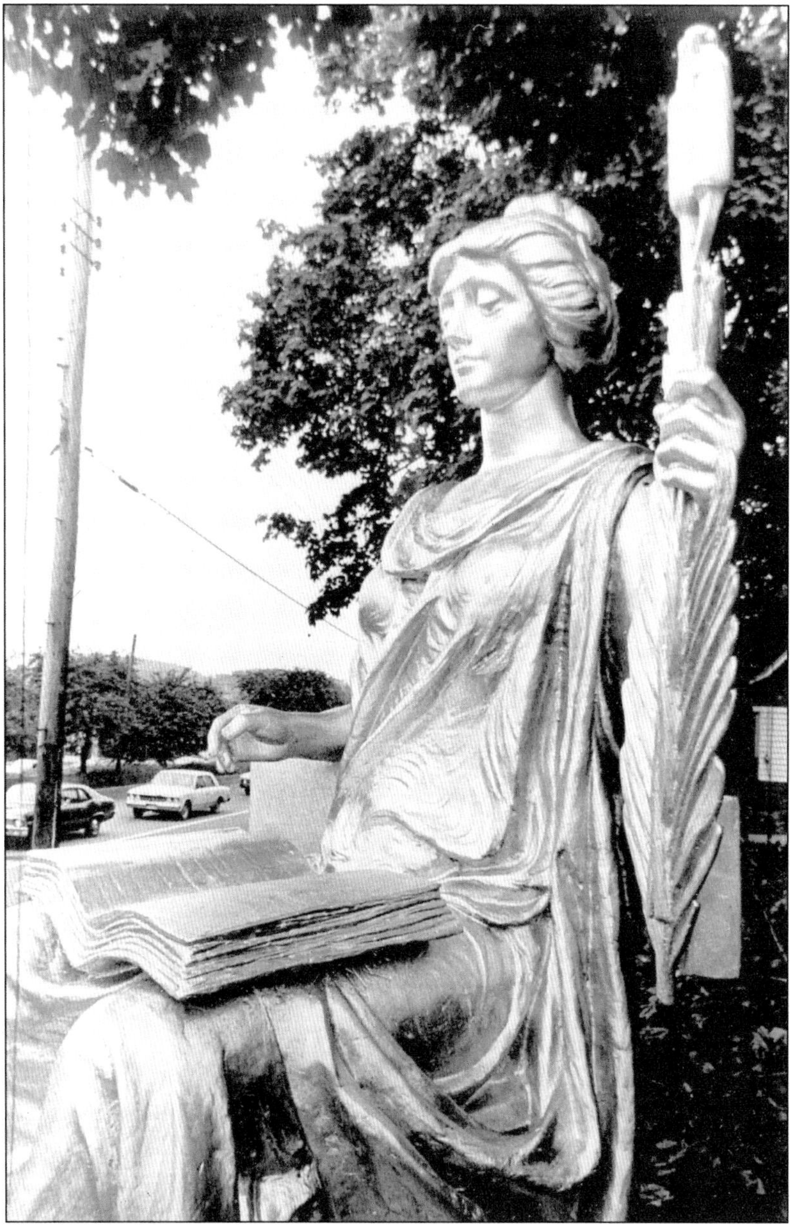

"Democracy holding the torch of Liberty in the left hand while on its knee rests a large book representing the great record of American Democracy past, present and future," reads the sculptor's description of the statue that is the centerpiece of the war memorial on the Oakmont Carnegie Library grounds at Allegheny River Boulevard and Pennsylvania Avenue. Local attorney Frank F. Canuti conceived the idea of a monument to memorialize Oakmonters who served in defense of the nation. In June 1922, Canuti organized the Oakmont Memorial Association to plan the monument. J. Vittori, a prominent Pittsburgh sculptor, was commissioned to design the monument and sculpt the figure of Democracy. The $7,000 cost of the memorial was raised by public subscription. To promote donations, the memorial association gave each subscriber an engraved copy of the memorial and the artist's description. The monument was dedicated in ceremonies held on May 25, 1924.

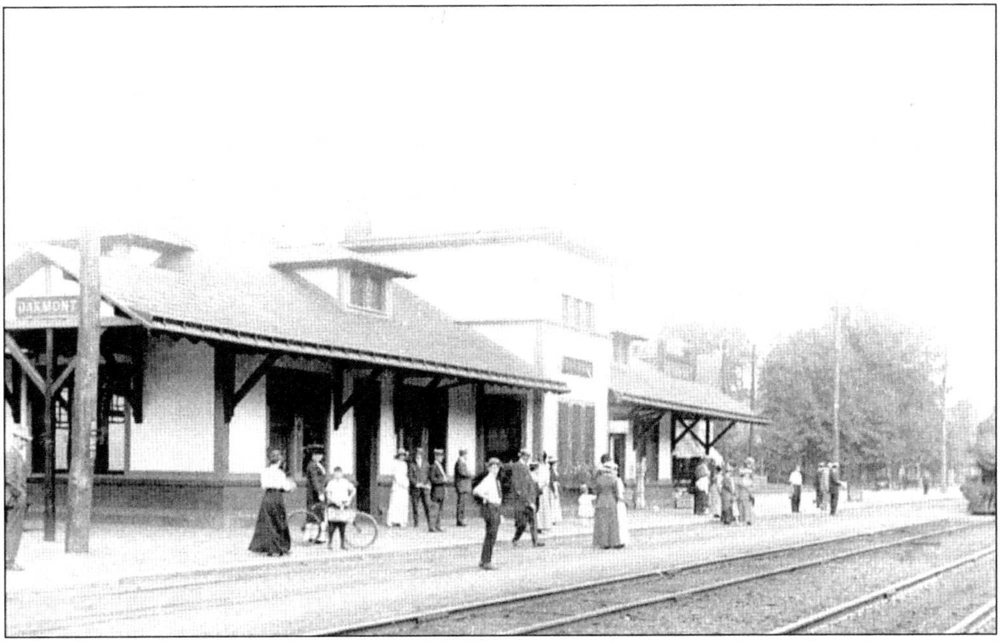

Oakmont once was served by three railroad stations. This station, located in the center of town between Delaware and Maryland Avenues, was the newest of the three stations and the last to survive. It served the town until passenger service on the Pennsylvania Railroad was discontinued in the 1960s and was demolished in June 1970.

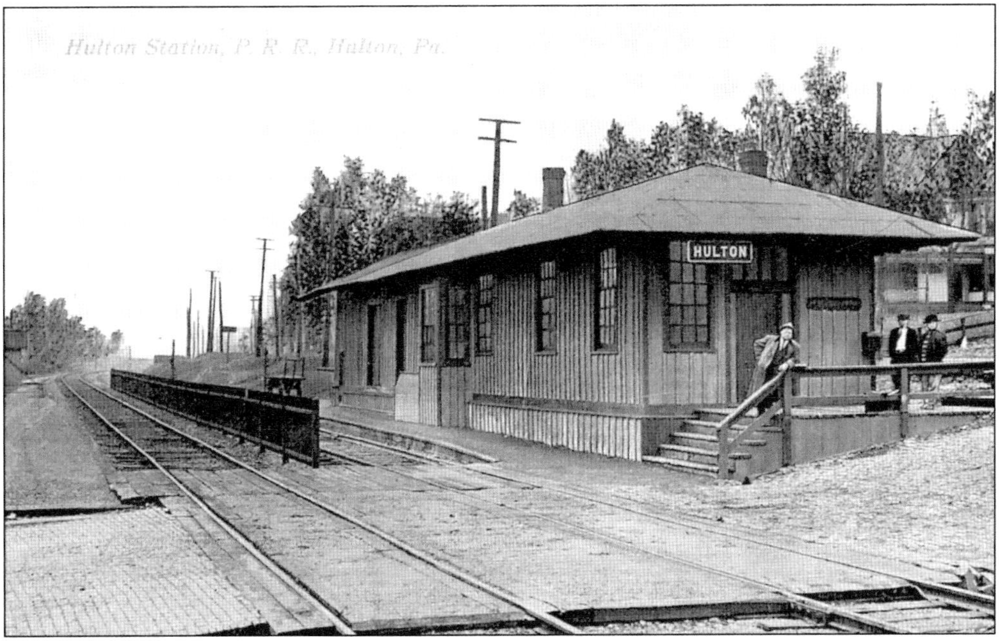

The Hulton station was on the north end of town, near Hulton Road. When passenger service was consolidated at the station in the center of town, the Hulton station was converted into a freight station. It closed in July 1933 and was moved to East Oakmont, where it served as a storage building before being destroyed by fire in the 1950s.

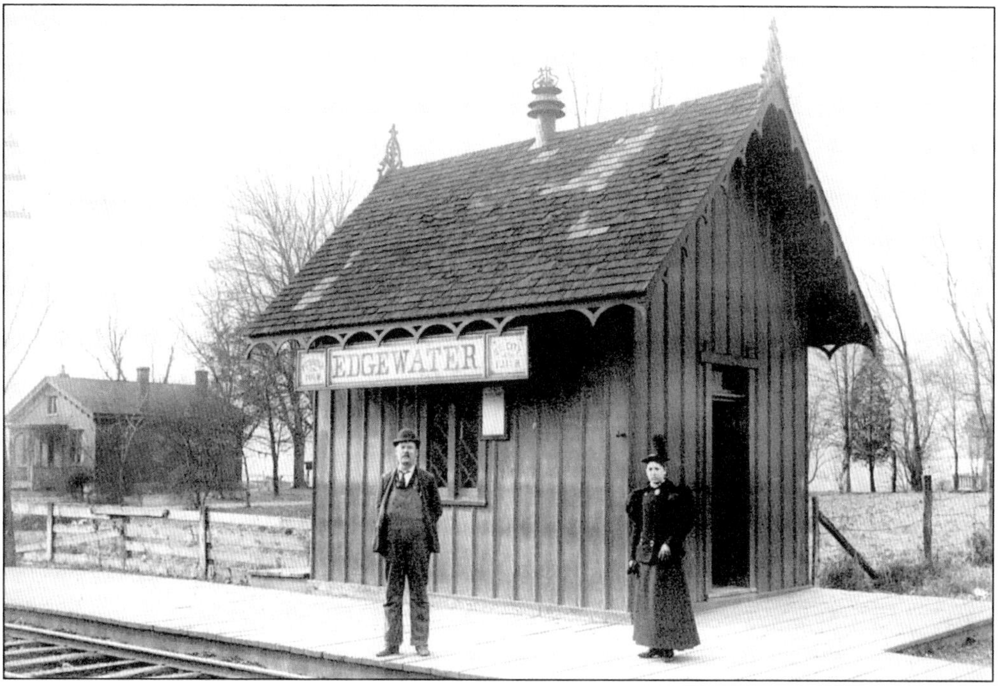

The Edgewater Railroad Station was at College Avenue near the Edgewater Steel plant. Behind the station was the riverside estate of John McD. Crossan, owner of the Monongahela House Hotel in Pittsburgh. The brick house on the left still sits on the Edgewater Steel property. The station sign carried the next train departures: 10:00 a.m. to Pittsburgh and 12:15 p.m. to Oil City.

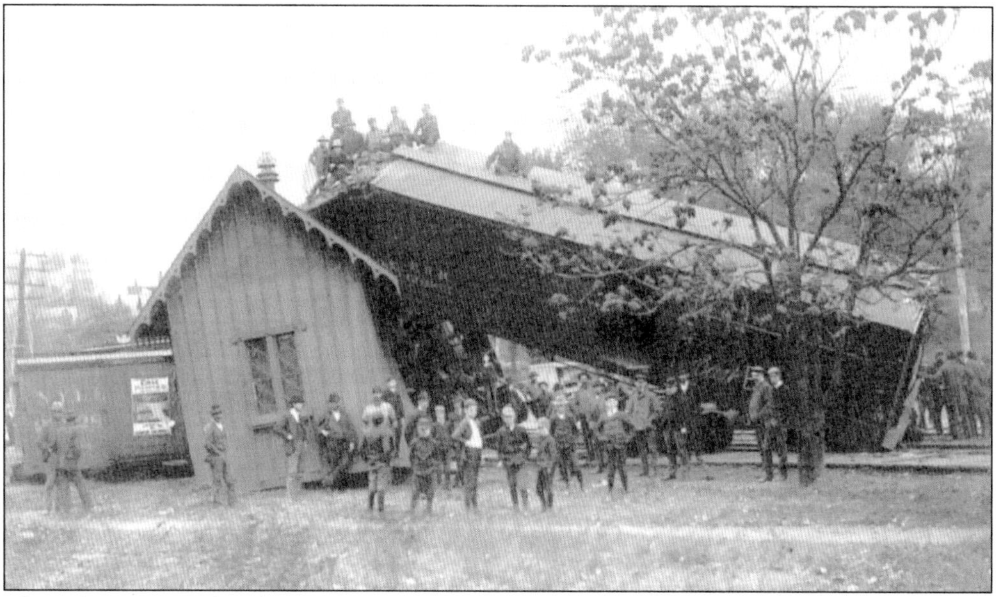

The Edgewater Railroad Station was almost totally destroyed when a freight train jumped the tracks and slammed into it. Some of the crowed attracted to the accident scene sat atop the precariously perched freight car to pose for the photographer. The accident so frightened Rebecca Fisher, the station agent, that after the station was rebuilt, she ran from the building every time a train passed by.

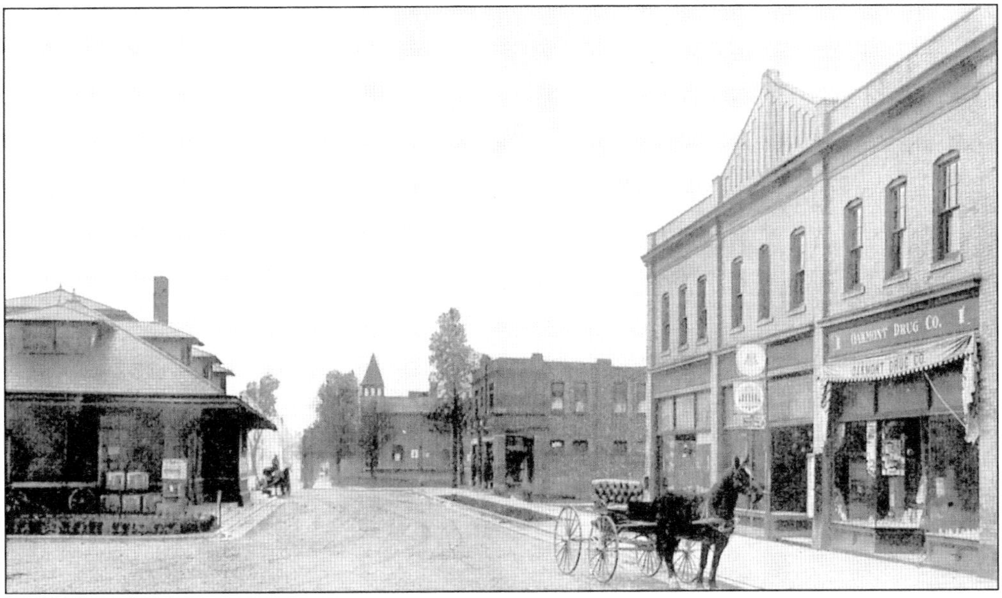

Except for horses and buggies, this part of West Railroad Avenue, now Allegheny Avenue, remained mostly unchanged until June 1970, when the railroad station (left) was demolished. The building on the right, now Hoffstot's Restaurant and Café Monaco, housed a drugstore and two shops. The building in the center now is Chelsea Grille. The spire of what now is the Riverside Community Church is seen in the background.

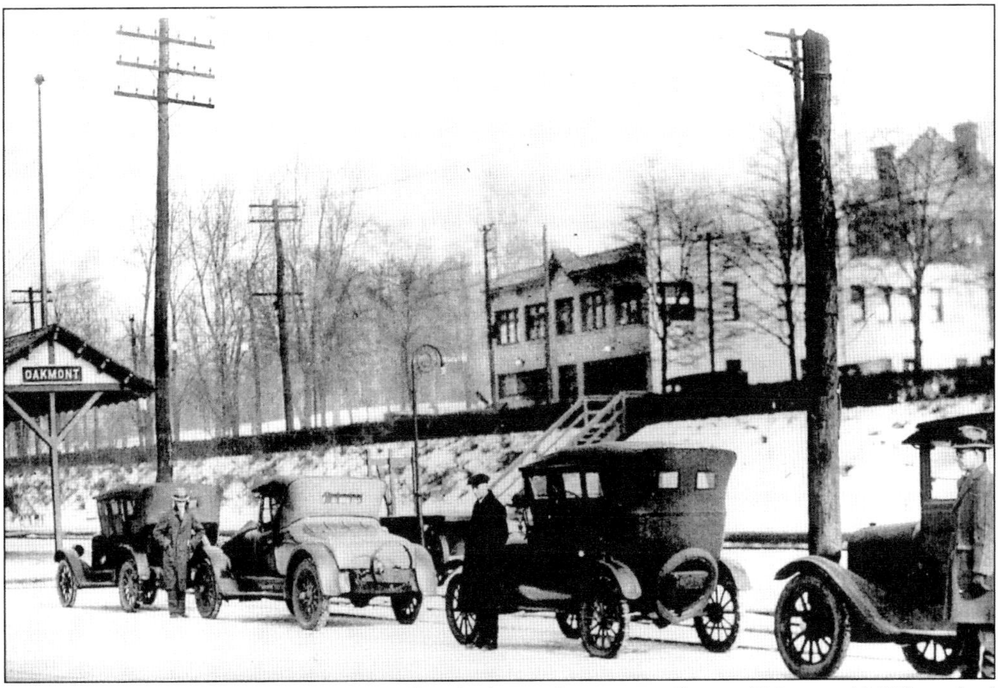

A fire that destroyed the Oakmont Bell Telephone Company office in February 1925 knocked out all telephone service in town. The telephone company was able to route calls to the Oakmont train station, where messengers, shown here standing next to their cars, picked up transcribed telephone messages and delivered them to the town's residents and businesses.

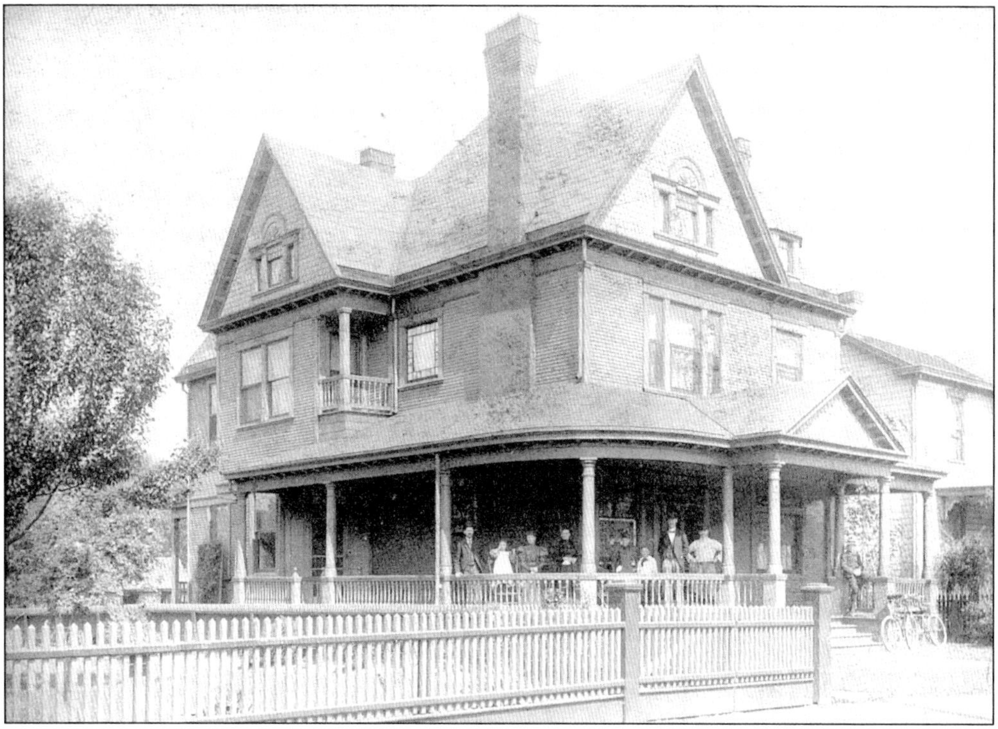

J.M. Witherspoon's family and friends pose on the wraparound porch of the Witherspoon home on West Railroad Avenue, which was renamed Allegheny Avenue in 1912. The bicycles near the front steps on the right were the preferred mode of local transportation at the time. The Witherspoon home was demolished in 1983.

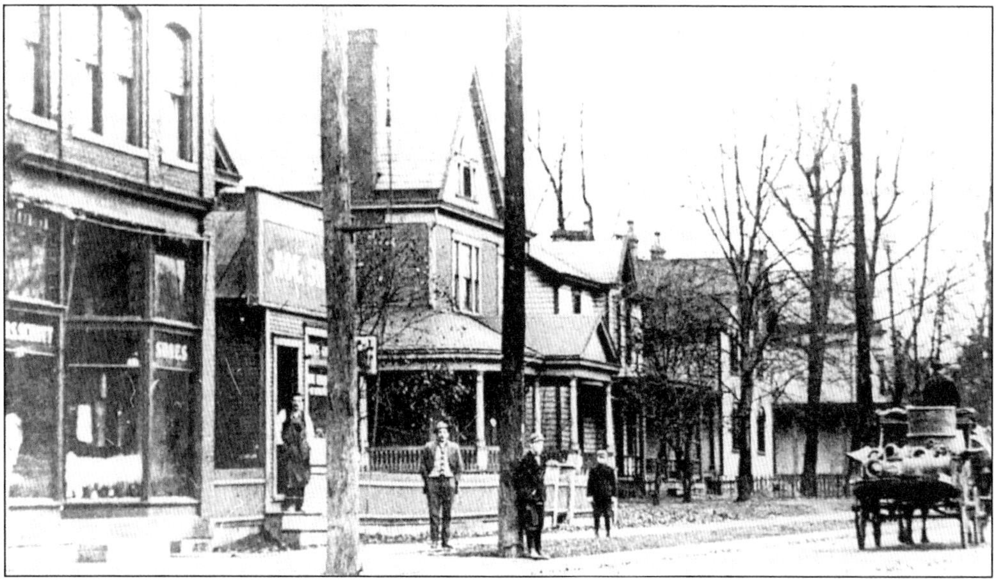

As the saying goes, location is everything, even on what was then West Railroad Avenue. The shop on the left is a shoe store and right next door is a shoe-repair and shoe-shine shop, with the apron-wearing proprietor waiting to serve customers. The J.M. Witherspoon family home is on the right of the shoe-shine shop.

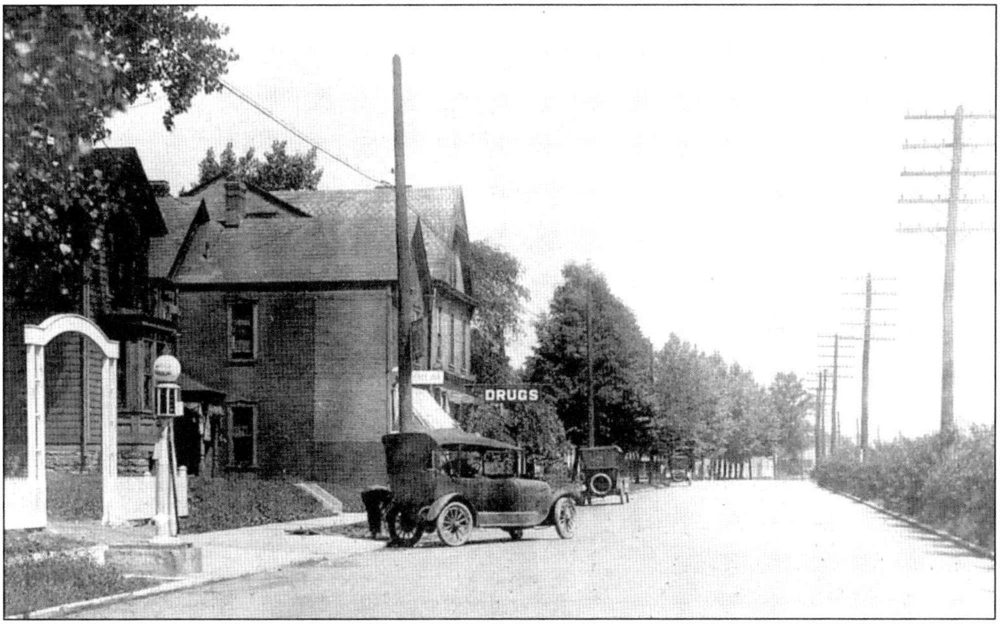

One of Oakmont's earliest gasoline stations was located on Allegheny Avenue. The curbside gas pump on the left dispensed Waverly gasoline, according to the name on its glass globe. The man bending behind his automobile is taking advantage of the free air advertised on the utility pole to inflate his tires.

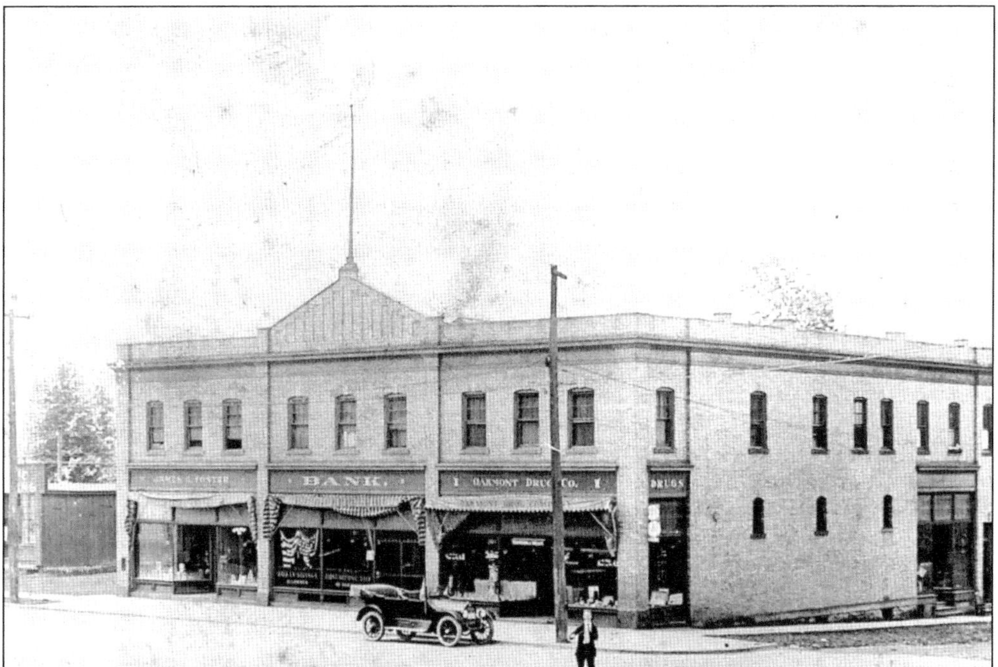

In 1910, when this photograph was taken, the building on Allegheny Avenue at Maryland Avenue that today is Hoffstot's Restaurant and Café Monaco, housed three businesses: James G. Foster's store (left), the First National Bank of Oakmont (center), and the Oakmont Drug Company.

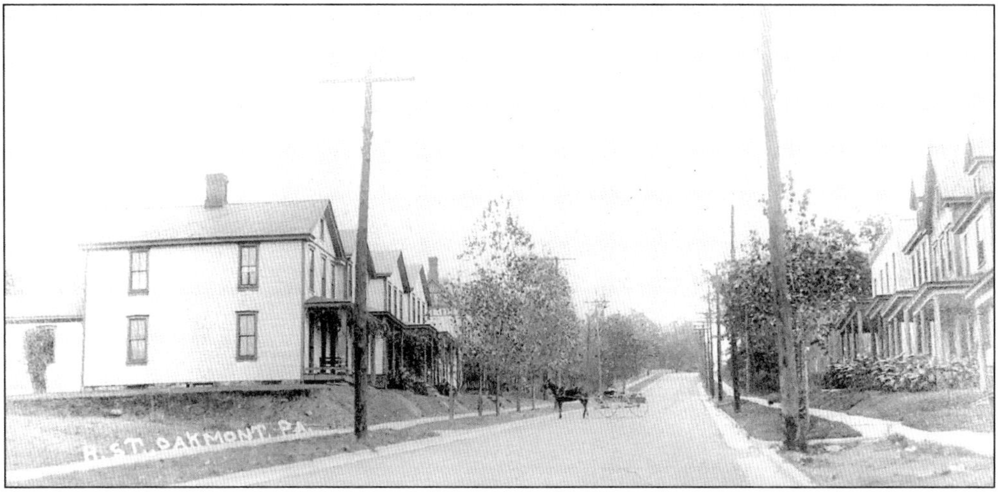

Busy Hulton Road, then called H Street, was not busy when this photograph was taken in 1912. Only one horse-drawn wagon can be seen. Today, there is a steady stream of cars, trucks, and buses here. Oakmont began putting up streetlights in 1912, but installation work had not yet reached Hulton Road at the time of this photograph.

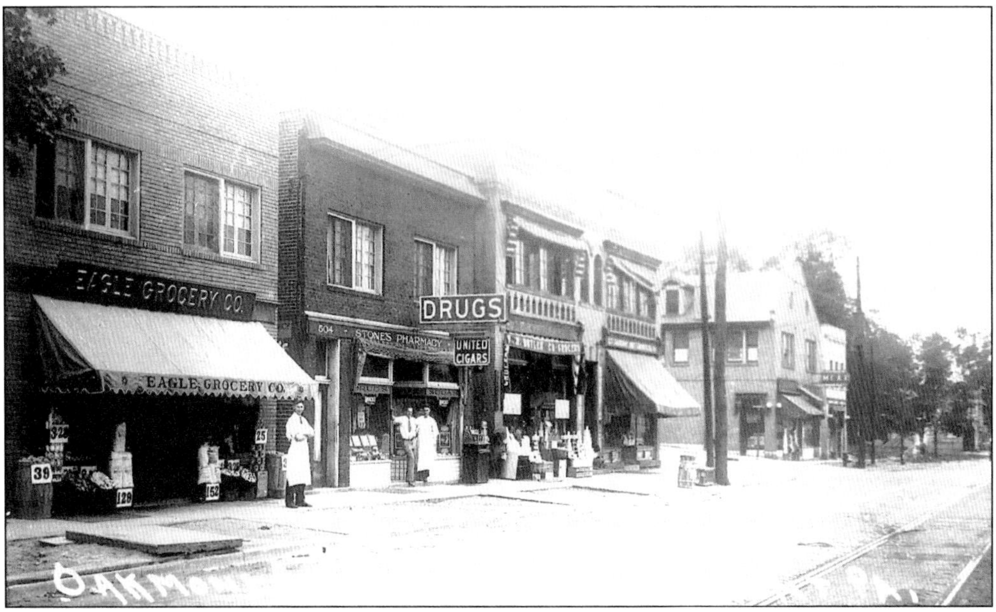

Some of Oakmont's main-street merchants pose in front of their stores near the intersection of Allegheny River Boulevard and Delaware Avenue in this 1928 photograph. The Eagle Grocery Company store is on the left, next to Stone's Pharmacy, which was still in business 50 years later. Notice the streetcar tracks that ran along the curb opposite the stores.

The Lehigh Theater on Delaware Avenue was called the Delmont when it opened as Oakmont's first motion picture house c. 1910. *Barbara Frietchie* was the featured movie when this photograph was taken. The Lehigh was owned by Stephen M. Rodnok, who later built and operated the Oaks Theater on Allegheny River Boulevard.

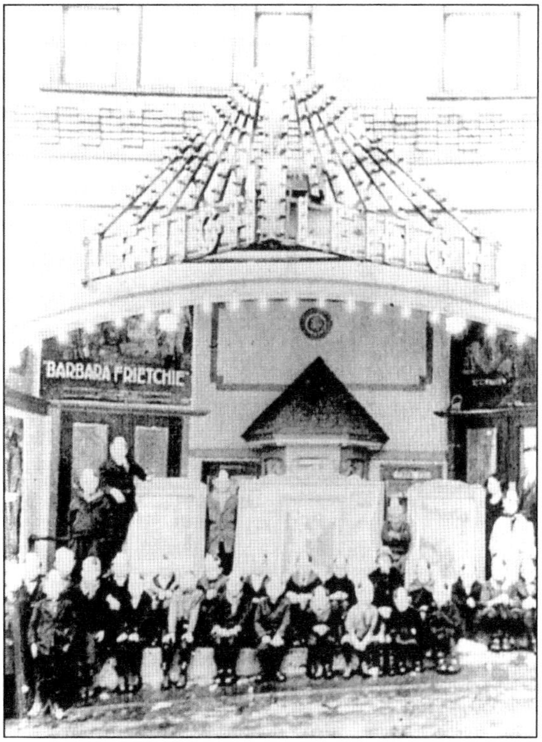

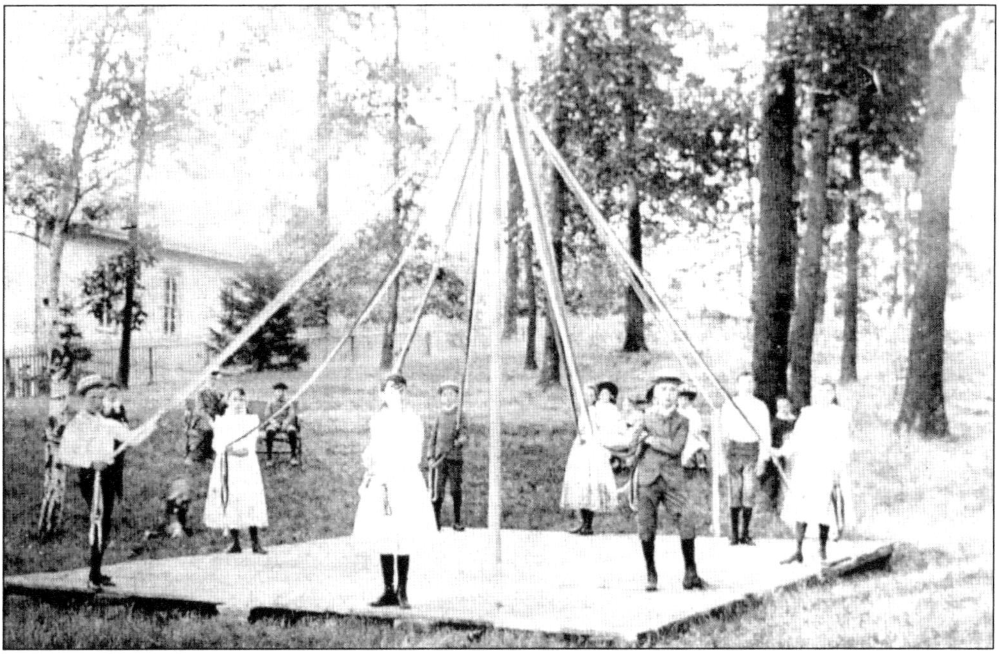

These children enjoyed a dance around a Maypole on the Arensberg family's property on Maryland Avenue between Allegheny River Boulevard and Fourth Street. When this photograph was taken, the building in the left rear, formerly the United Presbyterian Church, was the Oakmont Lyceum. It is now the Oakmont American Legion post. The Arensberg property was where the St. Irenaeus Catholic church and school now are located.

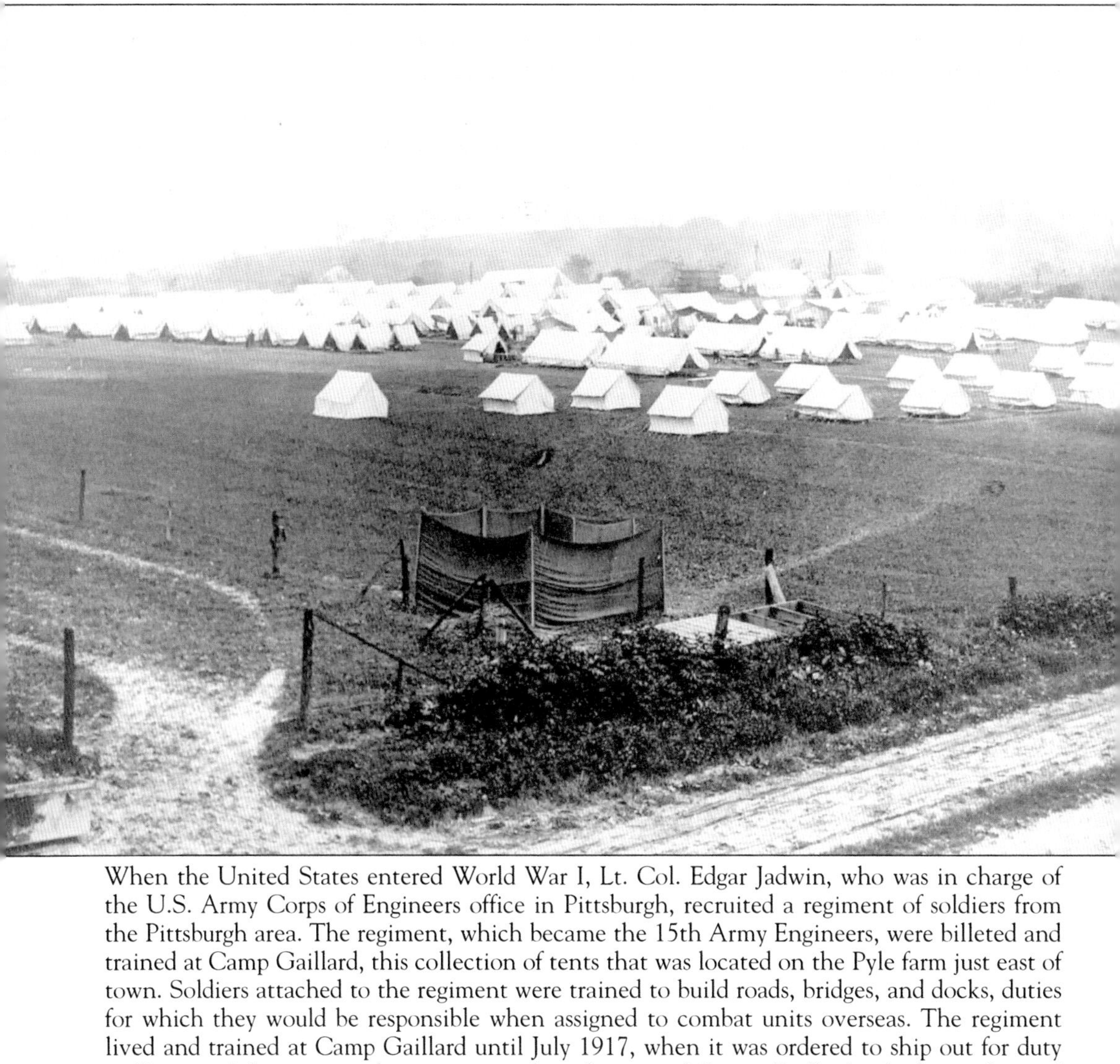

When the United States entered World War I, Lt. Col. Edgar Jadwin, who was in charge of the U.S. Army Corps of Engineers office in Pittsburgh, recruited a regiment of soldiers from the Pittsburgh area. The regiment, which became the 15th Army Engineers, were billeted and trained at Camp Gaillard, this collection of tents that was located on the Pyle farm just east of town. Soldiers attached to the regiment were trained to build roads, bridges, and docks, duties for which they would be responsible when assigned to combat units overseas. The regiment lived and trained at Camp Gaillard until July 1917, when it was ordered to ship out for duty in Europe. A historic marker was erected at the site of Camp Gaillard, which was located approximately where the Oakmont service plaza on the Pennsylvania Turnpike now stands.

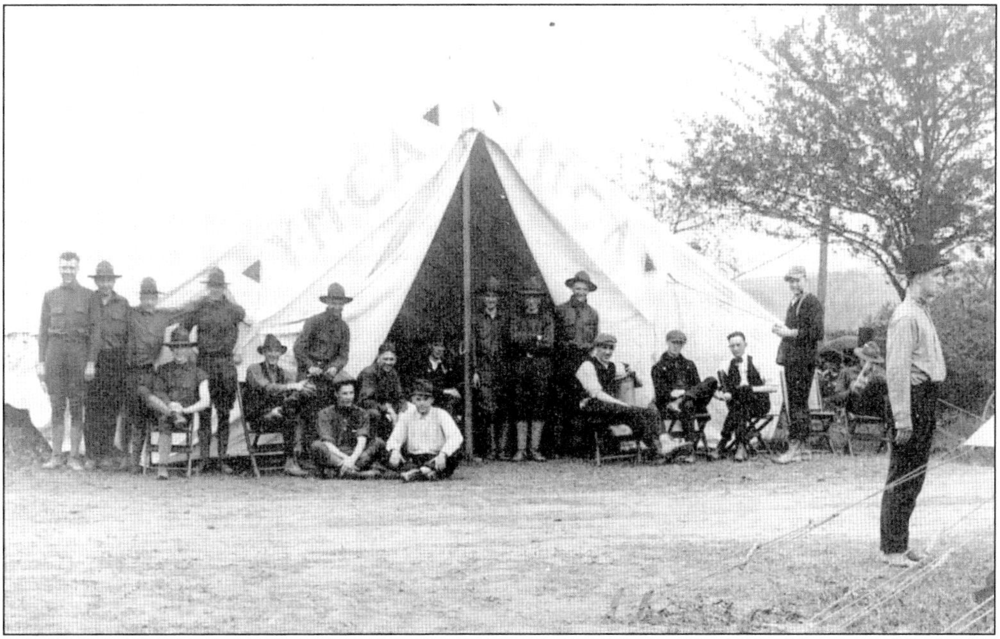

Area residents, groups, and associations rallied around the soldiers who were training at Camp Gaillard and frequently visited the camp. The YMCA maintained a tent at the camp to provide soldiers an opportunity to relax away from the rigors of training.

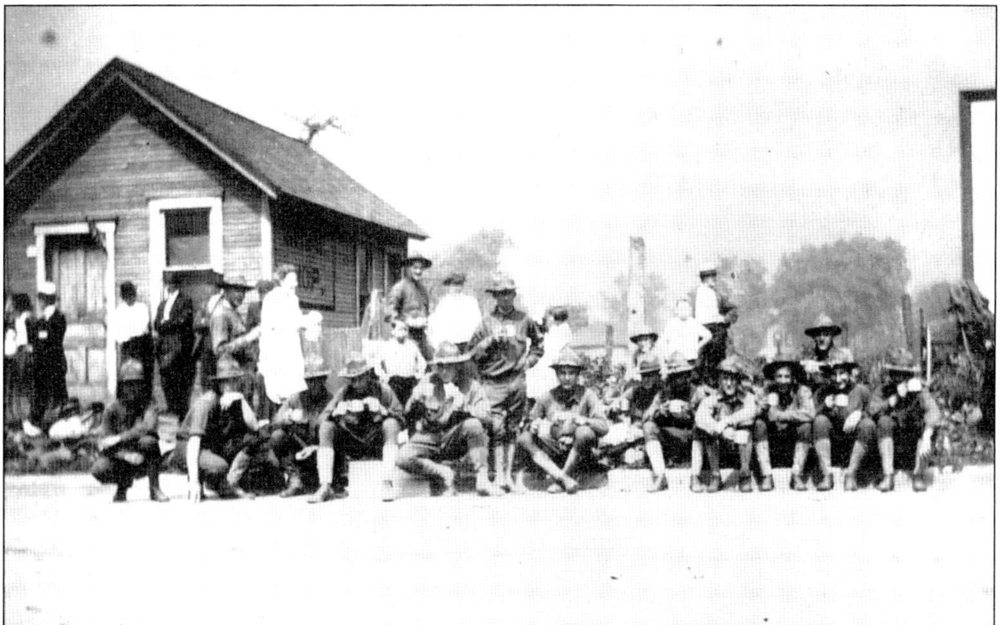

Oakmonters turned out to say goodbye to the soldiers of the 15th Army Engineers when they broke camp on the Pyle farm in July 1917 and assembled at the railroad station to await the train that would take them to their embarkation point for their journey overseas. Residents brought the men cold drinks and snacks and kept them company while they waited.

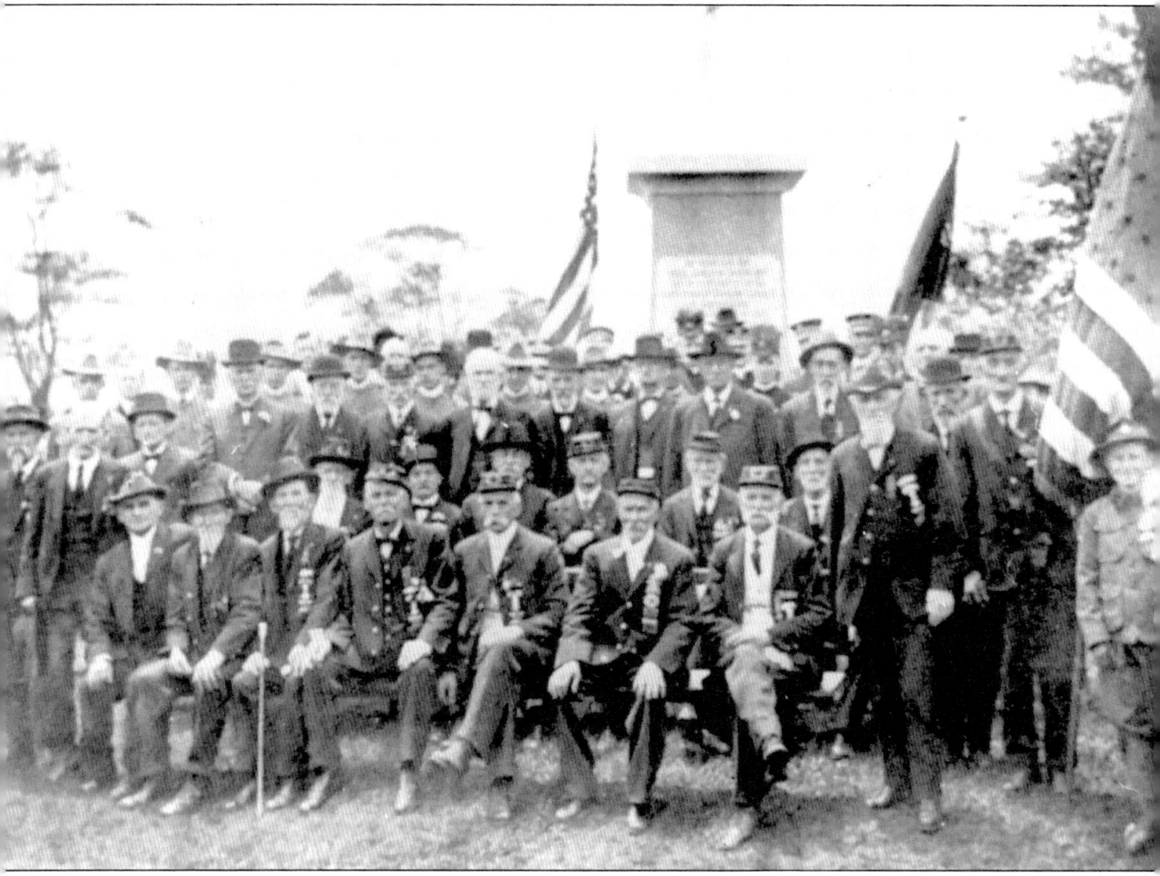

In 1917, Civil War veterans gathered for the town's celebration of what then was called Decoration Day and now is Memorial Day. They were photographed in the Verona-Oakmont Cemetery in front of the monument honoring Union Army soldiers. The monument was erected in 1915. The youngster in the Boy Scout uniform on the right likely was one of the marchers in the parade that preceded this gathering.

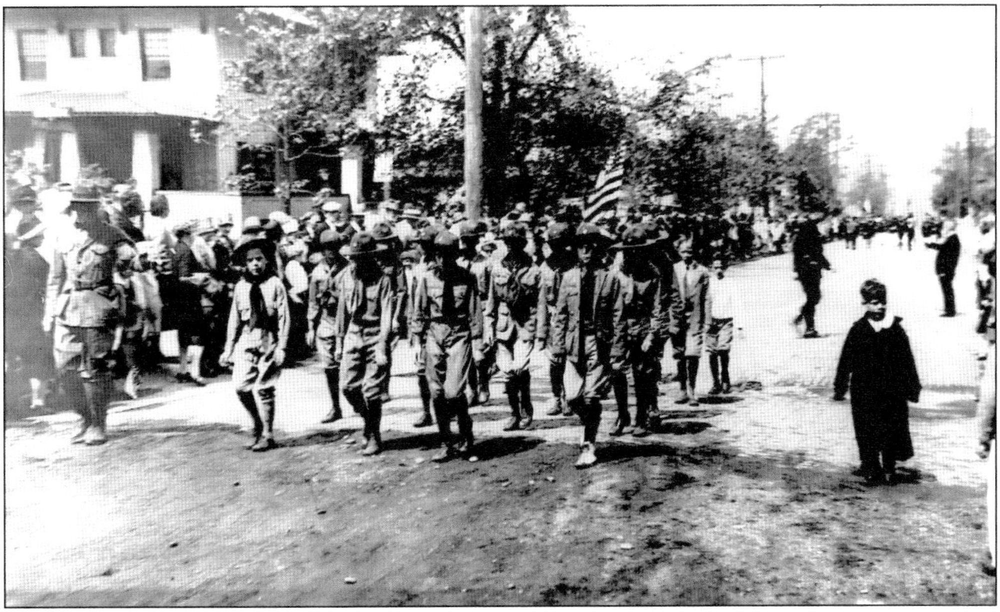

Boy Scouts marching in a Decoration Day parade approach Tenth Street after climbing steep Pennsylvania Avenue. They are probably relieved that the end of their march is just a few feet away. Note that the brick pavement on Pennsylvania gave way to dirt at the intersection. A continuing tradition, the parade began in Verona and ended with a memorial ceremony at the monument in the cemetery atop Pennsylvania Avenue.

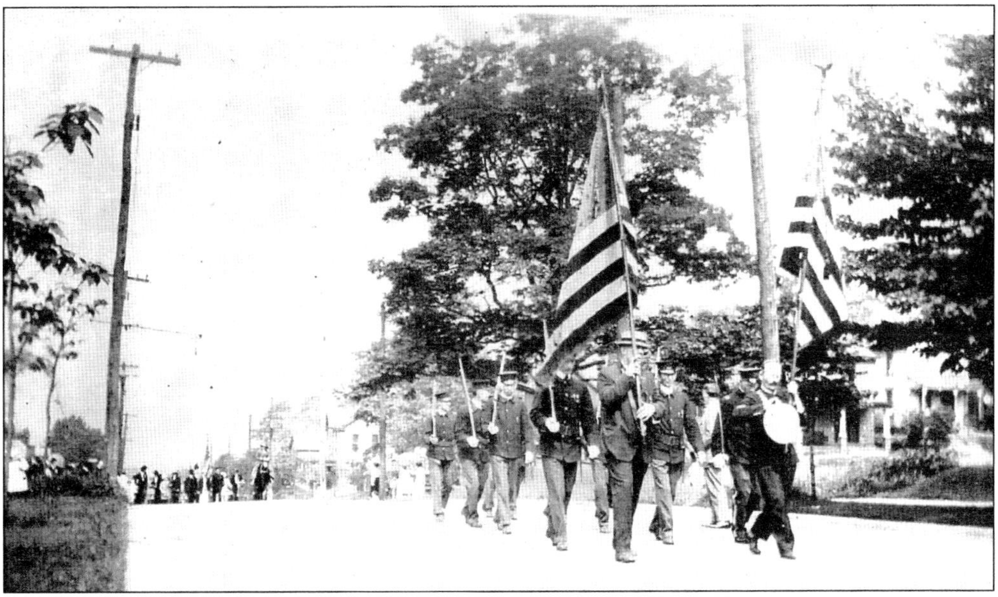

Marchers in the 1918 Oakmont-Verona Decoration Day parade have reached Ninth Street at the top of Pennsylvania Avenue after having marched from Verona. The parade then followed the same route as the annual Memorial Day parade does today. The next contingent of marchers, seen approaching the crest of the hill on the left, were led by a woman on horseback.

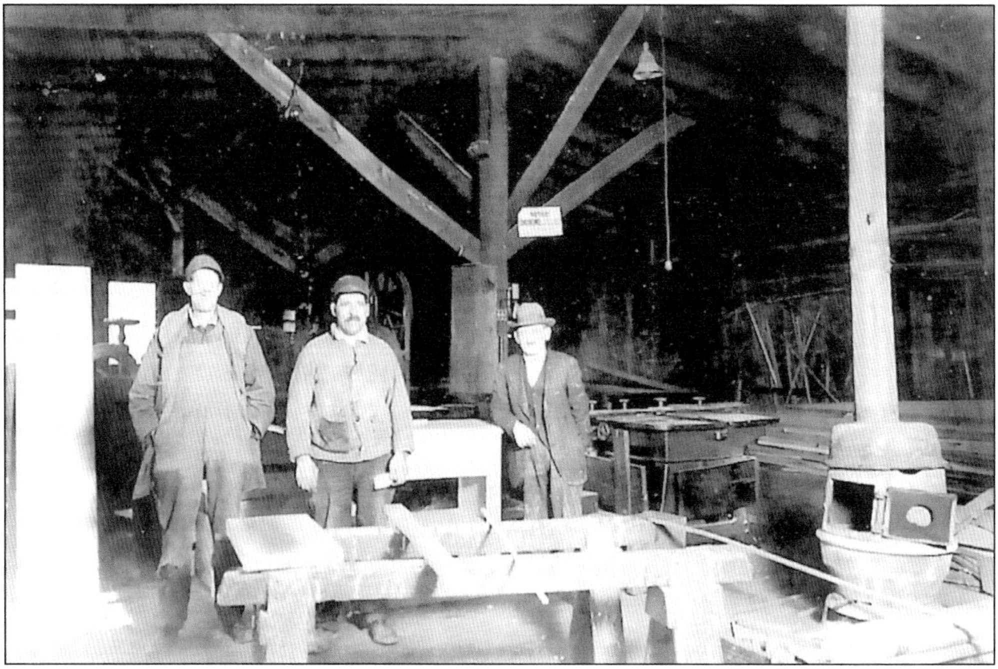

Reed's Lumber Mill was located on Cedar Way, behind where the Oakmont Water Authority building now stands. Mr. Reed, the owner, is shown on the right in this 1910 photograph. In the center is Frank Furko Sr., who worked at the mill for several years. The workman on the left is not identified. The potbelly stove was the only source of heat in the cavernous building.

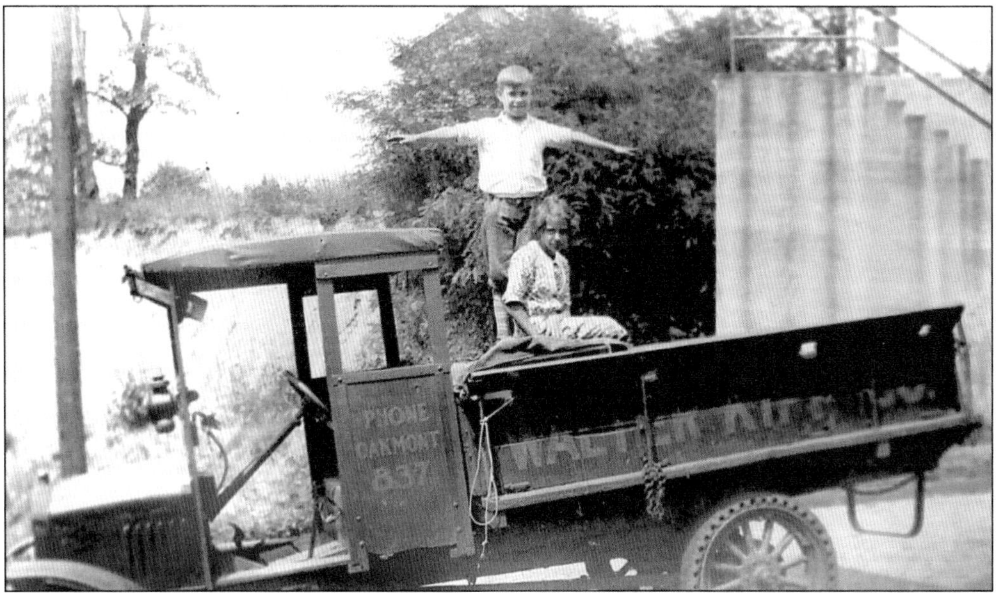

When they telephoned Oakmont 837 in the 1920s, local residents could order ice to be delivered to their homes and businesses by the iceman, Walter Kipp. When the Kipp delivery truck was not hauling ice around town, it sometimes served as a place to play for the owner's children, Janet and Walter Jr.

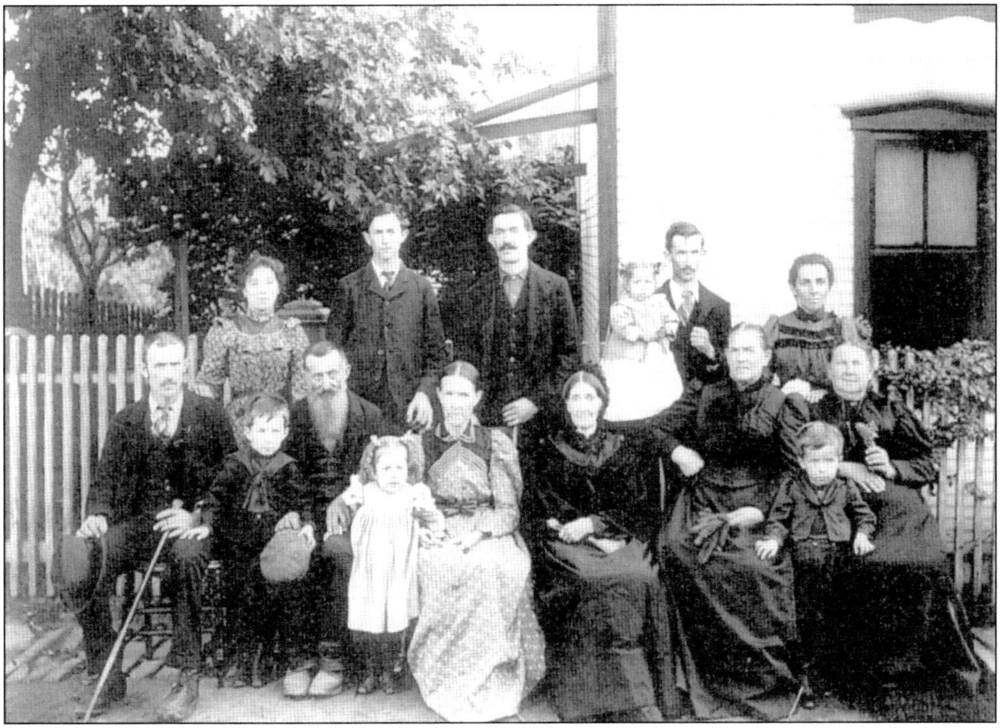

John King emigrated from Germany in the early 1900s. He built a house on D Street and ran a farm on the hill. The bearded family patriarch is shown with his wife Sarah (seated fifth from the left), his family, and friends. The group posed for this photograph in the yard of the King's home, which still stands at 914 Maryland Avenue.

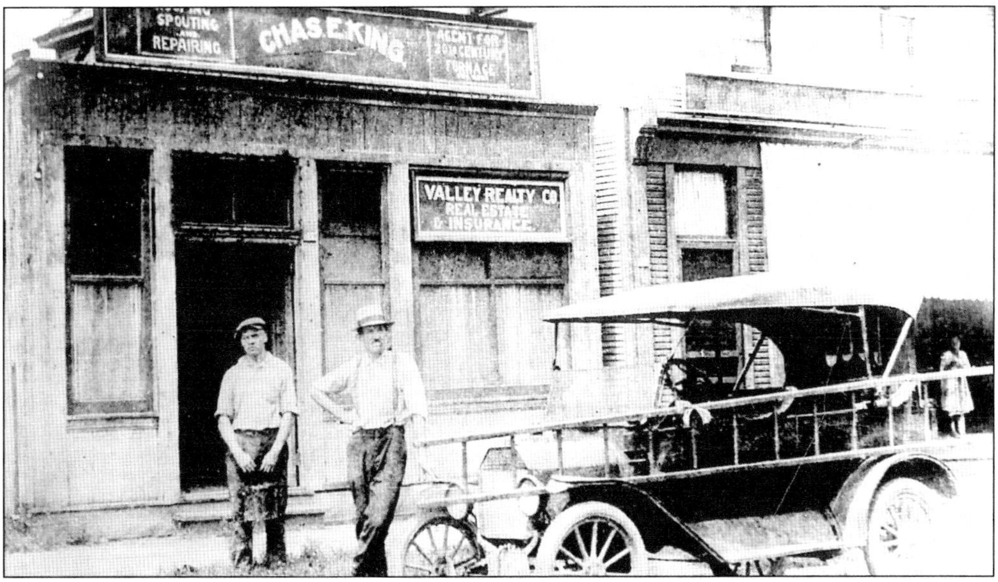

Charles E. King opened his heating and roofing business in 1918 at 761 Allegheny Avenue. Three generations of the King family operated the business until it closed in 1991, when it was located on Pennsylvania Avenue. King (right) and his brother-in-law, Charles Baxter, are shown with a Model T Ford that had been converted into a service truck.

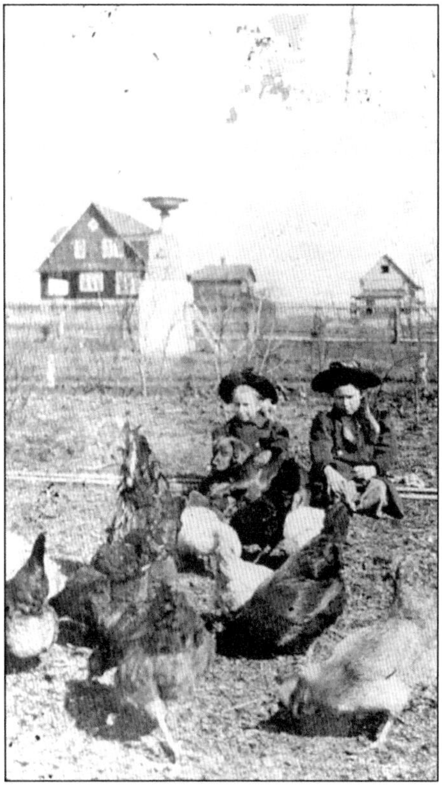

These photographs, taken years apart, are different views of the same property on Washington Avenue between Eighth and Ninth Streets, as evidenced by the presence in both of what appears to be a monument or an elaborate planter. In the photograph on the left, taken when the property was a chicken farm, the monument is behind the two children who are watching the chickens feed. In the later photograph, below, it is on the island in the lake that had been installed on the property. The home in the upper left corner of the photograph on the left still stands at 910 Washington Avenue. The roofed open building seen in the rear in the photograph below is a summerhouse that had several benches, an ideal place to sit, relax, and enjoy the idyllic setting.

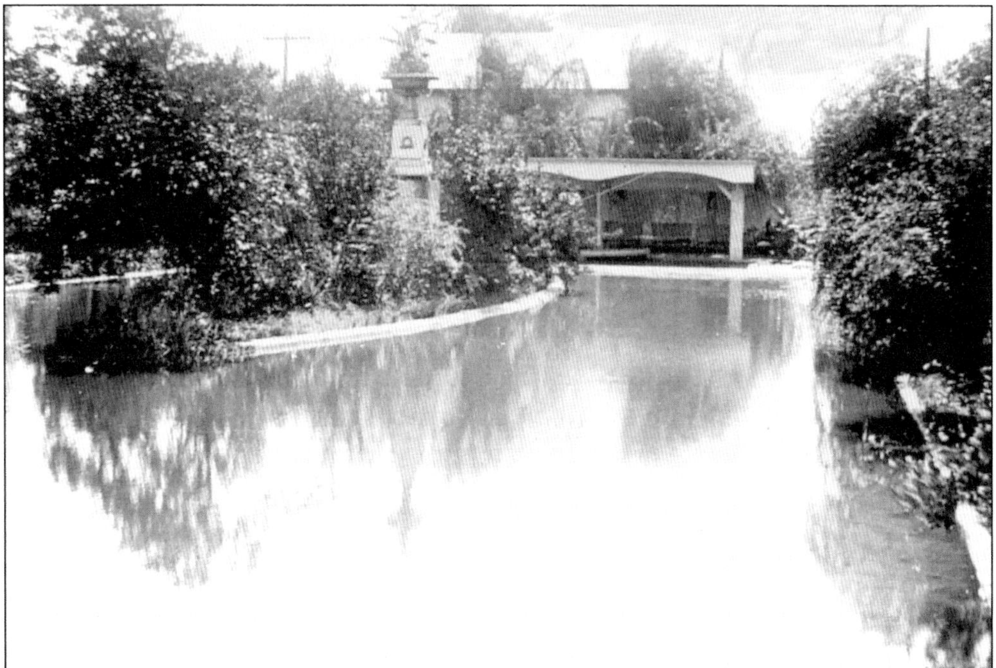

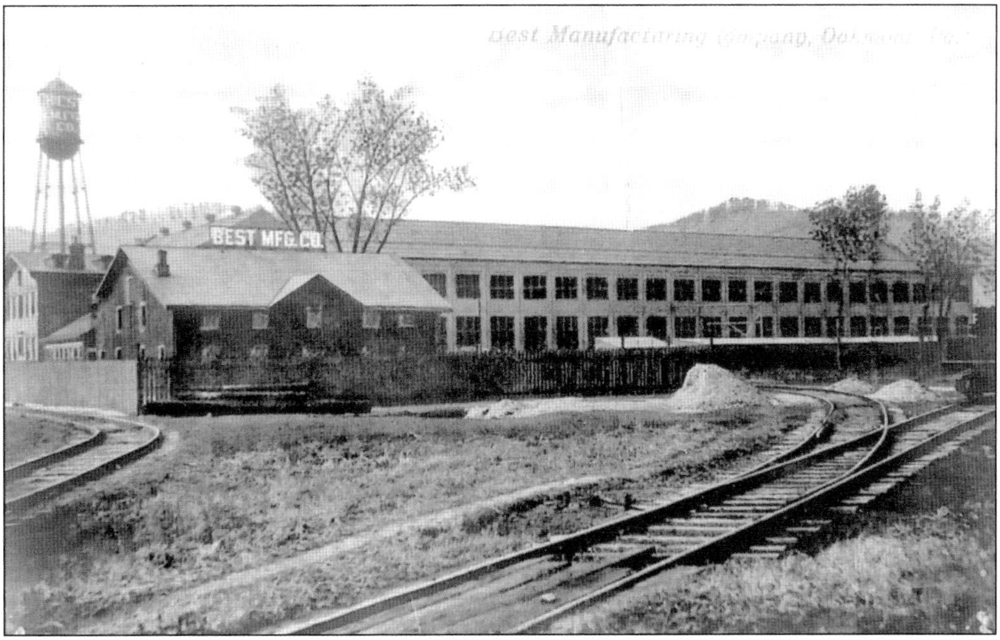

This plant was only partially completed when Best Manufacturing Company moved its pipe and fitting manufacturing operations from Pittsburgh to Oakmont in March 1910. Only six years later, in 1916, the plant on College and Allegheny Avenues was taken over by Edgewater Steel Company.

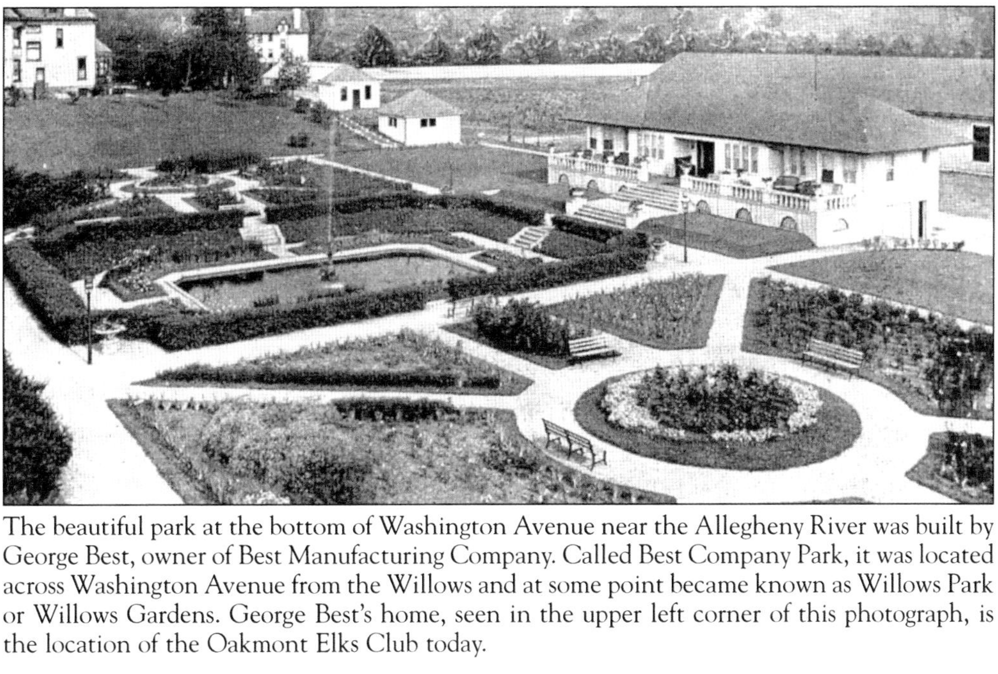

The beautiful park at the bottom of Washington Avenue near the Allegheny River was built by George Best, owner of Best Manufacturing Company. Called Best Company Park, it was located across Washington Avenue from the Willows and at some point became known as Willows Park or Willows Gardens. George Best's home, seen in the upper left corner of this photograph, is the location of the Oakmont Elks Club today.

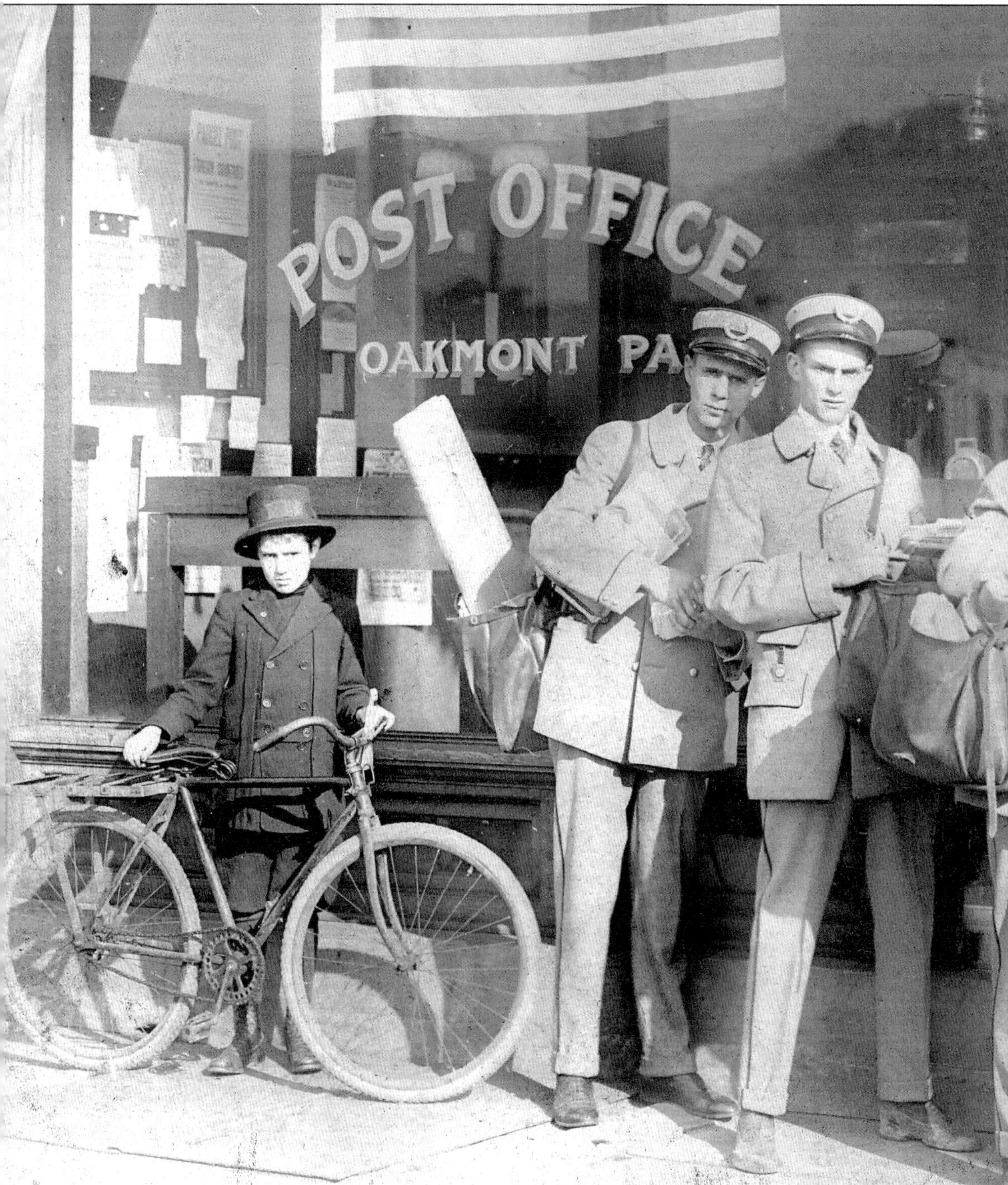

After the Oakmont post office moved from the old Hulton station, it occupied space in at least two other buildings in town before moving into its present building at Allegheny River Boulevard and Maryland Avenue. This photograph was taken in 1916, when the post office was housed in a building, located at today's Allegheny River Boulevard and Delaware Avenue, that earlier had housed the Central Drug Store. Dr. William H. Cooper, a physician and Oakmont's

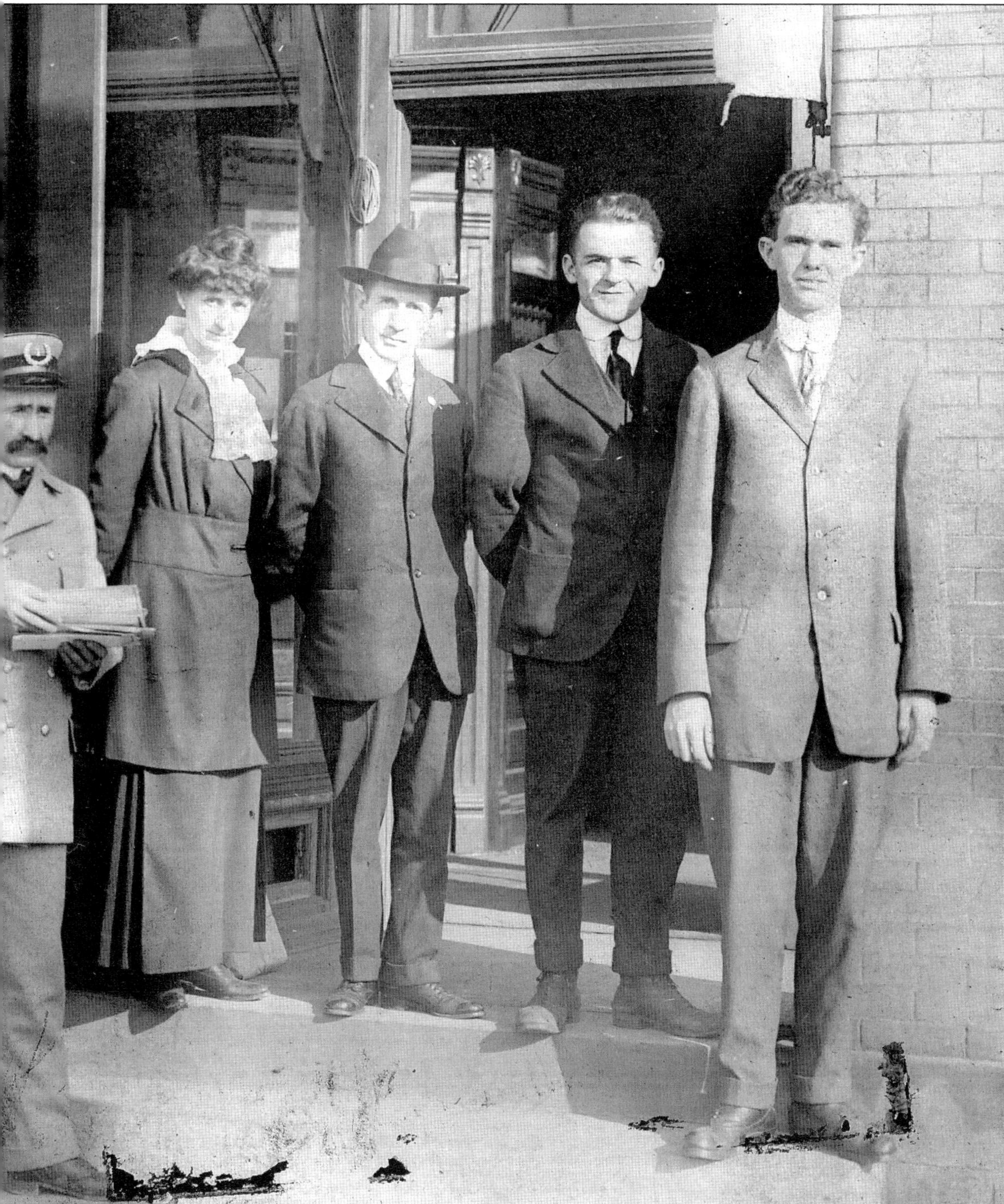

postmaster for many years, is third from the right in this photograph. The boy on the left, Franklin B. Cooper, later a U.S. Army medical doctor, was employed to deliver special delivery mail on his bicycle. Others pictured are, from left to right, mail carriers Frank Householder, Bruce Campbell, and Howard Woozley; and clerks Sara Hardy, John R. Fellows, and William Ashbaugh. The office location now is occupied by Mae's Hallmark greeting card shop.

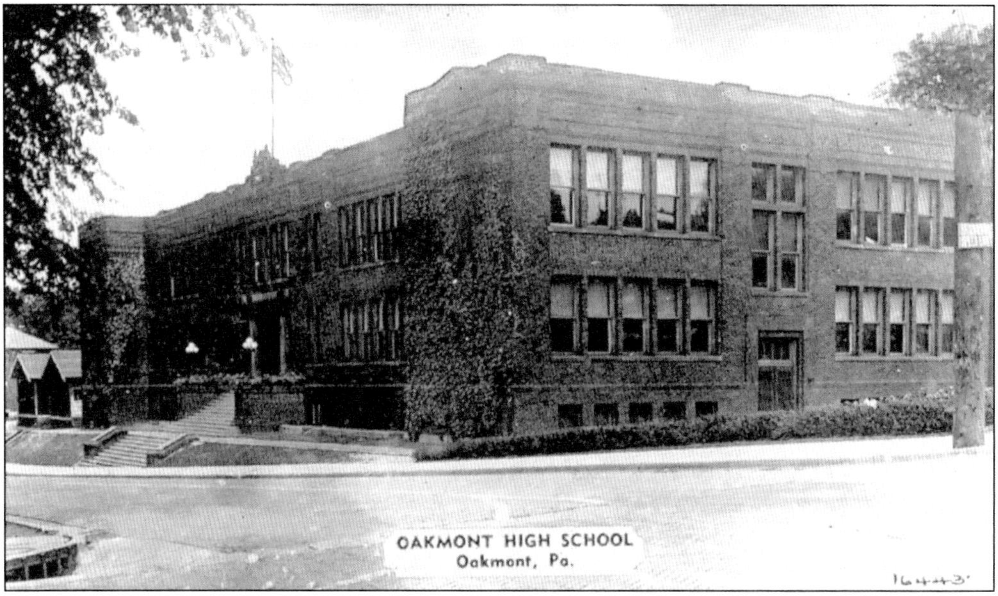

When Oakmont's first high school opened in 1912, 75 students were enrolled. The building at Fifth Street and Pennsylvania Avenue was converted to an elementary school in 1962 and renamed Gilmore School in honor of former superintendent Lee Gilmore. Its beautiful auditorium was the site for many years of stage shows and performances. The building was razed in 1977 to make room for the Angelan apartment complex.

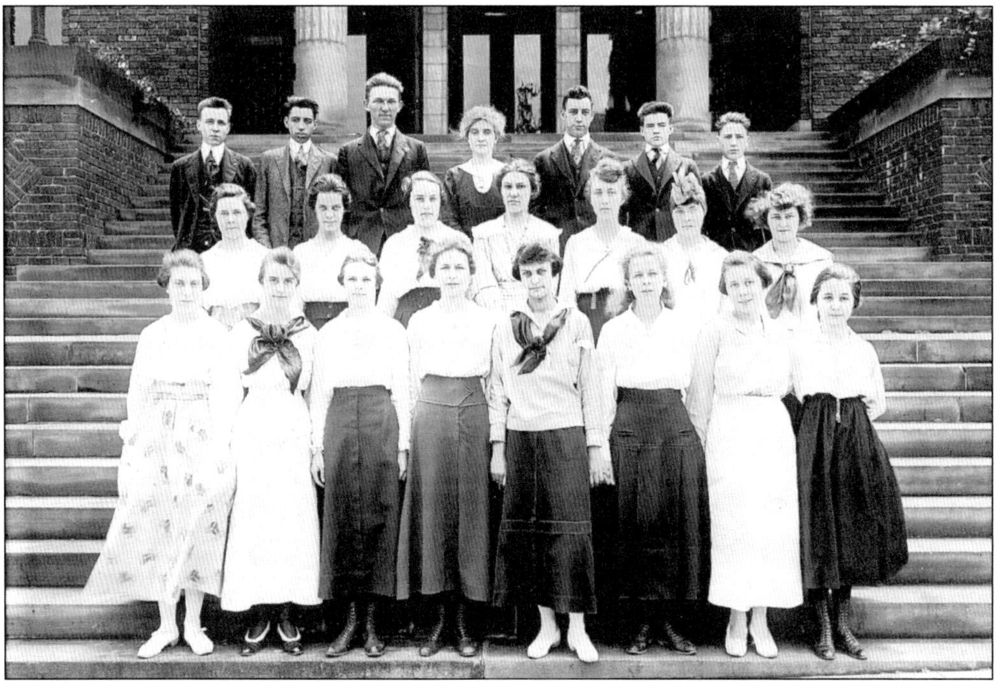

Young ladies outnumbered young men in the Oakmont High School Class of 1917. The class posed before the imposing entrance to the school, which then was located at Fifth Street and Pennsylvania Avenue. With the country's entrance into World War I in April 1917, many young men enlisted in the army or navy following high school graduation.

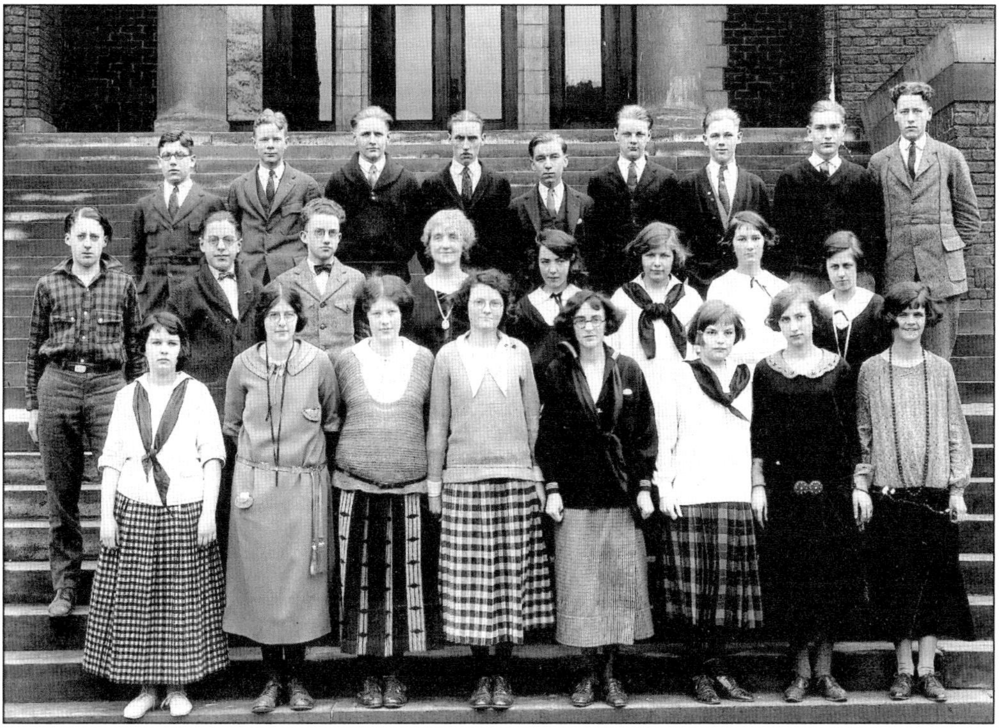

Members of Oakmont High School's Euclidean Society during the 1923–1924 school year looked properly serious and studious as they posed in front of the school at Pennsylvania Avenue and Fifth Street. The society's name indicates that its members were students of mathematics, particularly Euclidean geometry.

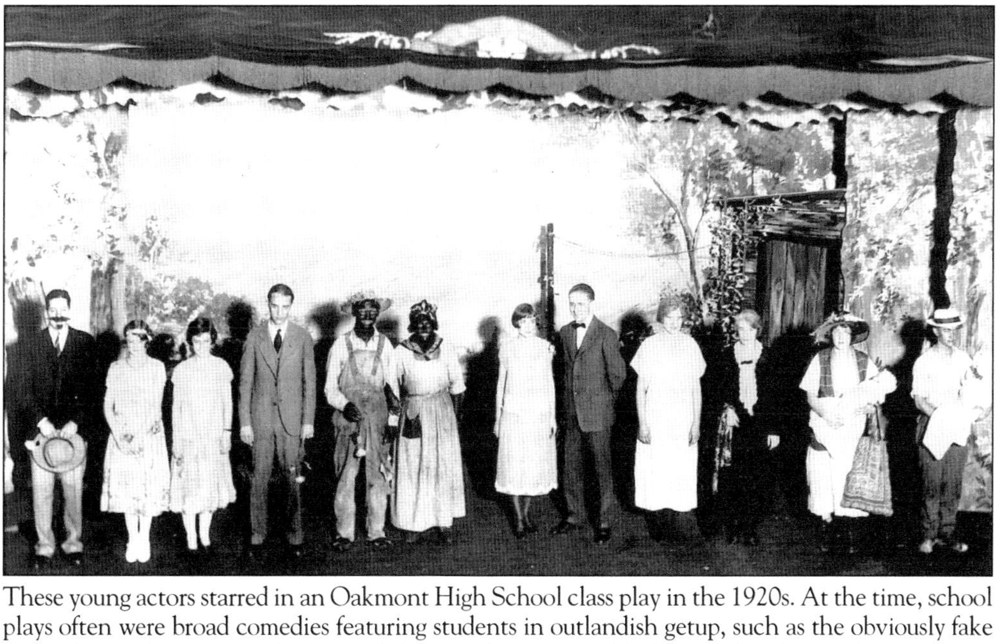

These young actors starred in an Oakmont High School class play in the 1920s. At the time, school plays often were broad comedies featuring students in outlandish getup, such as the obviously fake mustache on the actor on the left and the two characters in blackface. The plays at that time were staged in the school's beautiful auditorium at Fifth Street and Pennsylvania Avenue.

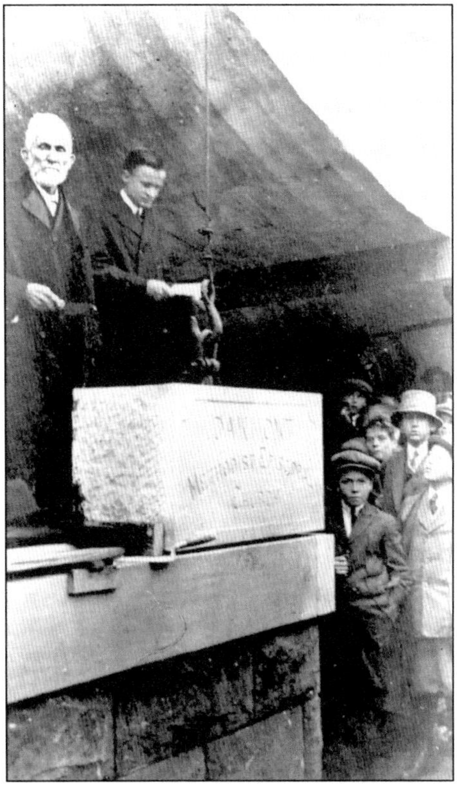

Rev. H.P. Kerr (left) and Rev. O.B. Emerson laid the cornerstone for the Oakmont Methodist Episcopal Church (today's Oakmont United Methodist Church) at 419 Maryland Avenue in 1914. The new church replaced a smaller structure on Fourth Street that now is the Highspire Apartments.

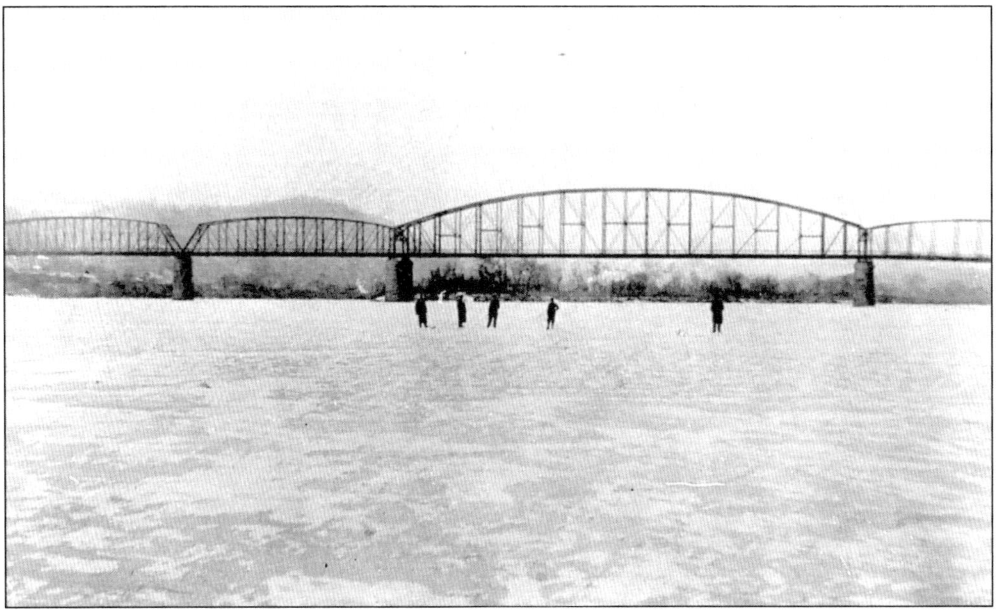

Boating and swimming were not the only activities that attracted Oakmonters to the Allegheny River. When the river was frozen solid from shore to shore from December 4, 1917, to the following February, skaters and ice hockey players took to the ice in large numbers for some wintertime fun.

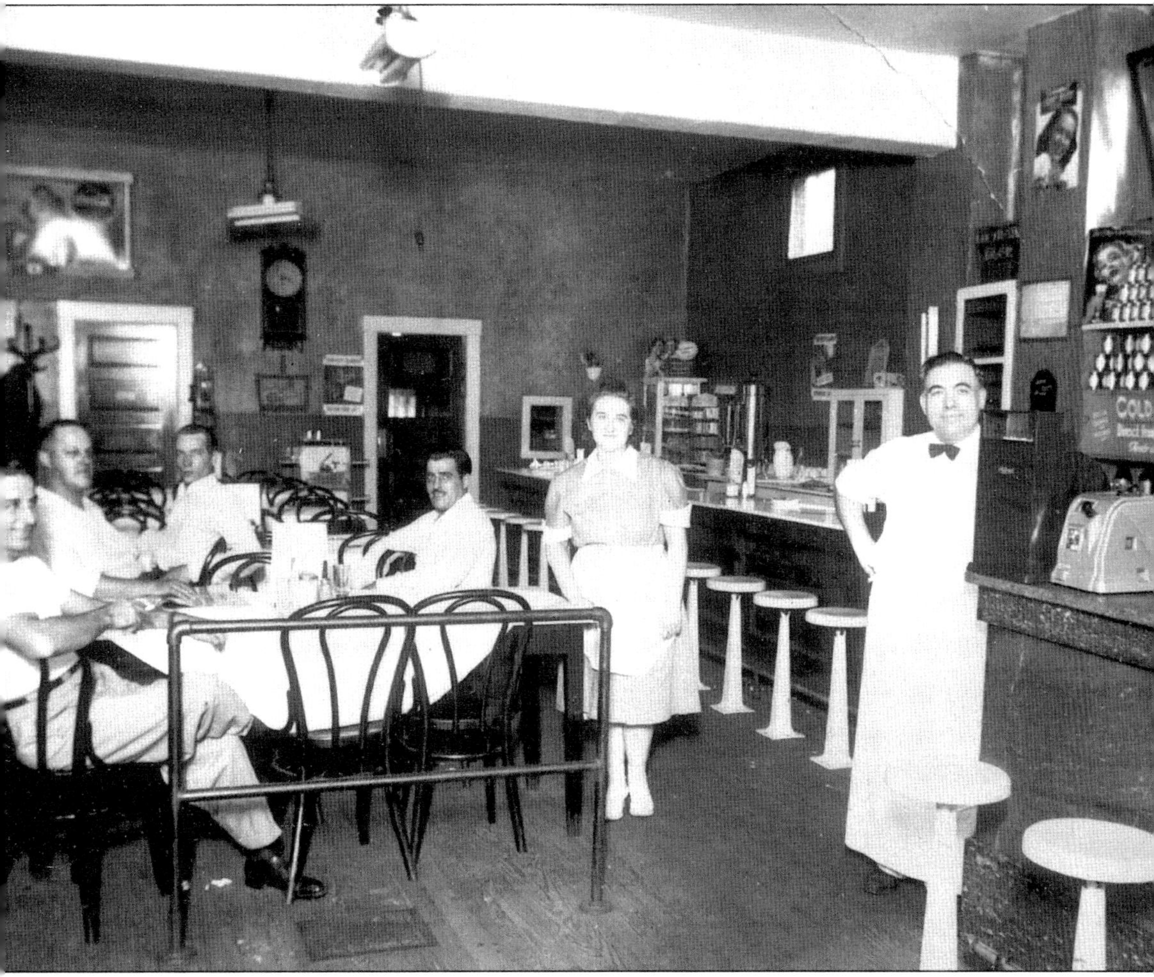

Peter Miller and John Argyros opened their Edgewater Restaurant at the corner of College Avenue and Allegheny River Boulevard in September 1922. Even though the restaurant was not located on the edge of the water, the Allegheny River, it faced the Edgewater Steel Company across the railroad tracks and much of its patronage came from the plant's employees. The sign, seen on the right, behind the counter, promised that the restaurant's cold draft beer was served "Brewery Fresh." The restaurant at College Avenue and Allegheny River Boulevard operated until 1977.

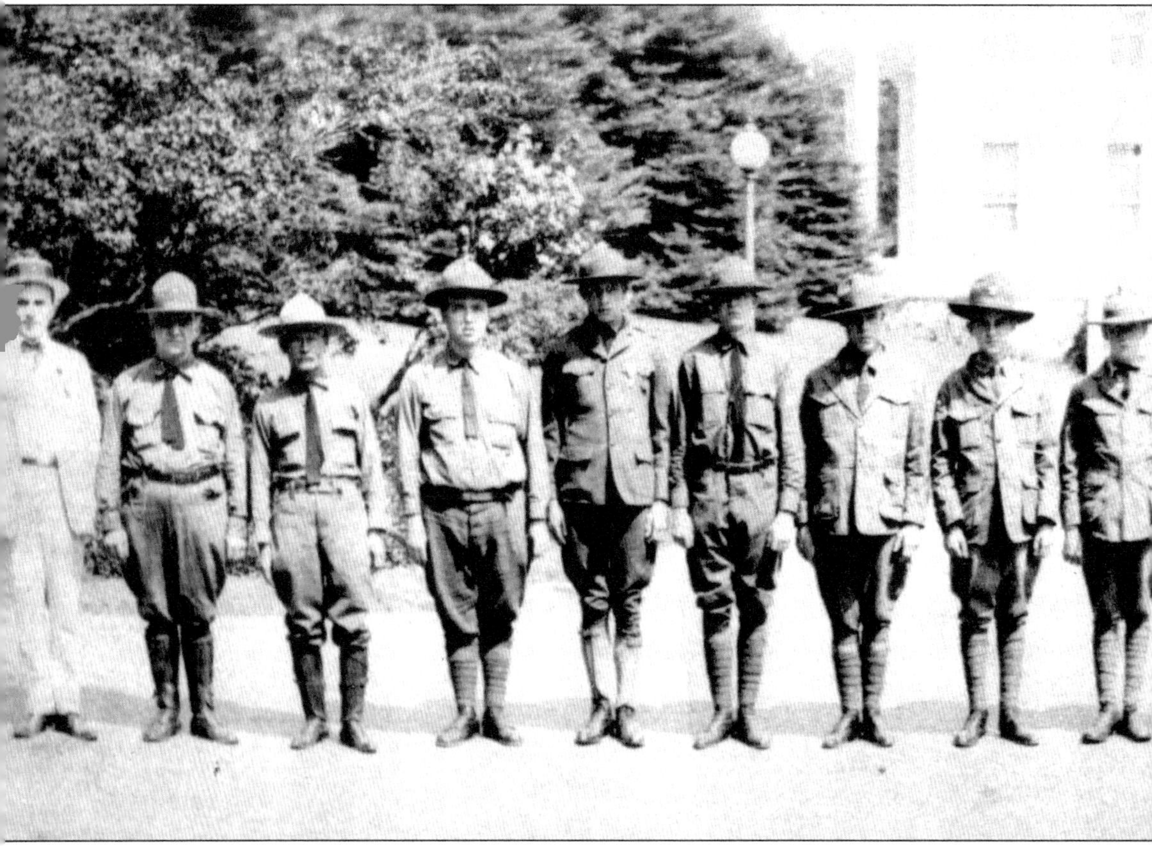

Oakmont Boy Scout Troop 3 was invited to the White House by Pres. Warren G. Harding in 1921 and honored for being the most decorated scout troop in the country. Pictured are, from left to right, Clyde Kelly (a congressman), Alfred Lee (the scoutmaster), unidentified (a scout official), ? D'Armidt (the assistant scoutmaster), James Verner, Kier Budd, Stewart Templeton,

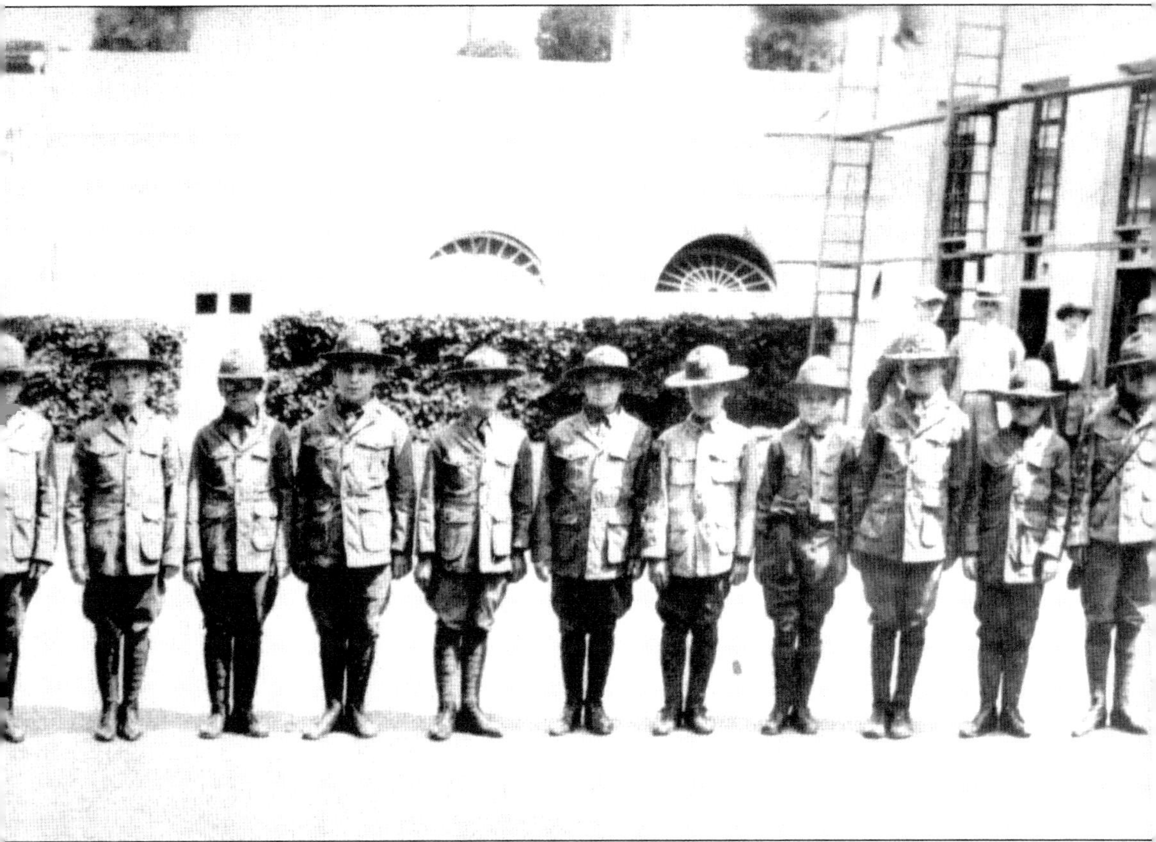

Alfred Lee Jr., Jim Budd, Donald McCandless, Merrill Stewart, Frank Foote, George Walker, Elmer Endrodi, George Lipman, James Bealey, Robert D'Armidt, Bud Fraser, Franklin Eves, and George Lee.

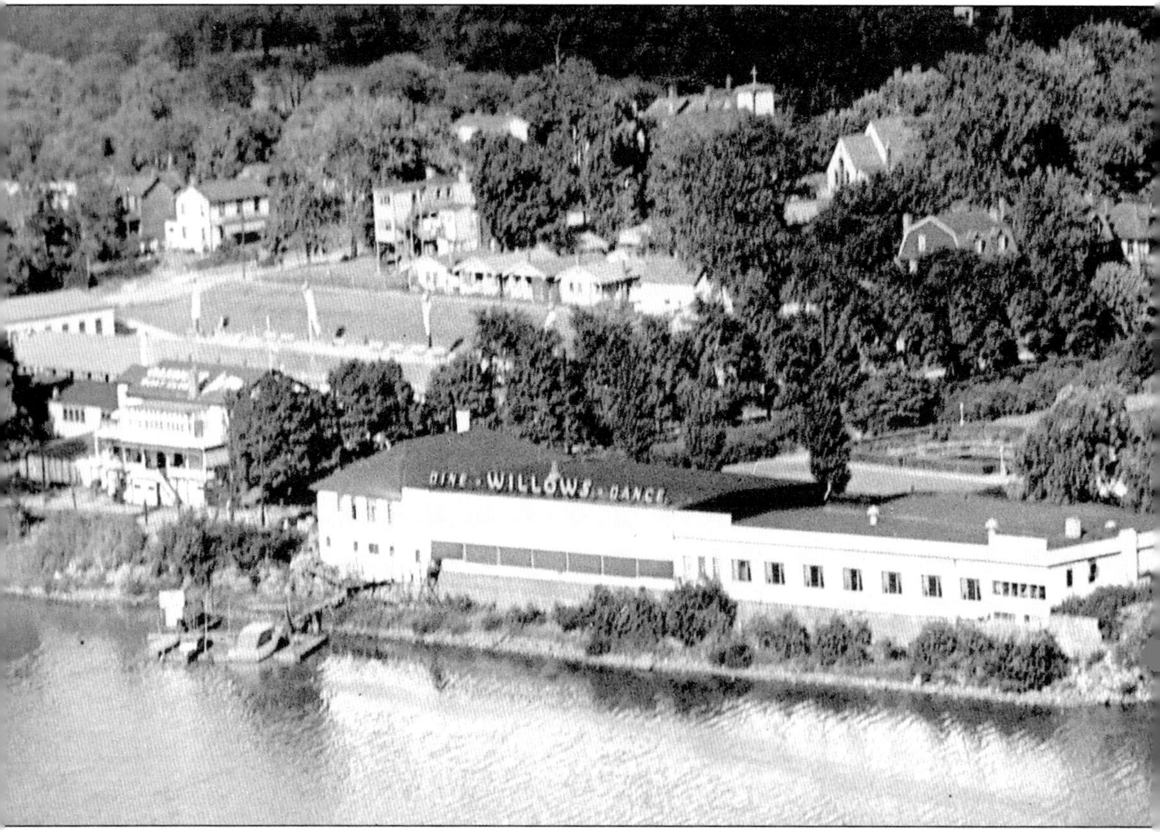

When Oakmonters roared in the Roaring Twenties, they did so at the Willows. The huge, block-long entertainment complex located on the river between Washington and California Avenues was a combination nightclub and river activity center. It featured fine dining, dancing in the spacious Dance Pavilion to the big-name bands of the day, and all manner of boating-related services, including rides, rentals, storage, and docking. Patrons at one time could take rides on an 11-passenger speedboat moored riverside. The Willows was destroyed by fire in 1925, with 100 canoes stored there lost in the blaze, but was rebuilt and reopened three years later. The swimming pool across Washington Avenue from the Willows was opened in 1926. The Willows prospered for years despite Prohibition, which banned the sale of alcoholic beverages, but fell victim to the hard economic times brought on by the Great Depression. It was closed and put up for sheriff's sale in 1931, but later reopened under new ownership.

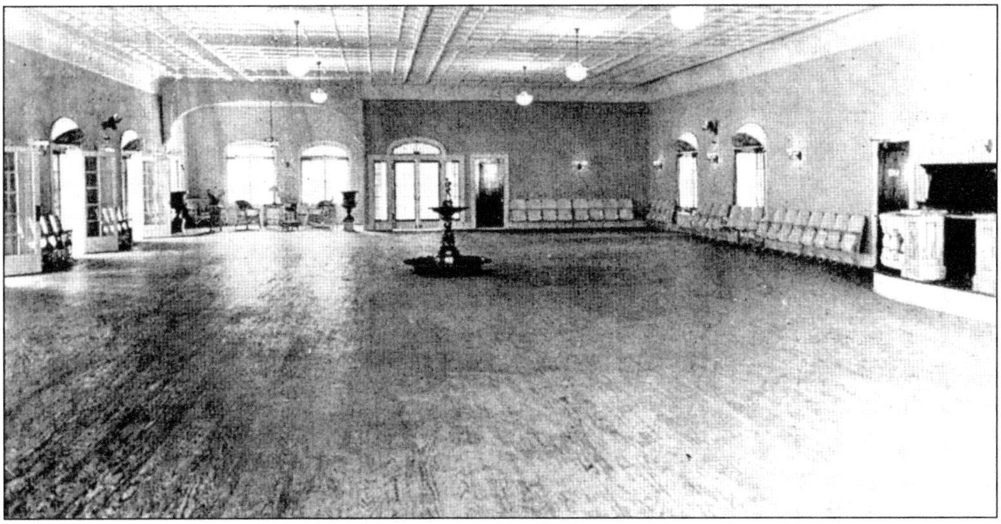

The spacious grand ballroom of the Willows was called the Dance Pavilion. Some of the biggest name bandleaders of the time, including Paul Whiteman, Woody Herman, Artie Shaw, Jimmy Dorsey, Hal Kemp, Fred Waring, and Guy Lombardo, played for the dancers who flocked to the Willows. The Dance Pavilion also served as a banquet hall on occasion.

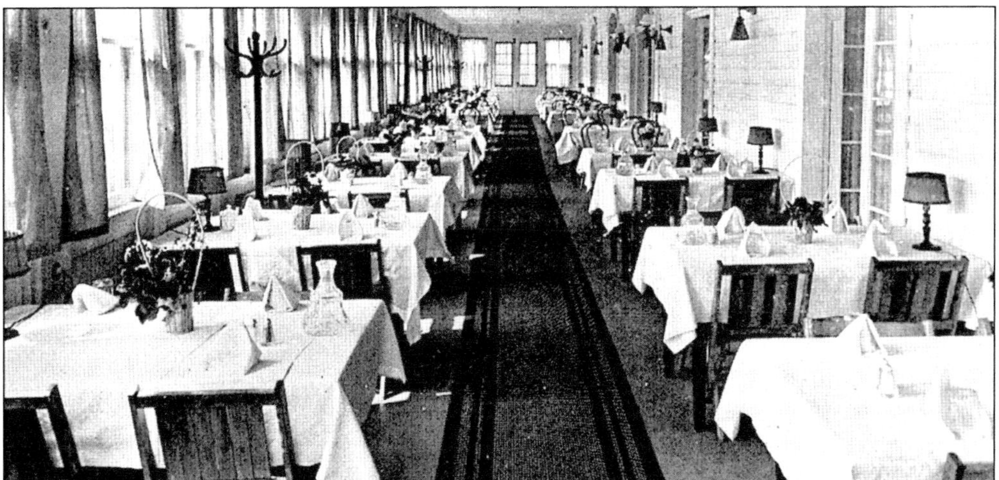

Visitors to the Willows had more than dancing to enjoy. The place also was known for fine dining. Its long, narrow riverside dining room afforded diners a splendid view of whatever was happening on the Allegheny.

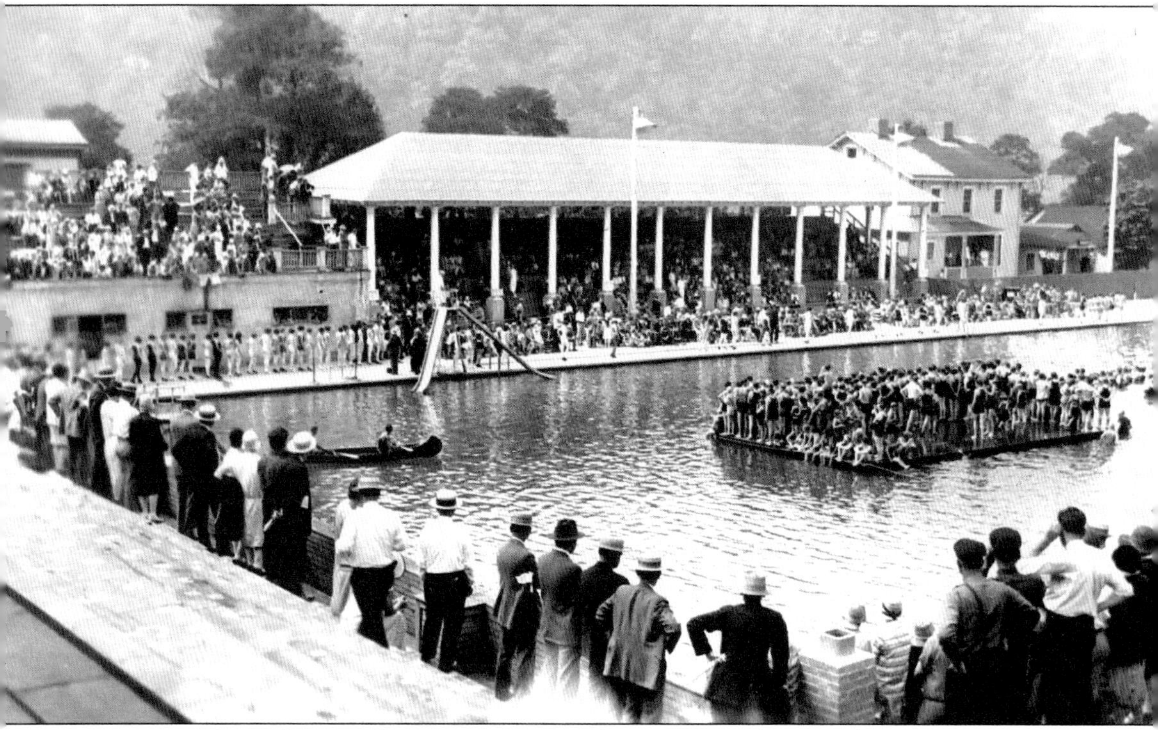

For years, the Willows pool was synonymous with summertime fun in Oakmont. Opened in June 1926, the gigantic, 335-foot-long and 225-foot-wide pool held 1.5 million gallons of water and covered a block-long stretch between Washington and Delaware Avenues across the street from the Willows nightclub. The pool was big enough to hold canoe races. Beauty pageants, like the one being held when this photograph was taken, were a common occurrence. The 1929 Miss Pittsburgh Pageant, affiliated with the Miss America competition, was held at the pool. To keep the popular pool open following the owners' bankruptcy in 1934, the borough bought it and operated it until 1947, when it was sold to new owners. Declining attendance and high maintenance costs brought an end to the Willows era in 1970. The pool site was sold to a Pittsburgh developer who constructed Oakmont Landing, an apartment complex, on the property.

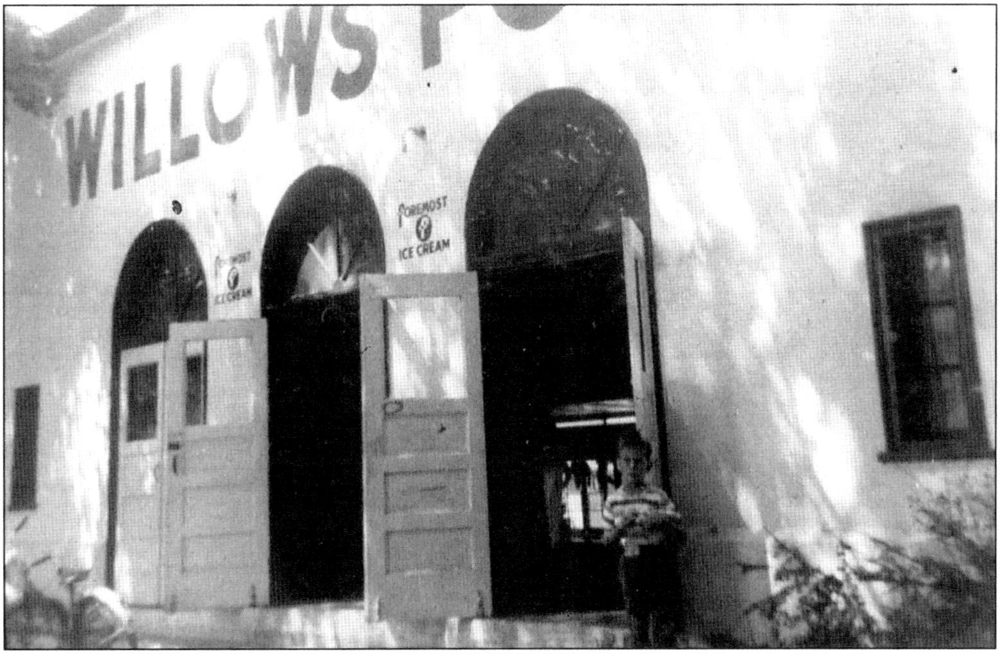

The entry to the Willows pool was the doorway to summertime fun for countless thousands of Oakmonters from when it first opened for swimming on June 15, 1926, to its still-lamented closing in 1970.

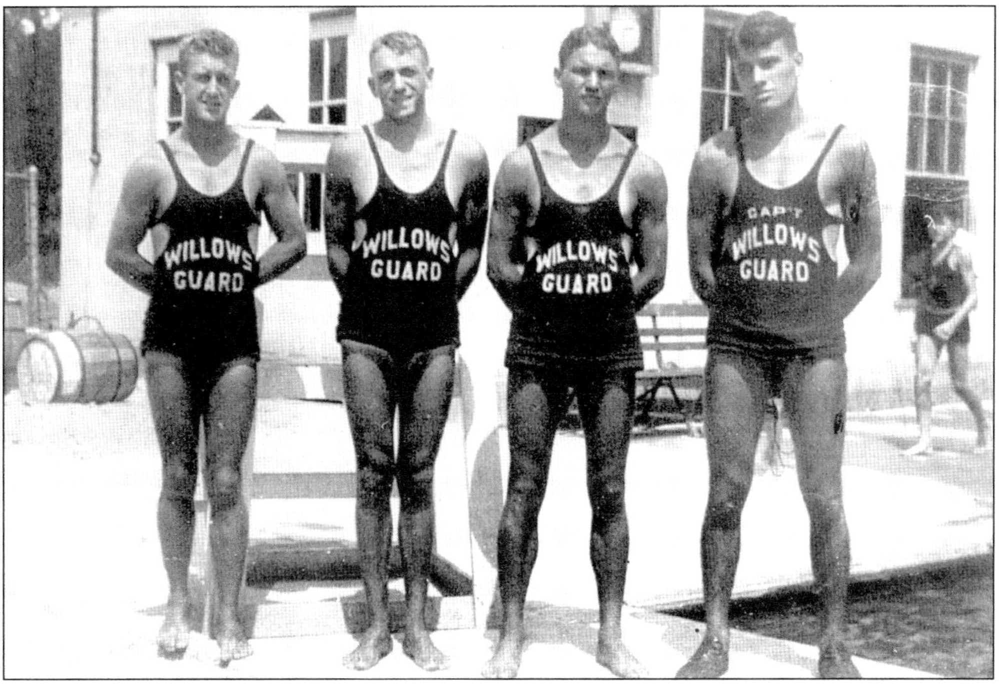

Swimmers at the Willows pool could take comfort that their safety was being looked after by strong and attentive lifeguards. Pictured here are four guards who served at the height of the pool's popularity. They are, from left to right, Bill Kennedy, Don McCandless, "Jet" O'Mara, and guards captain "State" Meckel.

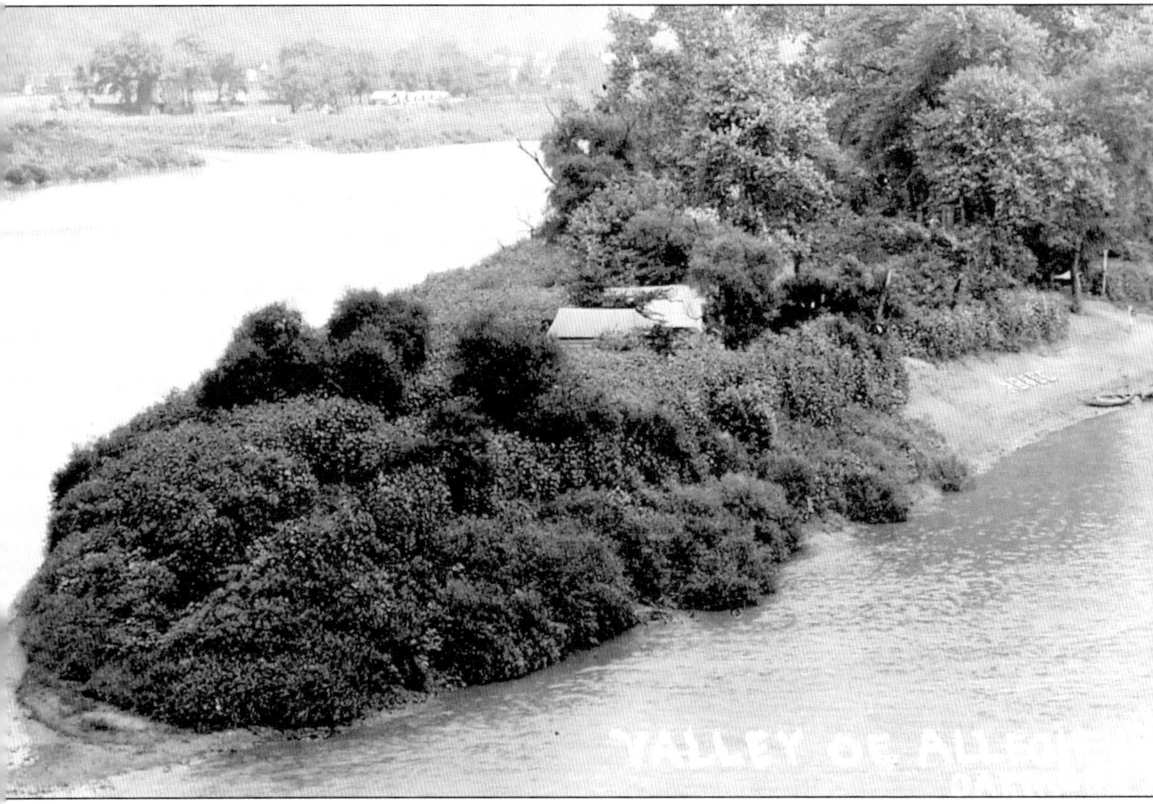

Twelve Mile Island, as seen here from the Hulton Bridge, has been a popular camping area for years. The island, located in the middle of the Allegheny River across from the Morris Camps section of town, once was owned by M.S. Verner of Oakmont, who sold it in 1919 to the J.K. Davidson Company. Accessible only by boat, the island once was served by a ferry. Twelve Mile Island is so named because it is about 12 miles upriver from Pittsburgh's Point, where the Allegheny and the Monongahela Rivers join to form the Ohio River.

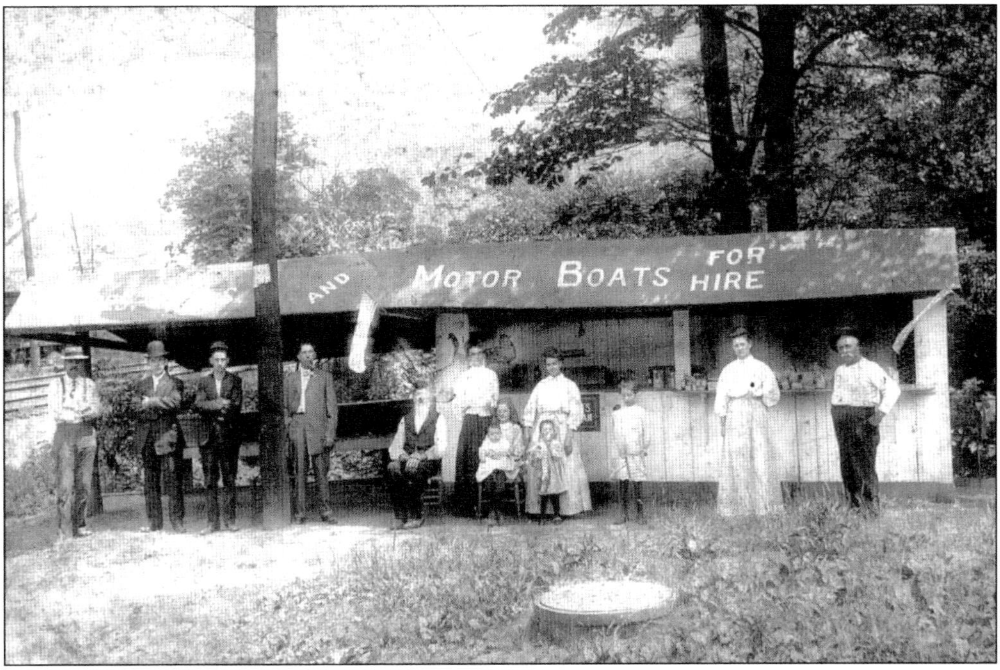

A savvy entrepreneur's stand offering "canoes, skiffs and motor boats for hire" was set up not on the riverbank, where other such businesses were located, but next to the railroad tracks on Allegheny Avenue. The location likely was chosen because it would be the first such stand encountered by weekend visitors when they got off the train from Pittsburgh.

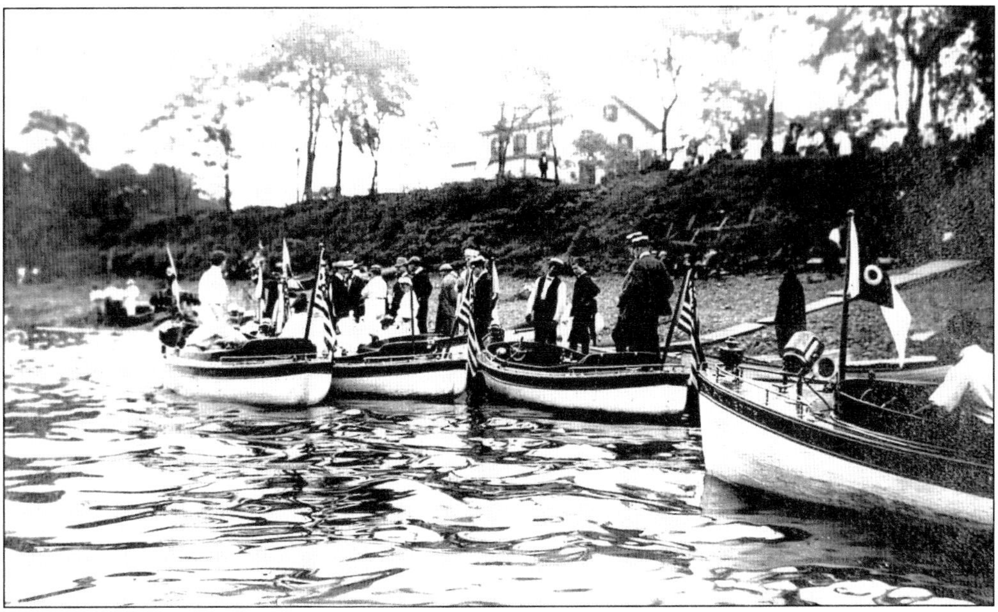

For years, Oakmonters have taken to the Allegheny River on warm-weather holidays. This Fourth of July outing in the 1920s was typical. It brought out men in coats, ties, and white-straw boaters, and many of the ladies wore white. The boat on the right flies the pennant of the Oakmont Yacht Club.

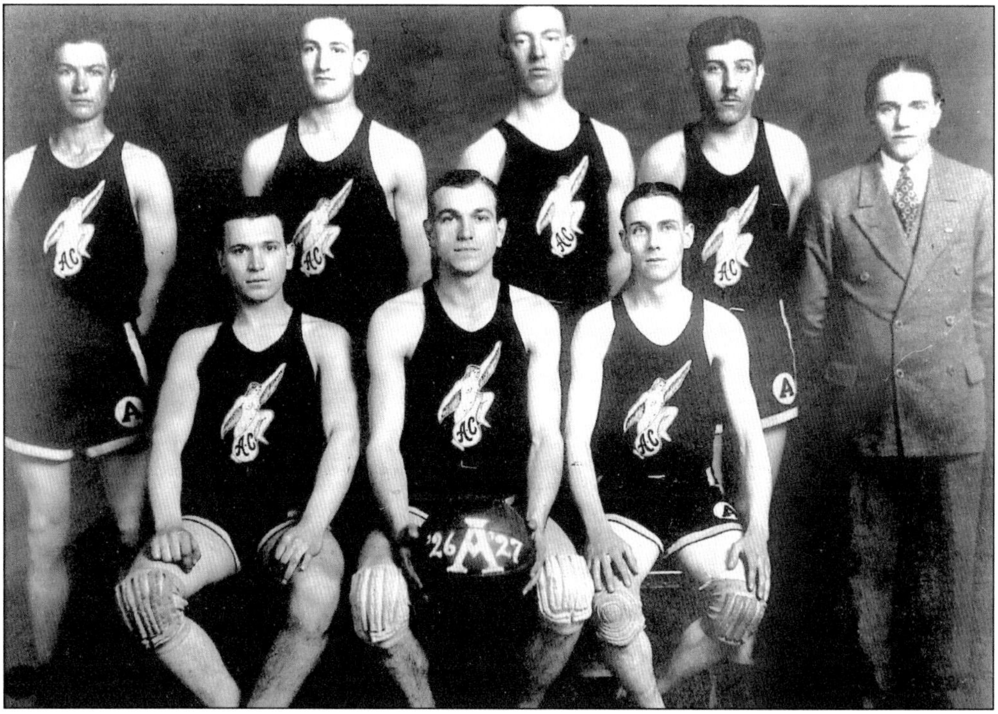

Members of the Atalanta Club's basketball team took their sport seriously, as this photograph shows. Only four members of the 1926–1927 squad are identified. Nick Aguzzoli and Joseph Aguzzoli are seated first and second from the left, respectively. Standing on the right is Frank Ruskewicz, and next to him is ? Mauro.

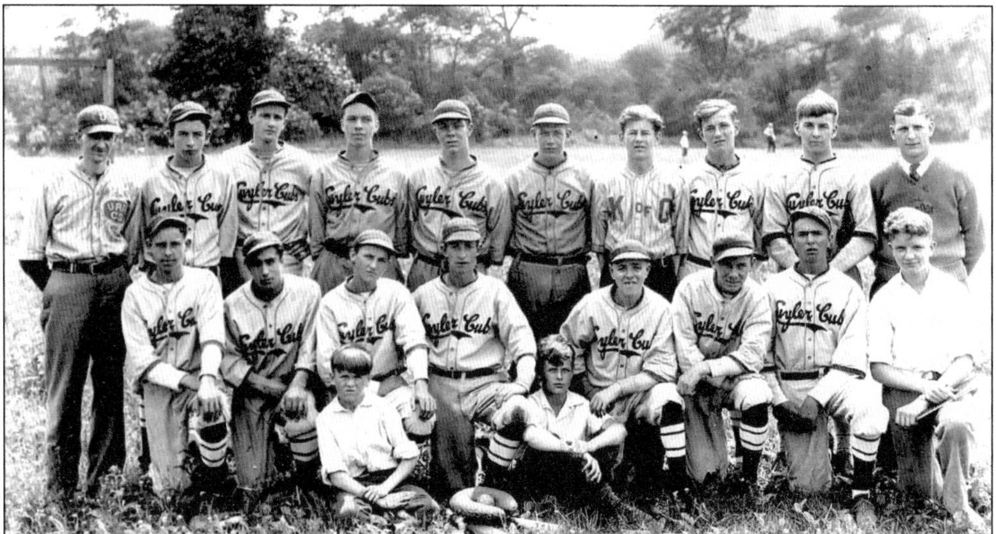

The 1928 Cuyler Cubs are shown at the baseball field on Ann Street. Seated are bat boys Hubert Sullivan and John Fowler. Seen here are, from left to right, the following: (front row) Frank Muir, Cel Mike, Glenon Sullivan, Mitch Hust, Charles Conway, Jim Malloy, Ray Kush, and Chuck Eker; (back row) Dick Wagner (coach), Bobby Fentzel, Roy Skinner, Ray Patrizio, Charles Denise, Clarence Hasson, Greg Asbee, Cletus Fowler, Jack Smith, and Joe Pemrick.

Oakmont's finest posed in front of the Hulton station for this 1914 photograph. Seen here are Henry Helwig (left), Alfred Evans (center), and James Beebe. At the time, those breaking the law in town were jailed in a one-room lockup at Fourth Street and Virginia Avenue. When a new borough building was constructed in 1917, it included the police station with three jail cells.

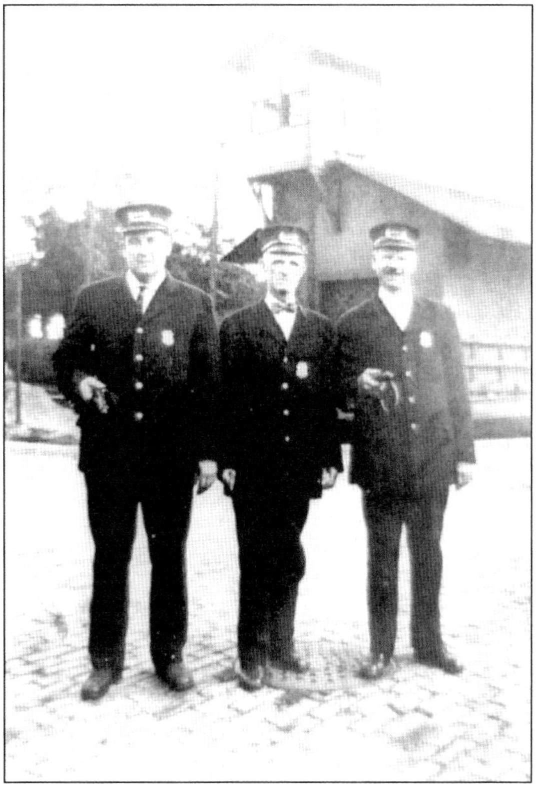

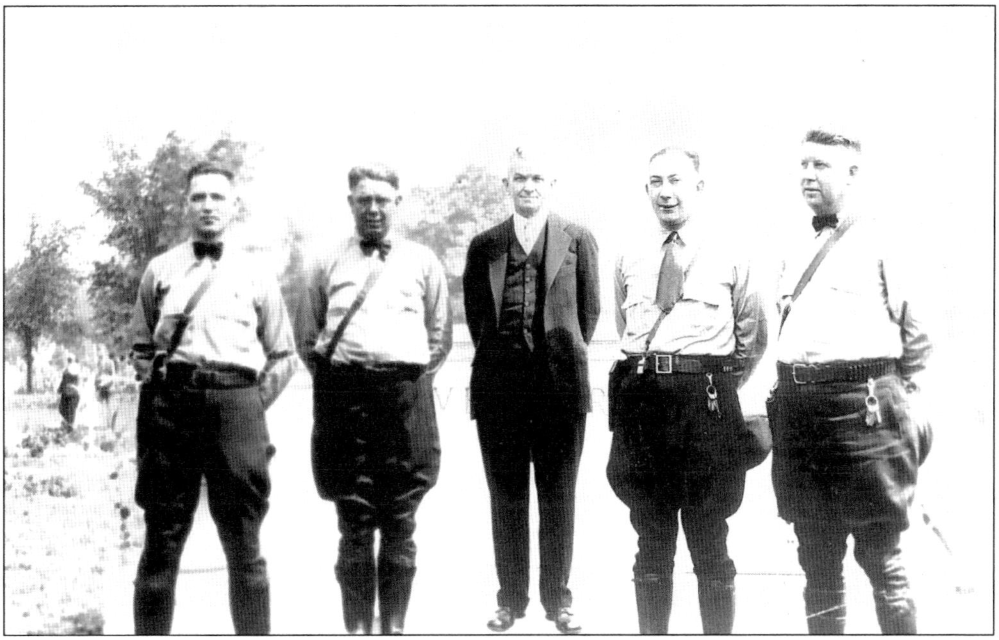

The Oakmont Police Department posed with Mayor James M. Bossert (center) in this 1928 photograph. The police officers are, from left to right, John Couch, Ed Helwig, Hugh Hammon, and Henry Helwig. Oakmont did not purchase its first police car until 1948—20 years after this photograph was taken.

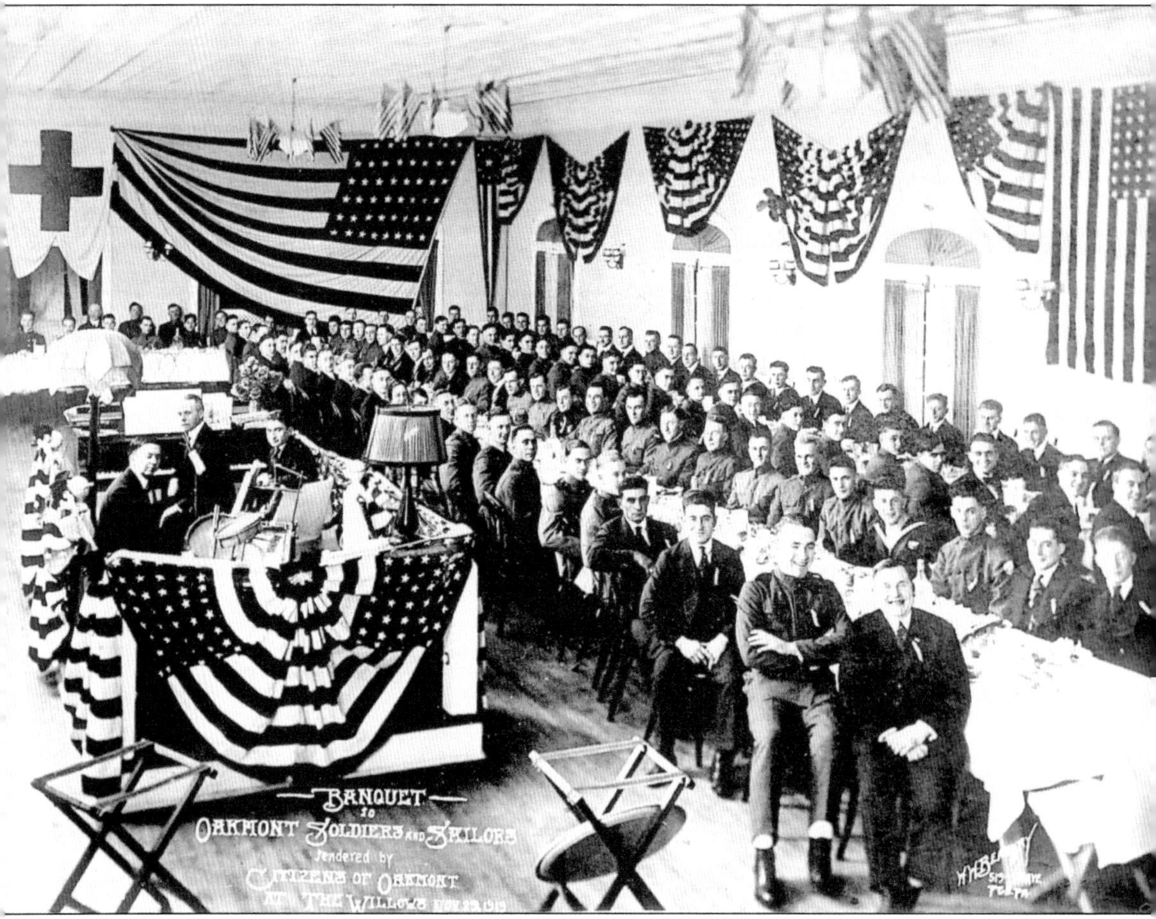

Oakmont welcomed home and honored local soldiers and sailors who had served in World War I with this gala banquet held in the flag-festooned grand ballroom of the Willows (known as the Dance Pavilion) on November 29, 1919. Returning veterans, most in uniform but many dressed in civilian clothes, filled the ballroom. A trio made music from what appears to be a portable bandstand in the center. The banquet was held a few weeks after the first anniversary of the signing of the armistice that ended what many hoped would be the war to end all wars.

Four

CHALLENGES AND CHANGE

The Depression and the 1936 St. Patrick's Day flood dominated most of the local news headlines during the 1930s. The Depression caused widespread unemployment, and the flood caused widespread destruction in town. Although the Depression and the flood pretty much defined the decade, there were other events and developments that helped in some small way to soften their impact.

The news, as it turned out, was not all bad. For example, census reports showed that Oakmont's population had grown by a third since 1920 and totaled 6,021. It was the largest percentage of population increase in Oakmont's brief history. In the first year of the decade, Edgewater Steel announced it would build a playground for the town's children next to its plant. Another new manufacturing plant was built that year on Pennsylvania Avenue to house operations of Walters Manufacturing Company.

Oakmont's main street got two new business addresses when the Pilgrim Building and Grubbs Arcade were built in 1931. In that same year, the owners of the Woodings Forge and Tool Company felt confident enough in an eventual economic recovery to buy the long-established Verona Tool Works.

Budgets were being slashed, businesses were closing, people were losing jobs, and teachers' salaries were being cut in 1932, but the owner of the Lehigh Theater invested $5,000 to make improvements to his movie house by installing a new screen and sound system. The investment, he said, was made possible by the community's loyal patronage.

The Oakmont Boat Club held the town's first regatta on the Allegheny River in 1934, the same year the Willow pool's mortgage was threatened with foreclosure. Answering the threat in hopes of retaining a valuable community asset, the borough bought the pool for $23,000 and the Suburban Water Company agreed to operate the pool's filter plant without charge.

The *Advance Leader*, a consolidation of the Allegheny *Advance* and the Verona *Leader*, was first published in 1937. And, during the remaining years of the 1930s, it had some very good news to report. In 1938, the paper covered the opening of the new Oaks Theater, the opening of a Ben Franklin store in a new building next to the Grubbs Arcade, and the biggest event of the year, the opening of the viaduct linking Oakmont and Verona, which signaled the completion of Allegheny River Boulevard. The following year, Oakmont Avenue was renamed Allegheny River Boulevard.

Oakmont ended the troubled decade of the 1930s in style by celebrating its 50th anniversary.

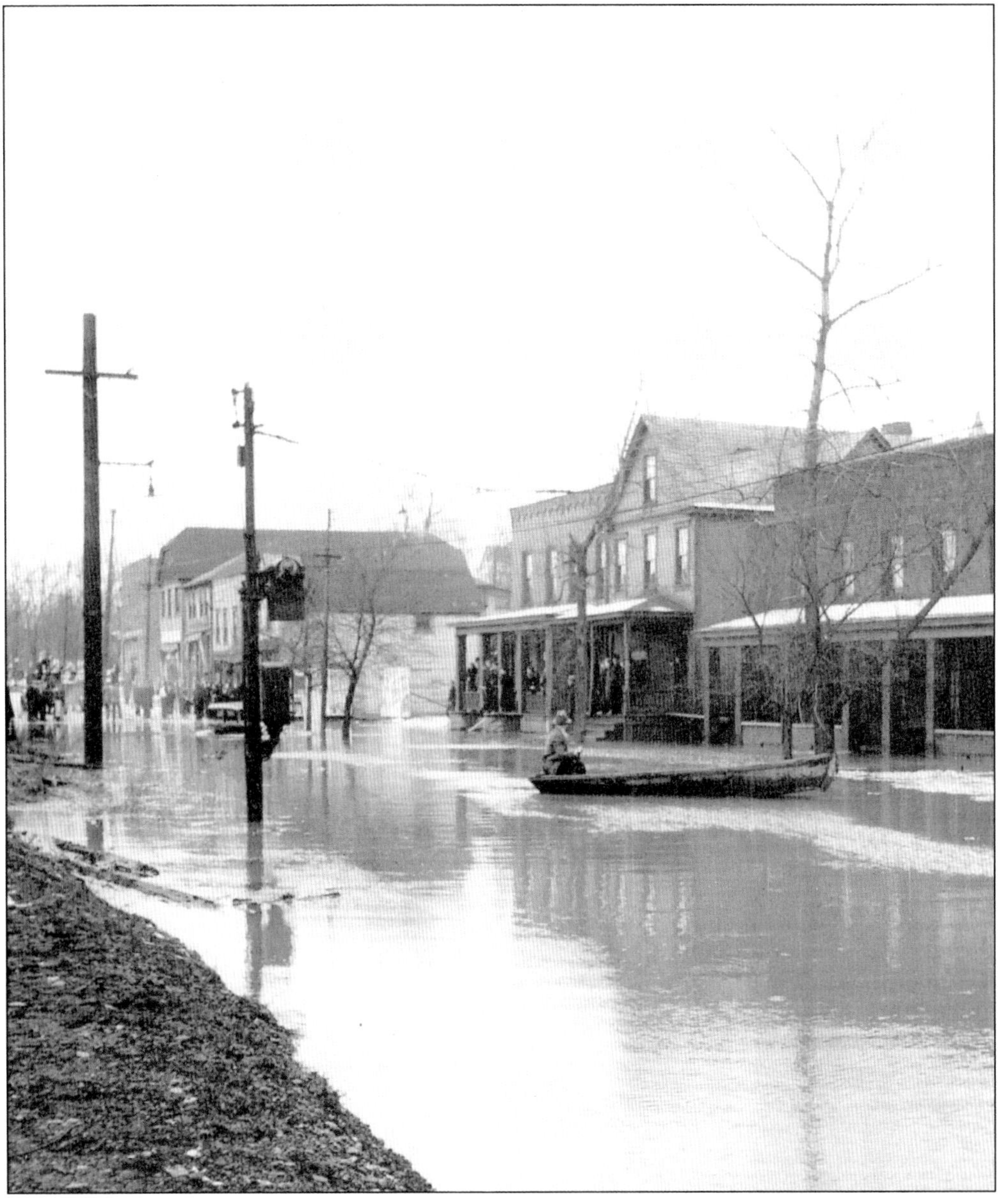

The 1936 St. Patrick's Day flood caused extensive damage in Oakmont, as it did in all towns along the Allegheny River. Reportedly, 130 homes and buildings in Oakmont were flooded. Hardest hit by the March 17 flood were the sections of town adjacent to the river. On higher ground inland, the area near where Plum Creek enters the river also flooded. Especially hard hit were Plum Street, which borders the creek, and the southern end of Oakmont Avenue, now Allegheny River Boulevard. People living along the road between Plum Street and College Avenue can be seen on their porches watching the rising waters and likely waiting to be rescued from their homes, which, like all of Oakmont, were without gas or electricity. A would-be rescuer in the boat surveys the scene. Also shown is a submerged automobile visible between the two utility poles on the left. Notice people standing in the roadway at the rear of the stranded automobile. In the area where they stood, the road rises slightly as it approaches the Edgewater Restaurant on College Avenue.

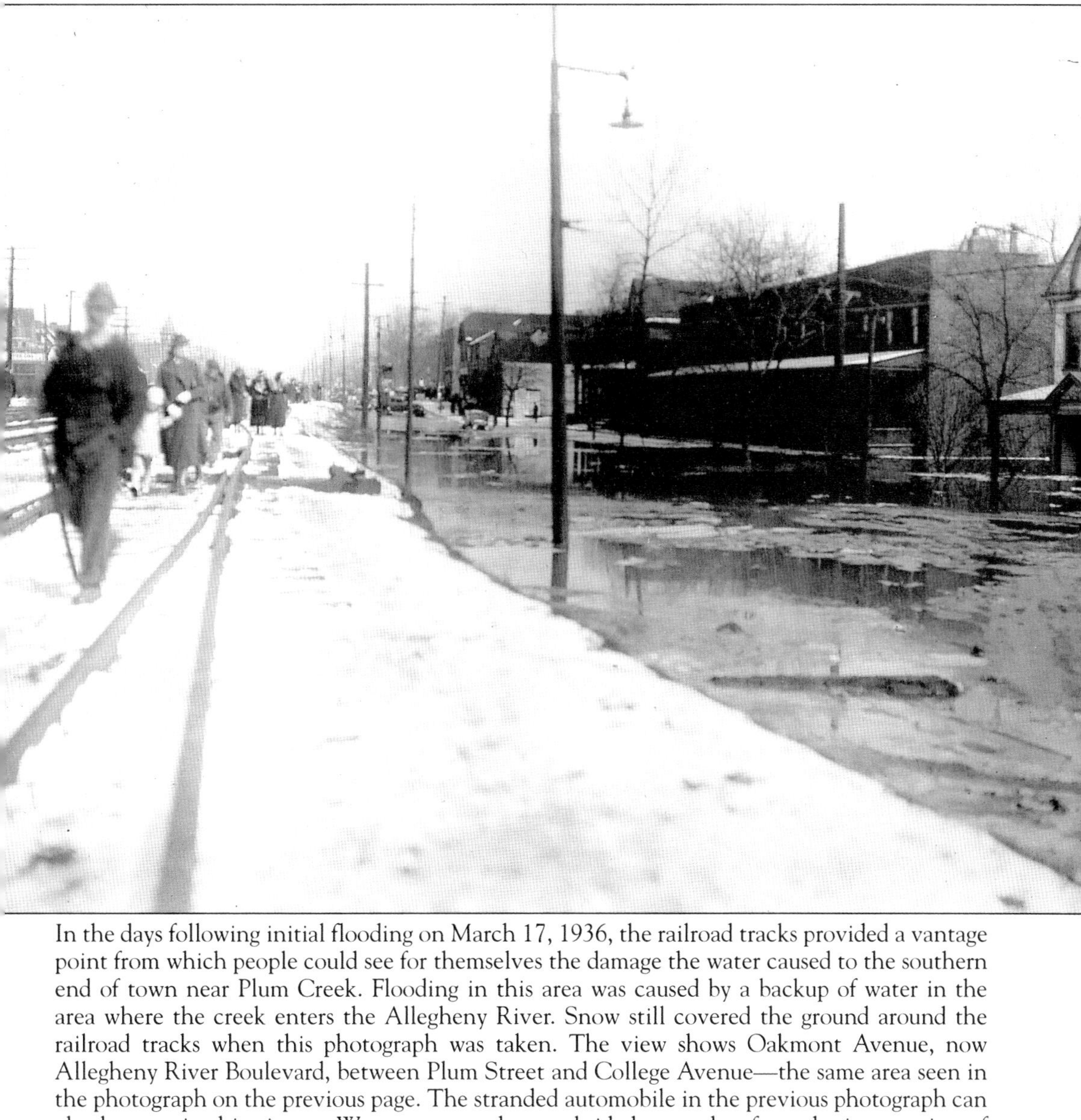

In the days following initial flooding on March 17, 1936, the railroad tracks provided a vantage point from which people could see for themselves the damage the water caused to the southern end of town near Plum Creek. Flooding in this area was caused by a backup of water in the area where the creek enters the Allegheny River. Snow still covered the ground around the railroad tracks when this photograph was taken. The view shows Oakmont Avenue, now Allegheny River Boulevard, between Plum Street and College Avenue—the same area seen in the photograph on the previous page. The stranded automobile in the previous photograph can also be seen in this picture. Water seems to have subsided somewhat from the intersection of the road and College Avenue, enough to allow some vehicles easier access to the area.

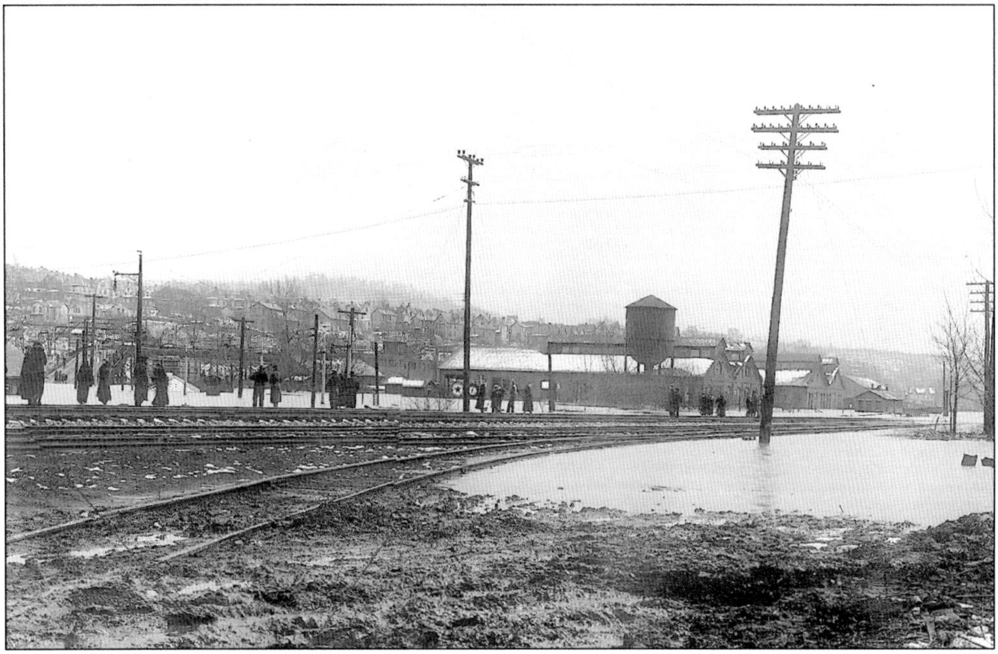

This view of the St. Patrick's Day flooding is from in front of the Edgewater Steel plant looking towards Verona. The wooden streetcar bridge linking the two towns is barely visible on the left, behind the group of walkers. The industrial buildings in the center are the Pennsylvania Railroad shops in Verona.

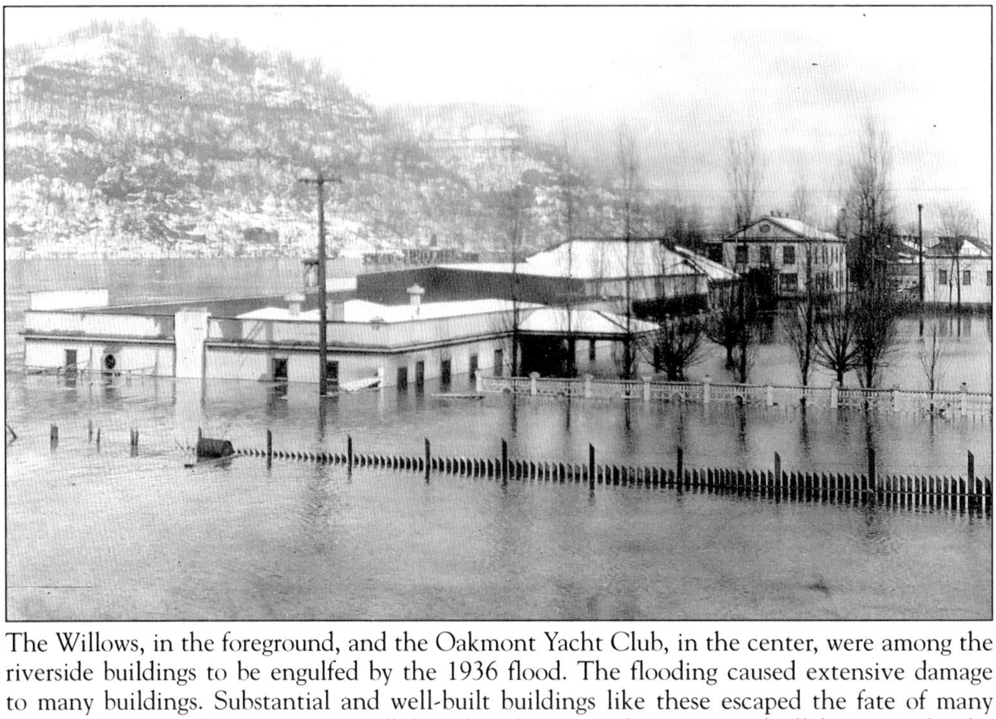

The Willows, in the foreground, and the Oakmont Yacht Club, in the center, were among the riverside buildings to be engulfed by the 1936 flood. The flooding caused extensive damage to many buildings. Substantial and well-built buildings like these escaped the fate of many smaller structures that were swept off their foundations and even carried off downriver by the turbulent Allegheny.

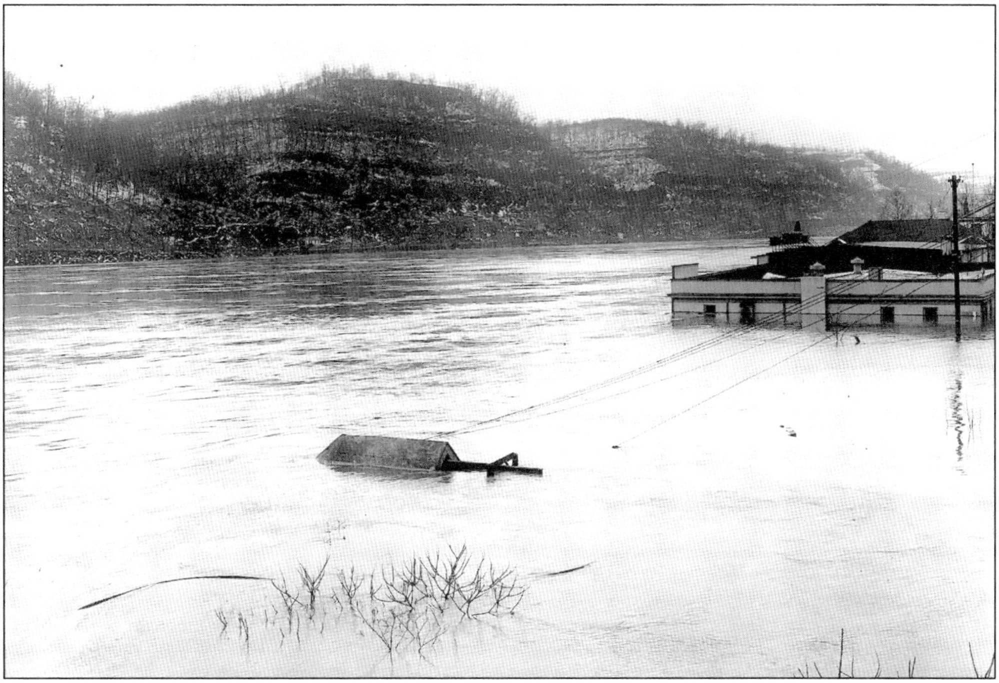

That is the pump house of the Edgewater Steel Company plant in the foreground, the swollen waters of the Allegheny River lapping at its rooftop. Production at riverside manufacturing plants from the upper reaches of the Allegheny down to Pittsburgh's Point was curtailed for extended periods after the 1936 flood until buildings were cleaned up and equipment was refurbished.

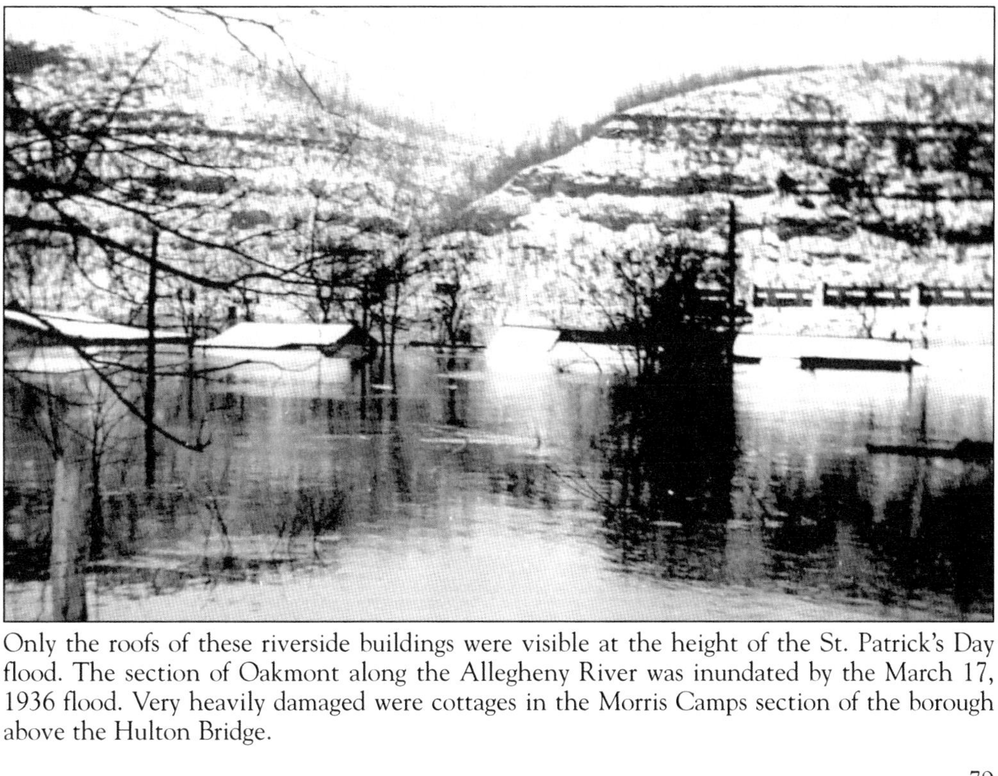

Only the roofs of these riverside buildings were visible at the height of the St. Patrick's Day flood. The section of Oakmont along the Allegheny River was inundated by the March 17, 1936 flood. Very heavily damaged were cottages in the Morris Camps section of the borough above the Hulton Bridge.

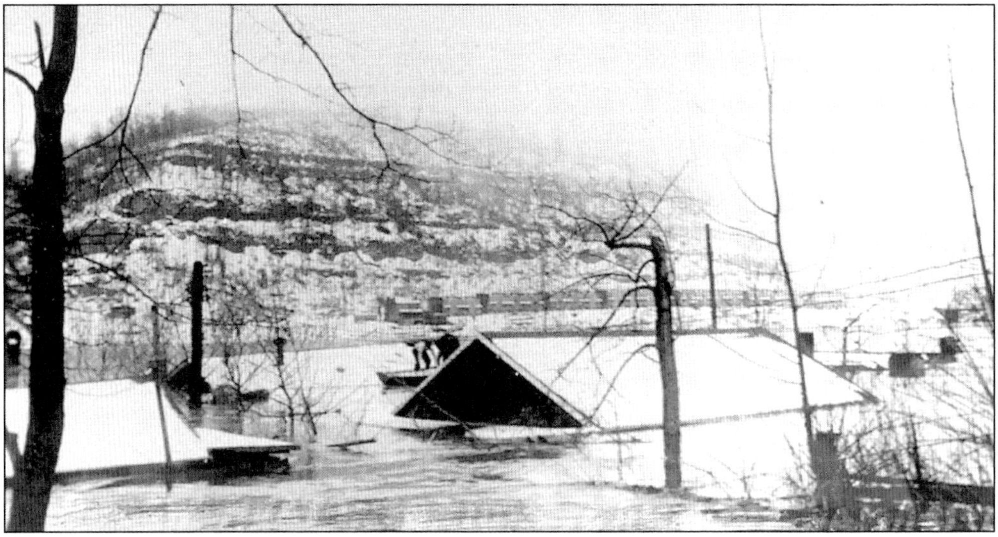

Two men in a boat attached lines to a cottage to prevent it from being swept down the Allegheny River during the 1936 flood. One of the men has been identified as Bill "Hutch" Bauman. Such rescue efforts were common occurrences in the flood, as people attempted to protect their riverside properties.

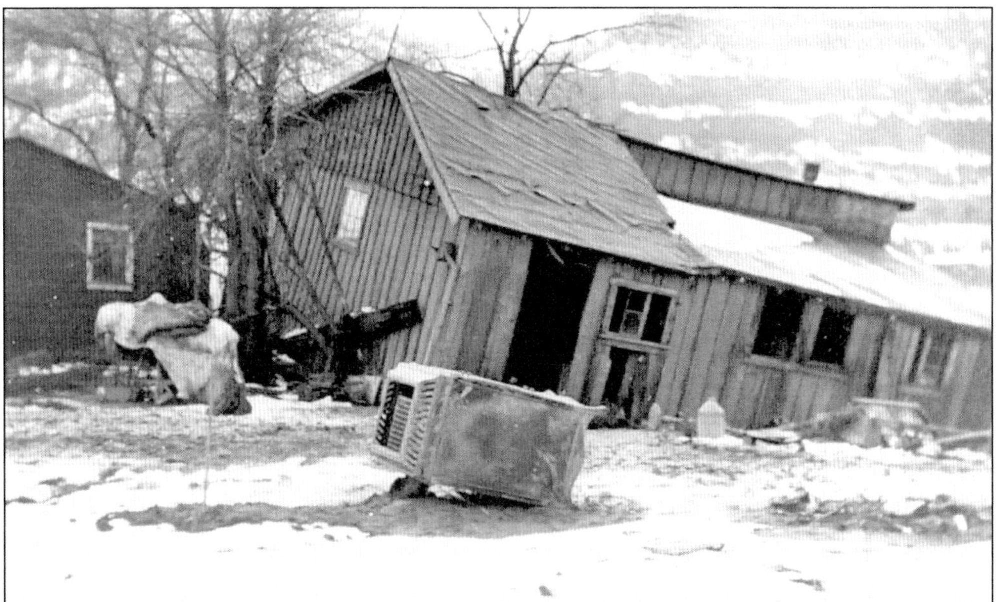

Fortunately for some, much of the Allegheny River's bank around Oakmont was tree lined. Sturdy trees growing alongside the river stopped Bert Fisher's house and saved it from being swept into the Allegheny during the flood. Although extensively damaged, the house at least escaped being completely destroyed by the floodwaters.

Could the woman in an upstairs window of this house on the southern end of Oakmont Avenue be talking about the possibility of rescue with the man in the rowboat? During the 1936 flood, water rose to the middle of the first floor of the house in the 100 block of what now is Allegheny River Boulevard. It was one of 130 structures in town flooded.

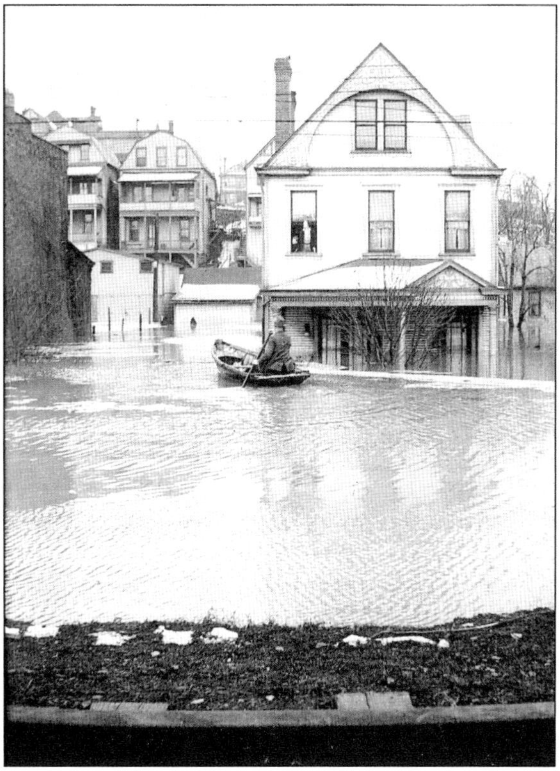

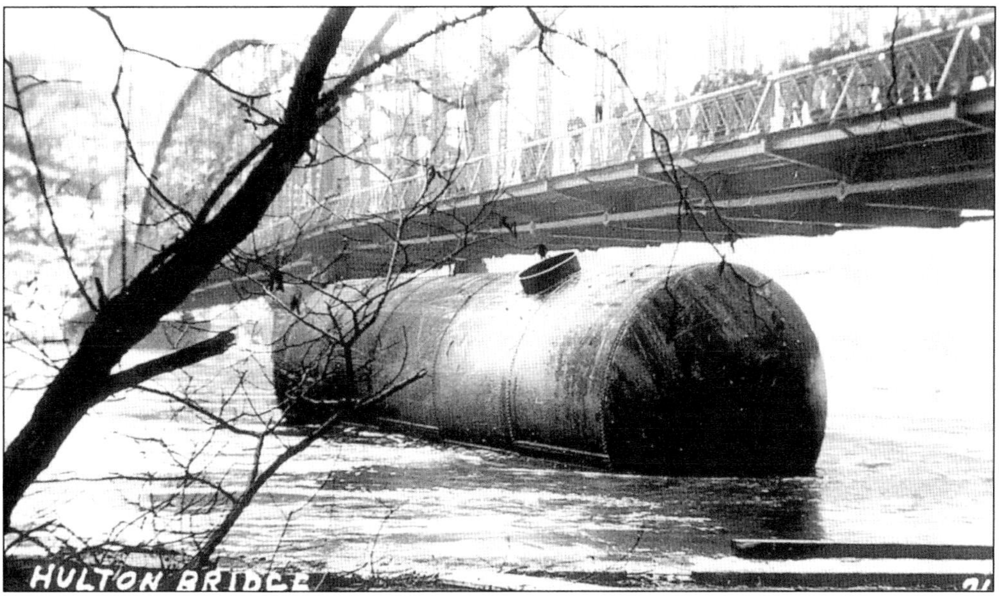

During the St. Patrick's Day flood, people stood on the Hulton Bridge to watch the Allegheny River carry away small cottages, barges, trees, and all manner of debris. Here, they see a massive tank swept away from a petroleum refinery in Oil City, many miles upriver from Oakmont, finally run aground on the riverbank near the Bradley Children's Home on Hulton Road.

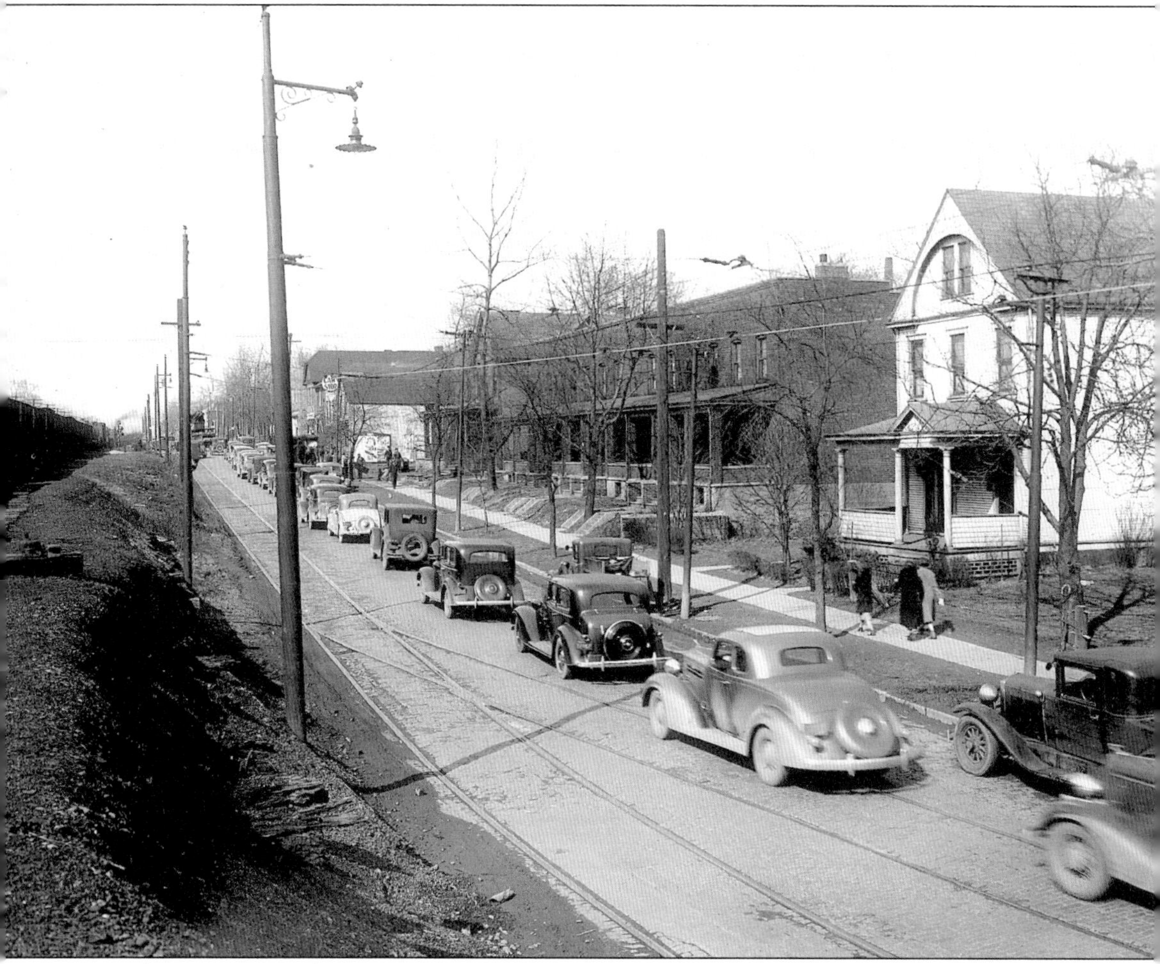

Traffic jams on Oakmont's main street are nothing new, as this lineup of automobiles on Oakmont Avenue between College Avenue and Plum Street attests. Streetcars often disrupted the flow of automobile traffic in areas like this, where two streetcar tracks merged into one, and the cars traveling in either direction ran on the single track.

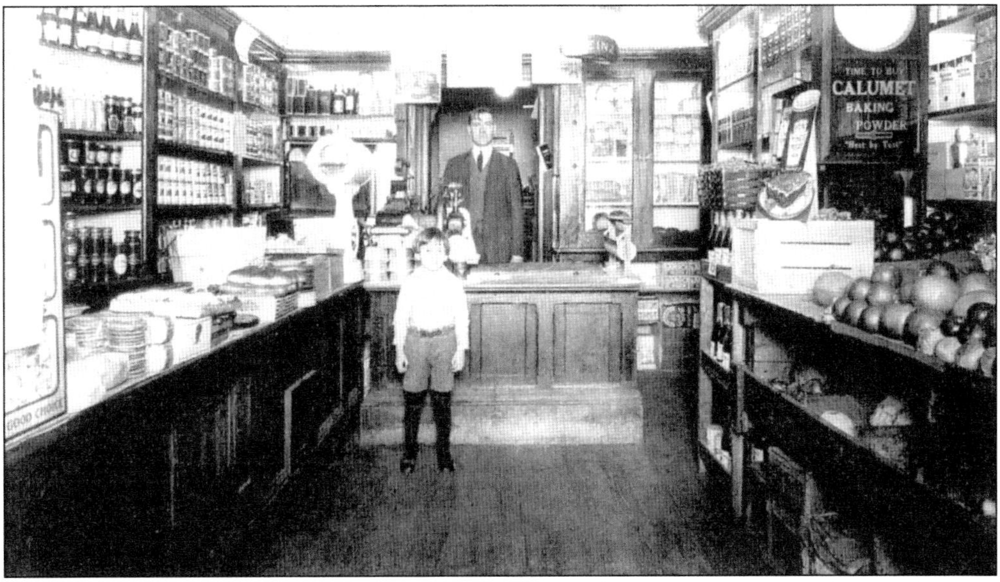

This photograph shows the interior of Hastings' dry goods and grocery store. The brand names of many of the articles on the store shelves are still familiar today. The store, originally opened at Sixth Street and Maple Way in 1875, occupied several locations around town before the business closed in 1941.

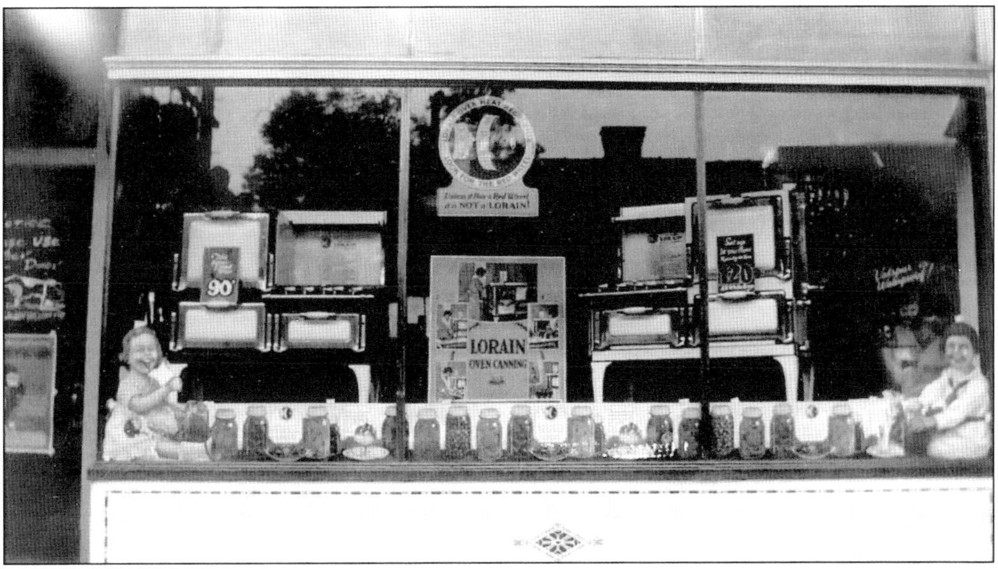

Bossert's hardware store displayed the latest gas ranges in its front window in the 1930s, along with preserved fruit and an advertising poster for ice cream. Begun as a tin shop in 1884, the business moved to this location at the corner of Fourth Street and Maryland Avenue in 1885.

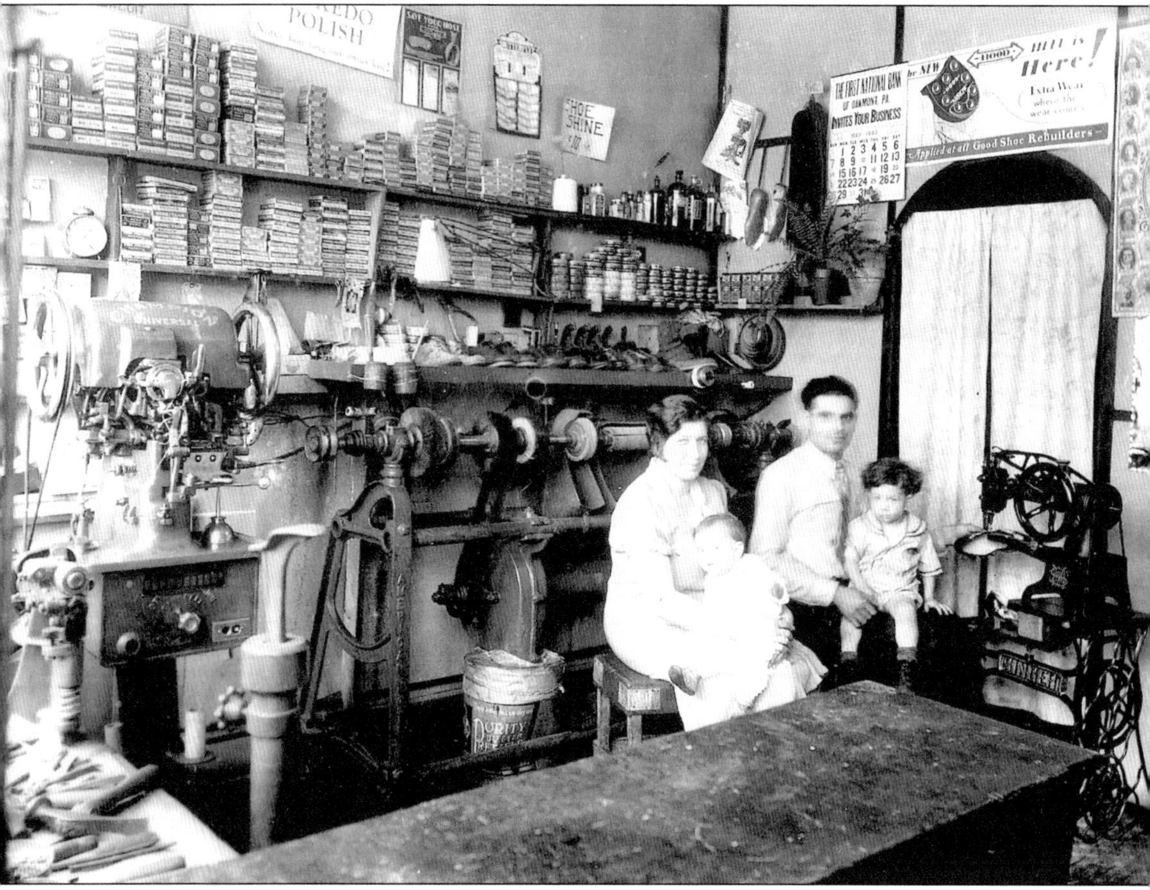

Vincent Provenza's shoe-repair shop was on West Railroad Avenue, now Allegheny Avenue, when this photograph of him, his wife, Lucy Liberto Provenza, and his children Mary and Charles, was taken in May 1933. The shop later moved to Maryland Avenue. Besides repairs, customers also could get their shoes shined. The sign above the counter offers shines for only 10¢.

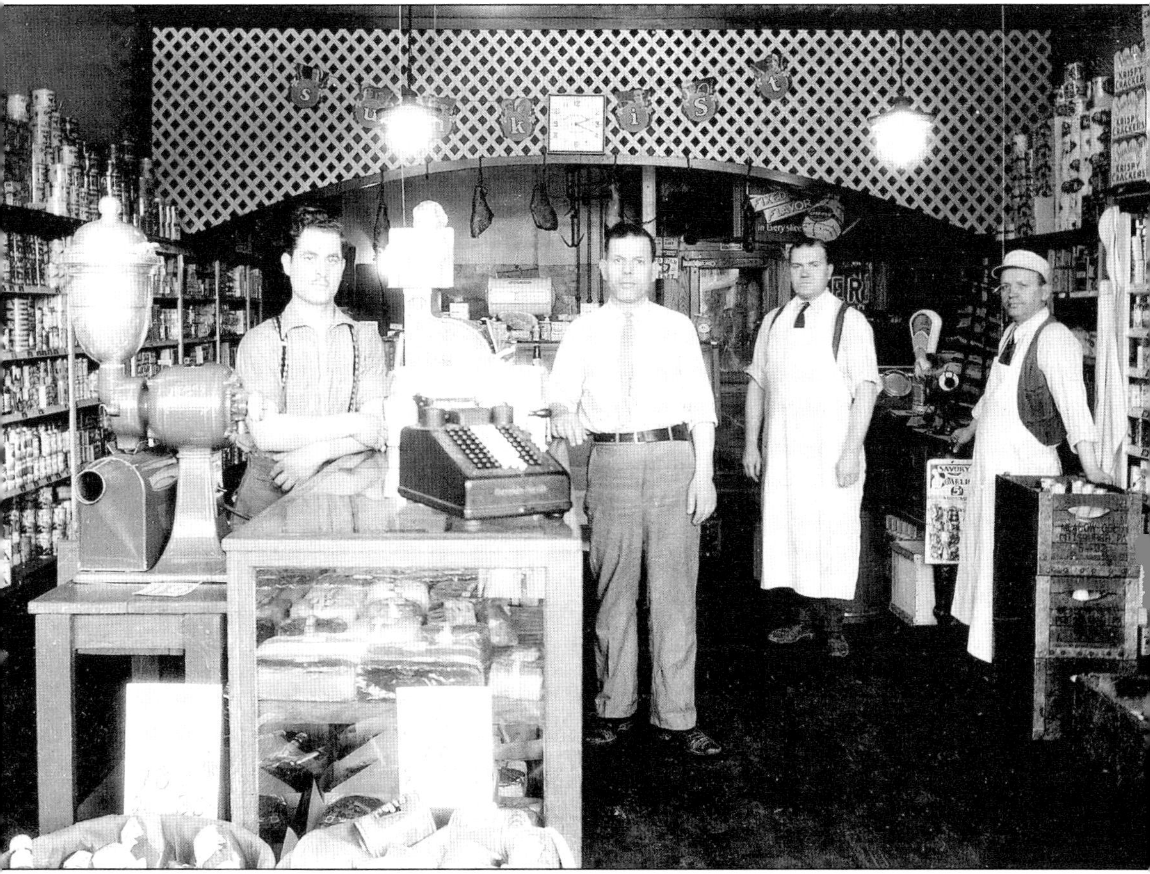

The Kokales family operated a meat and grocery store on Allegheny River Boulevard from 1921 to 1979. This photograph of the store's interior was taken in the early 1930s. Seen here, the store's staff included, from left to right, George N. Kokales, John G. Kokales, Mr. Glasser, and Gus Kokales. Notice the cured hams hanging on hooks from the lattice work.

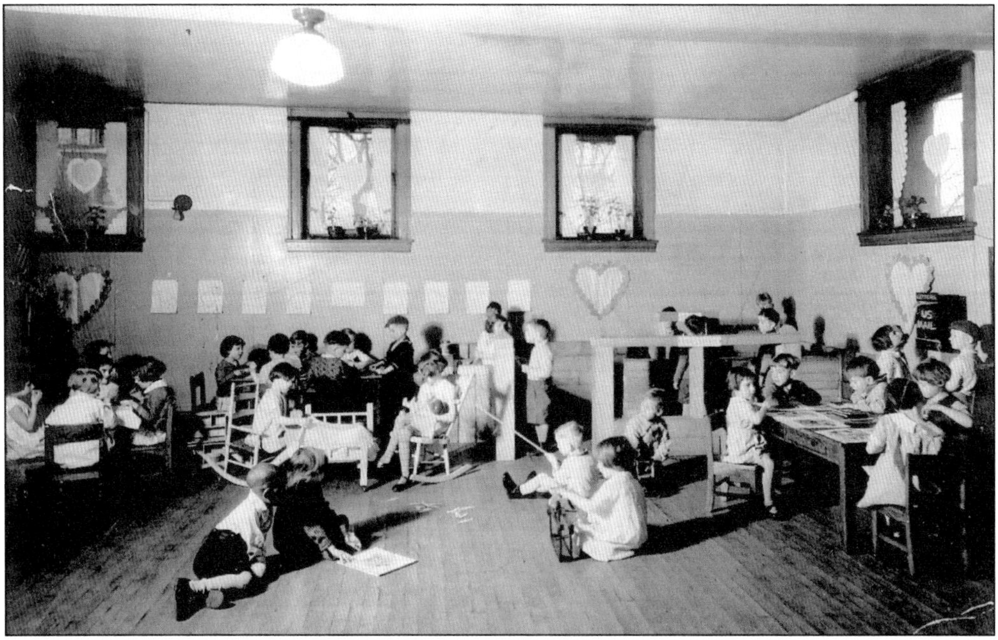

The basement of the Oakmont Carnegie Library served several purposes over the years. It was the location of the first office of the First National Bank of Oakmont when the bank was founded in 1903. Early kindergarten classes in town were held in the basement. Here, the 1931 kindergarten class gets ready for Valentine's Day. Oakmont's school board maintained the library until 1966.

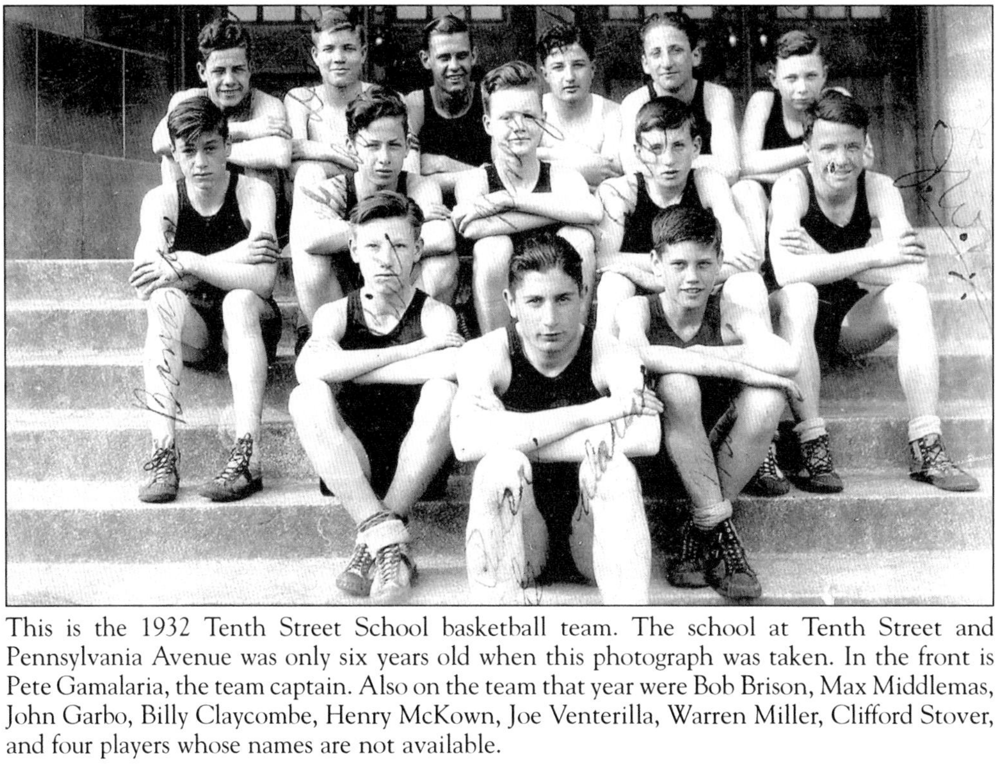

This is the 1932 Tenth Street School basketball team. The school at Tenth Street and Pennsylvania Avenue was only six years old when this photograph was taken. In the front is Pete Gamalaria, the team captain. Also on the team that year were Bob Brison, Max Middlemas, John Garbo, Billy Claycombe, Henry McKown, Joe Venterilla, Warren Miller, Clifford Stover, and four players whose names are not available.

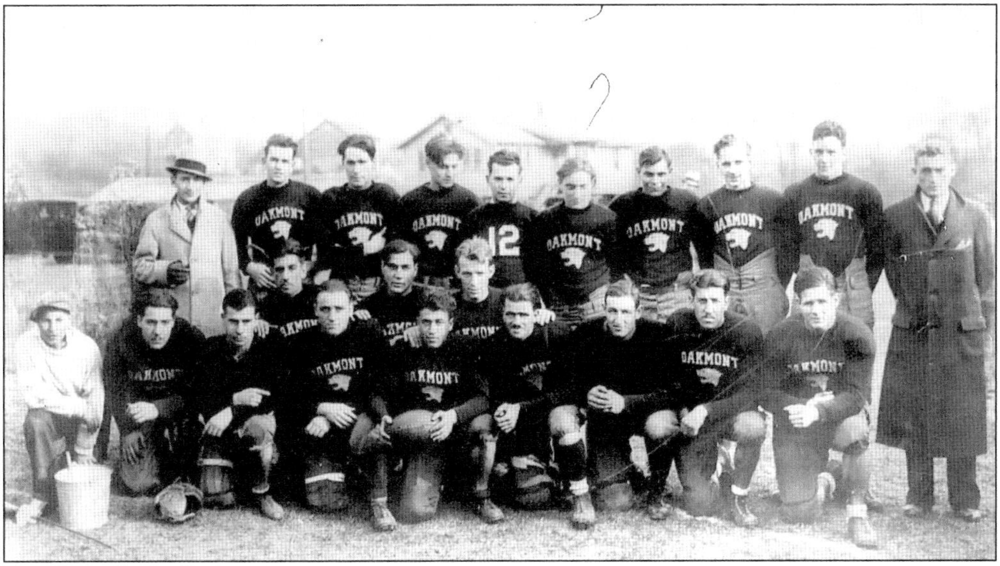

This 1931 Oakmont sandlot football team played its home games at Scaife Field on Ann Street. Unfortunately, the names of the players, coaches, and water boy (the young lad in the cap, kneeling on the left) could not be furnished. Sandlot and club football, baseball, and basketball leagues gave young men who had played on high school and college teams the opportunity to continue competing.

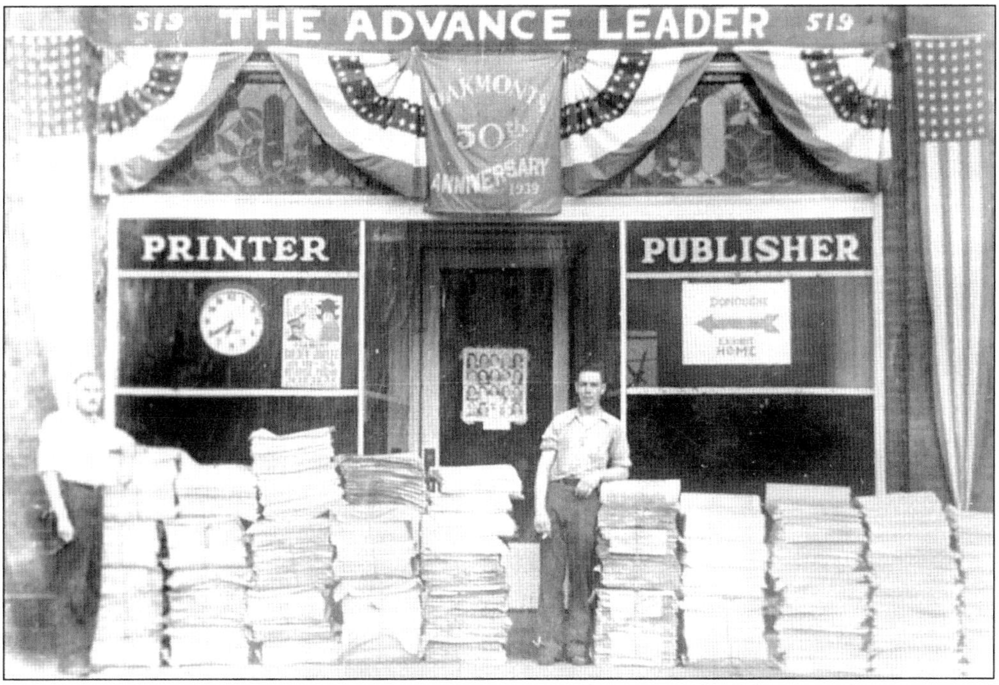

When Oakmont marked its 50th anniversary in 1939, the news of celebrations, banquets, and other happenings in town were reported in Len Anderson's newspaper, the *Advance Leader*. Here, the week's papers are stacked outside the newspaper's decorated office, awaiting the delivery truck. During the 1936 St. Patrick's Day flood, the newspaper was printed in this building by candlelight.

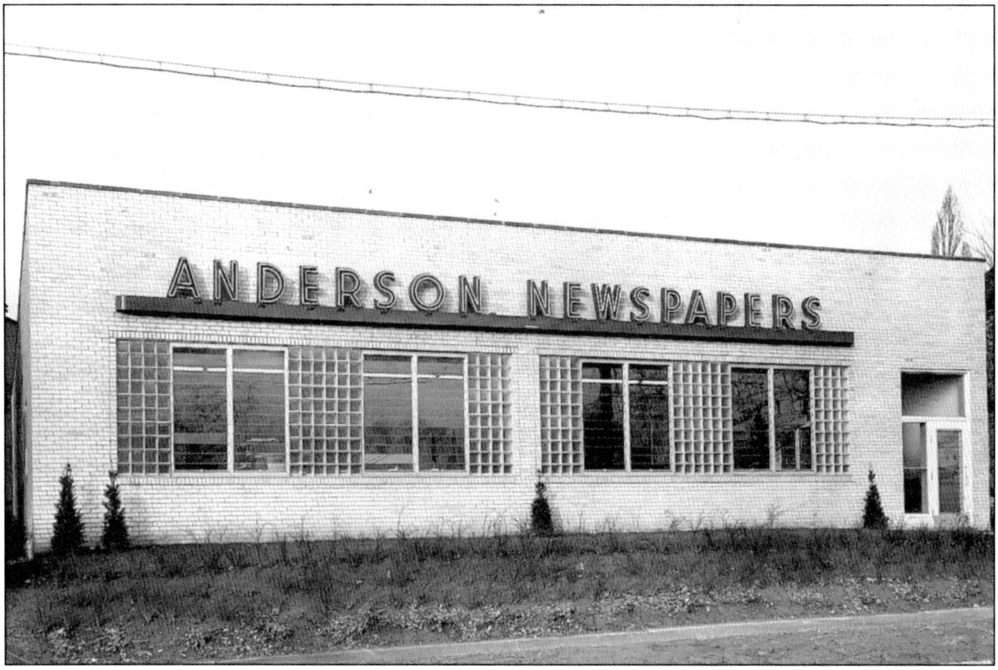

Anderson Newspapers operated out of this modern plant in the 200 block of Allegheny Avenue from March 1953 until Len Anderson sold the company in 1959. At the time of the sale, Anderson published 13 weekly newspapers out of this building, including the Oakmont-Verona *Advance Leader*.

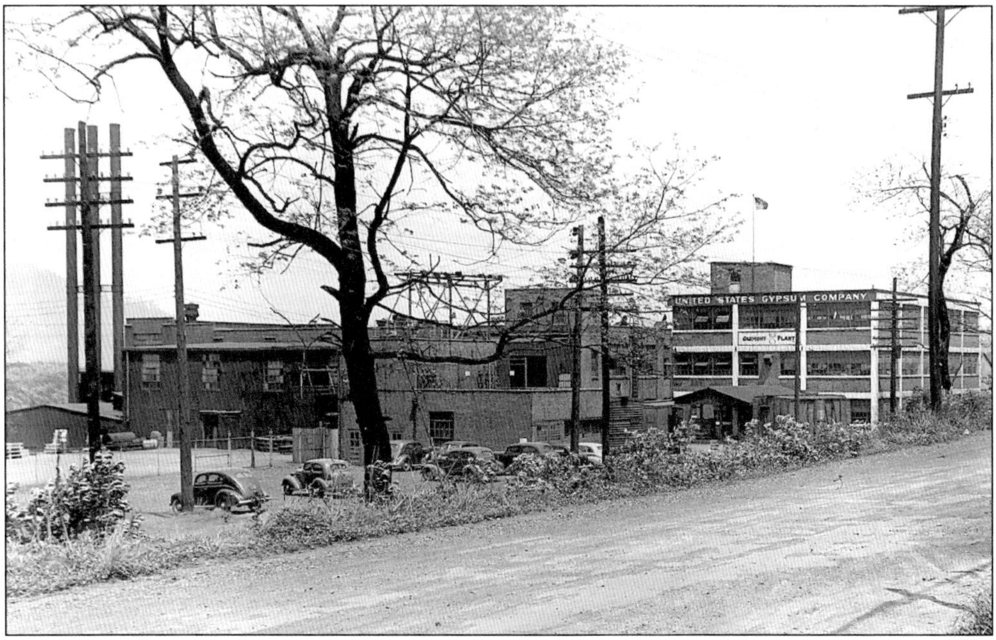

One of the more positive happenings in town in 1936 was the opening on March 7 of the paper and bag plants of United States Gypsum Company, then the largest manufacturer of building materials in the world. This photograph, taken in 1944, shows the plant and parking lot along Allegheny Avenue above the Hulton Bridge.

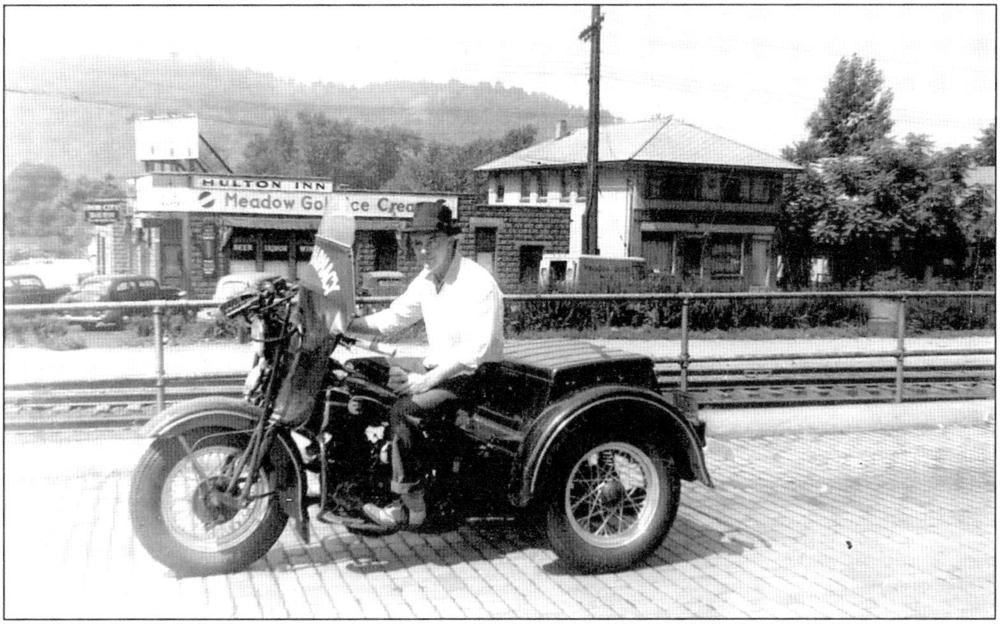

A motorcyclist delivered medicines and other goods to customers of the Oakmont Pharmacy, which was located on Allegheny River Boulevard. This photograph was taken at the intersection of Allegheny River Boulevard and Hulton Road. Signs of the Hulton Inn in the background advertised both Meadow Gold ice cream and Fort Pitt beer.

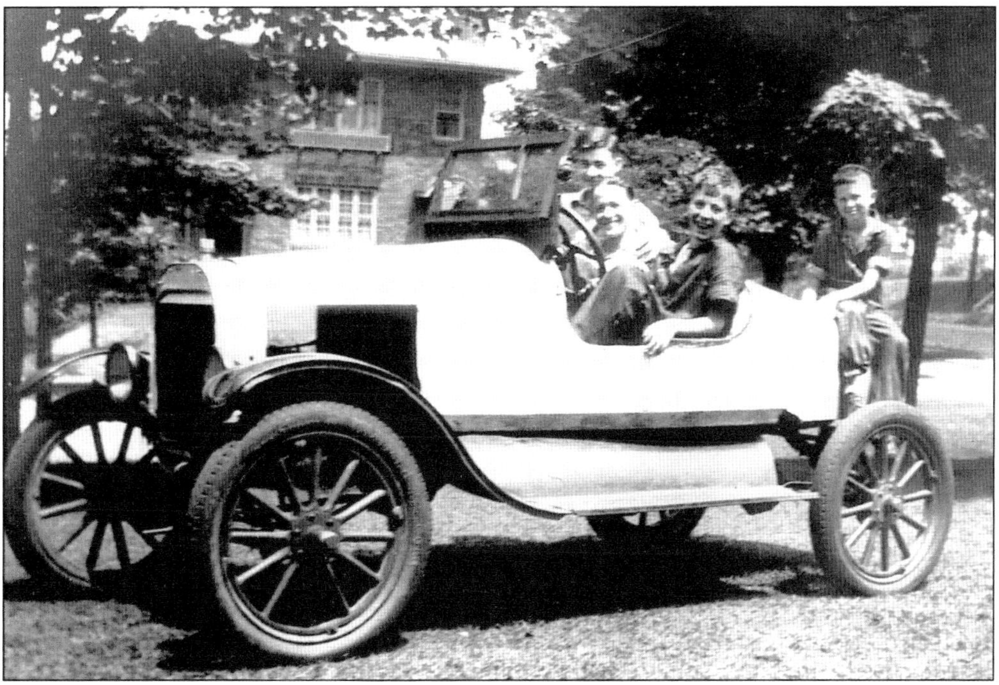

Dick Rowand and some of his friends got together for some warm-weather fun and acted all grown-up when they posed for this picture in the summer of 1931 at Fourth Street and California Avenue. Shown taking a pretend joyride in a vintage automobile are, from left to right, Bob Campbell, Don McCauley, Dick Rowand, and Laney Foreman.

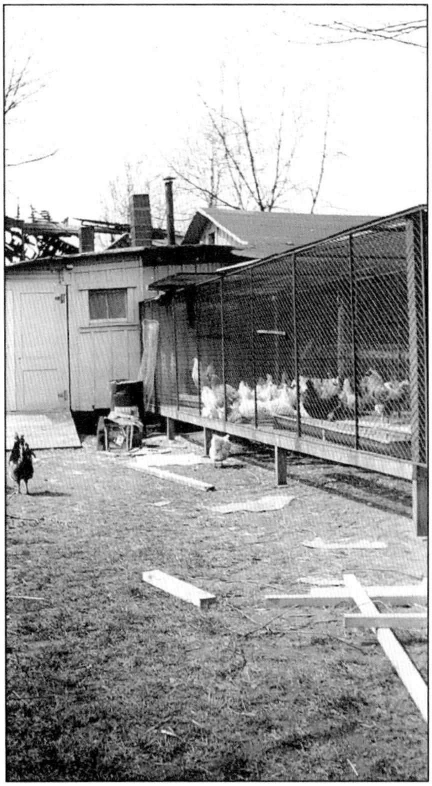

Chicken farming was a profitable venture when done on a large enough scale. Hite's Chicken Farm, located on the Allegheny River at the foot of Pennsylvania Avenue, was a large-scale operation. The farm prospered until it was heavily damaged by a fire in the 1930s. These chickens, in their outdoor coops away from the farm's main building, survived the blaze.

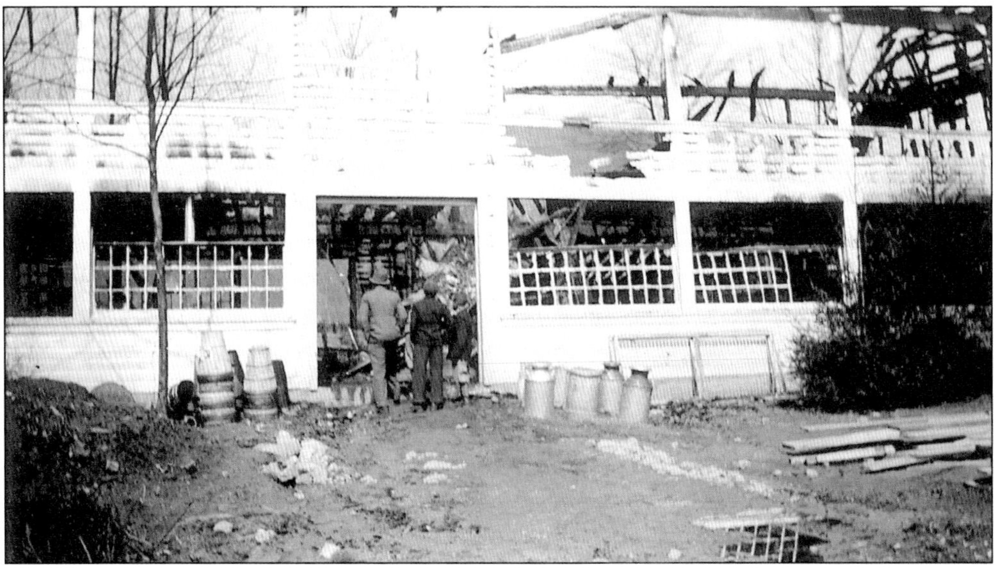

A group of men are shown inspecting the main building of Hite's Chicken Farm, which was almost completely gutted in the early 1930s fire. The Hites operated the chicken farm for many years. Several homes and an office building now occupy the area along the river at the bottom of Pennsylvania Avenue, where the farm was located.

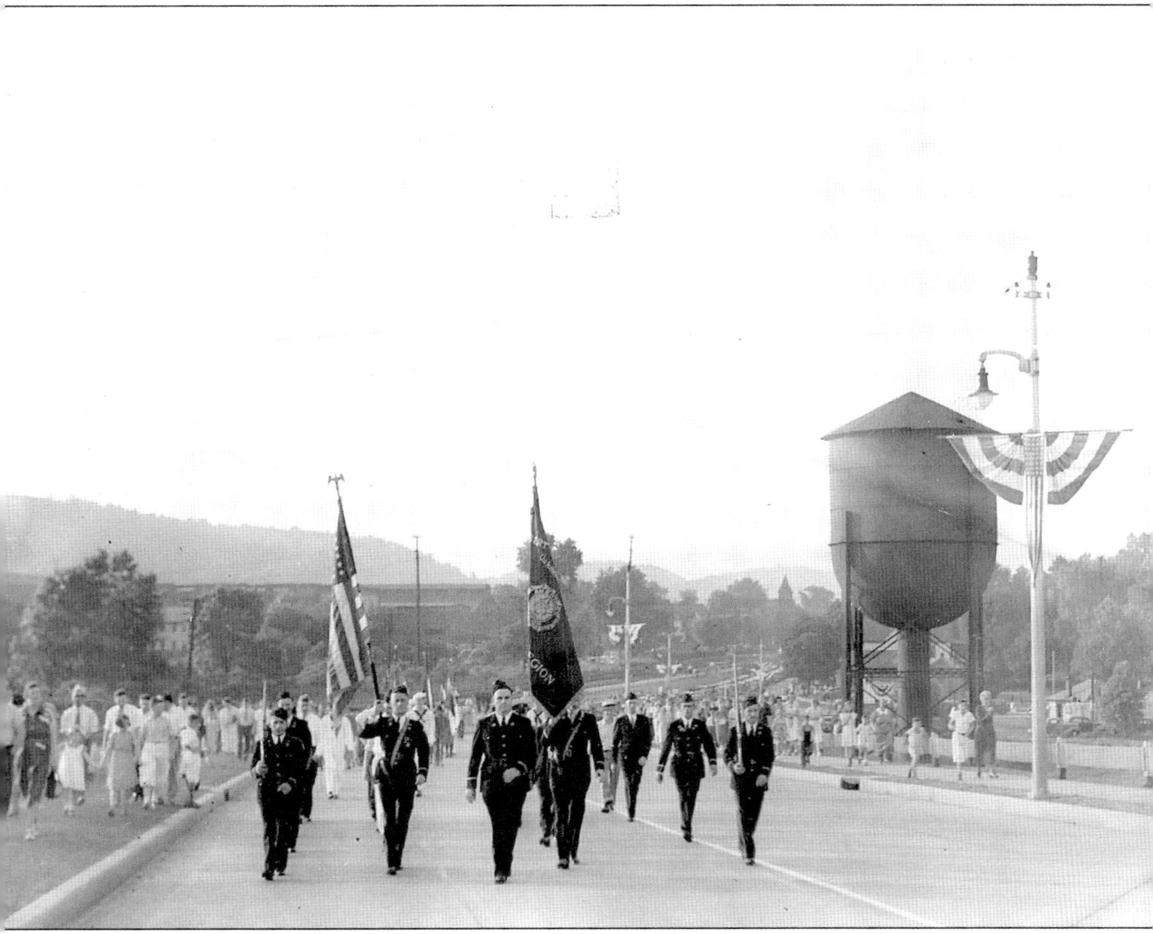

The Oakmont American Legion Post 600 was one of many marching units that took part in the parade on June 21, 1938, celebrating the opening of the new viaduct linking Oakmont and Verona and the dedication of the last section of Allegheny River Boulevard. Some 5,000 people attended the ceremonies. The viaduct replaced a wooden streetcar bridge between the towns and opened Allegheny River Boulevard for its entire length, from Washington Boulevard in Pittsburgh to Hulton Road in Oakmont. With the completion, the name of Oakmont's main street was changed from Oakmont Avenue to Allegheny River Boulevard. The first section of Allegheny River Boulevard, from Washington Boulevard to Verona, had been completed in 1931. The water tower on the right served the Verona Pennsylvania Railroad shops, which were located where the Daily Juice Products and Lamagna Cheese plants now stand.

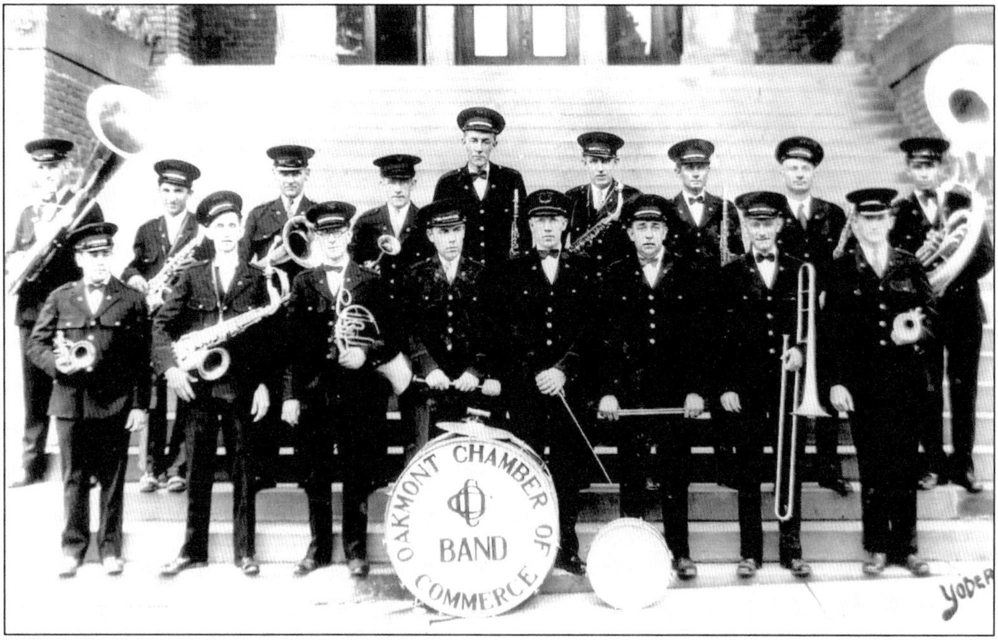

The Oakmont Chamber of Commerce Band was a very popular participant in parades and shows in the area. The musicians are shown here on the steps of Oakmont High School, where they performed regularly in the auditorium. The band also performed outdoor concerts in the park on summer evenings, and the concerts drew sizable crowds.

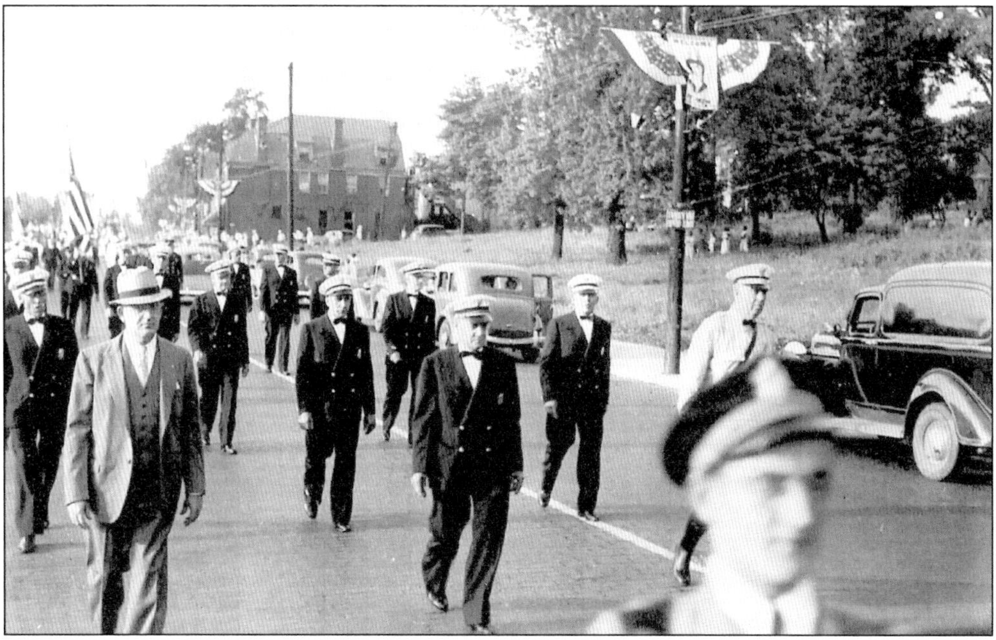

In 1939, the town's 50th anniversary, Oakmont and Verona co-hosted the Allegheny County Firemen's Convention. The convention parade, with 50 fire company units, was watched by 6,000 people. Members of the host Oakmont Fire Department were led in the parade by Mayor Wilbur Stopp (left) and Police Chief Charles Helwig (right) as they marched on Allegheny River Boulevard between Virginia and Pennsylvania Avenues.

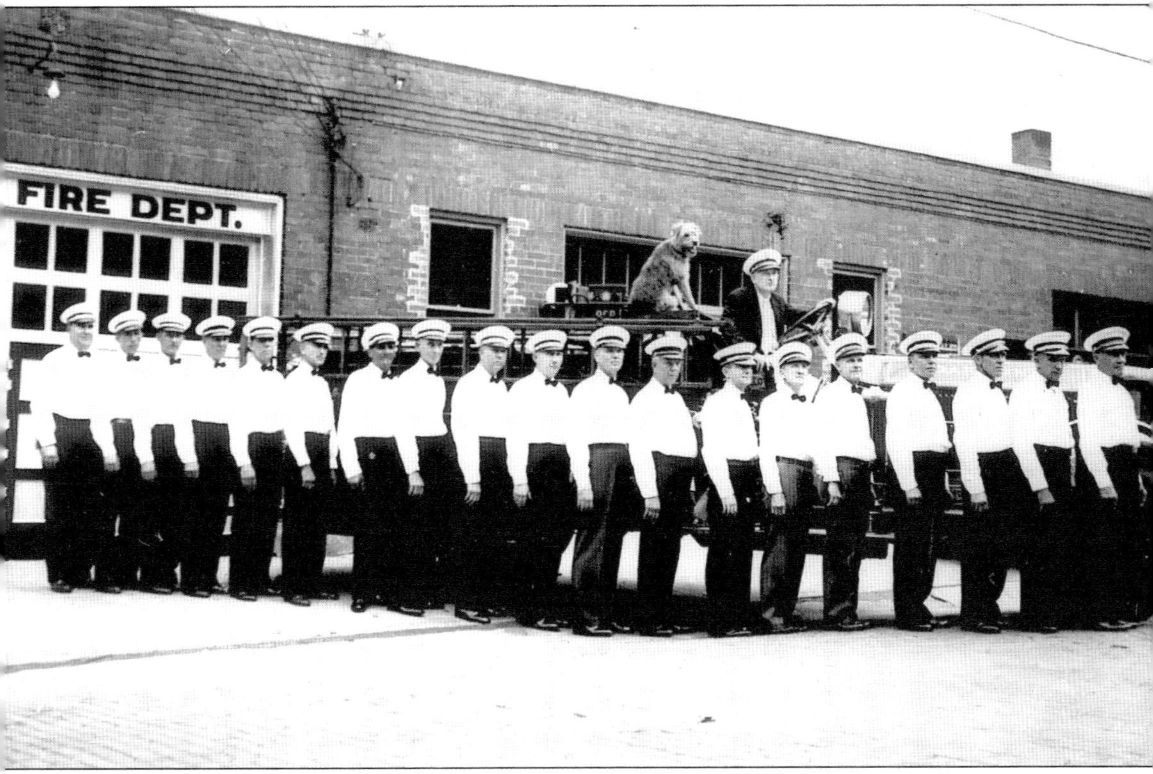

Members of the Oakmont Volunteer Fire Department are shown lined up before the fire station, which, when this picture was taken in 1938, was on Fifth Street where the borough offices now are located. Sitting behind the fireman in the driver's seat of the 1929 American LaFrance fire truck is Junior, the department's mascot. Junior ran to the station when the fire whistle blew and rode to every fire atop the truck. The dog was so faithful that when he failed to show up for a fire in January 1938, the *Advance Leader* reported his absence as a news bulletin.

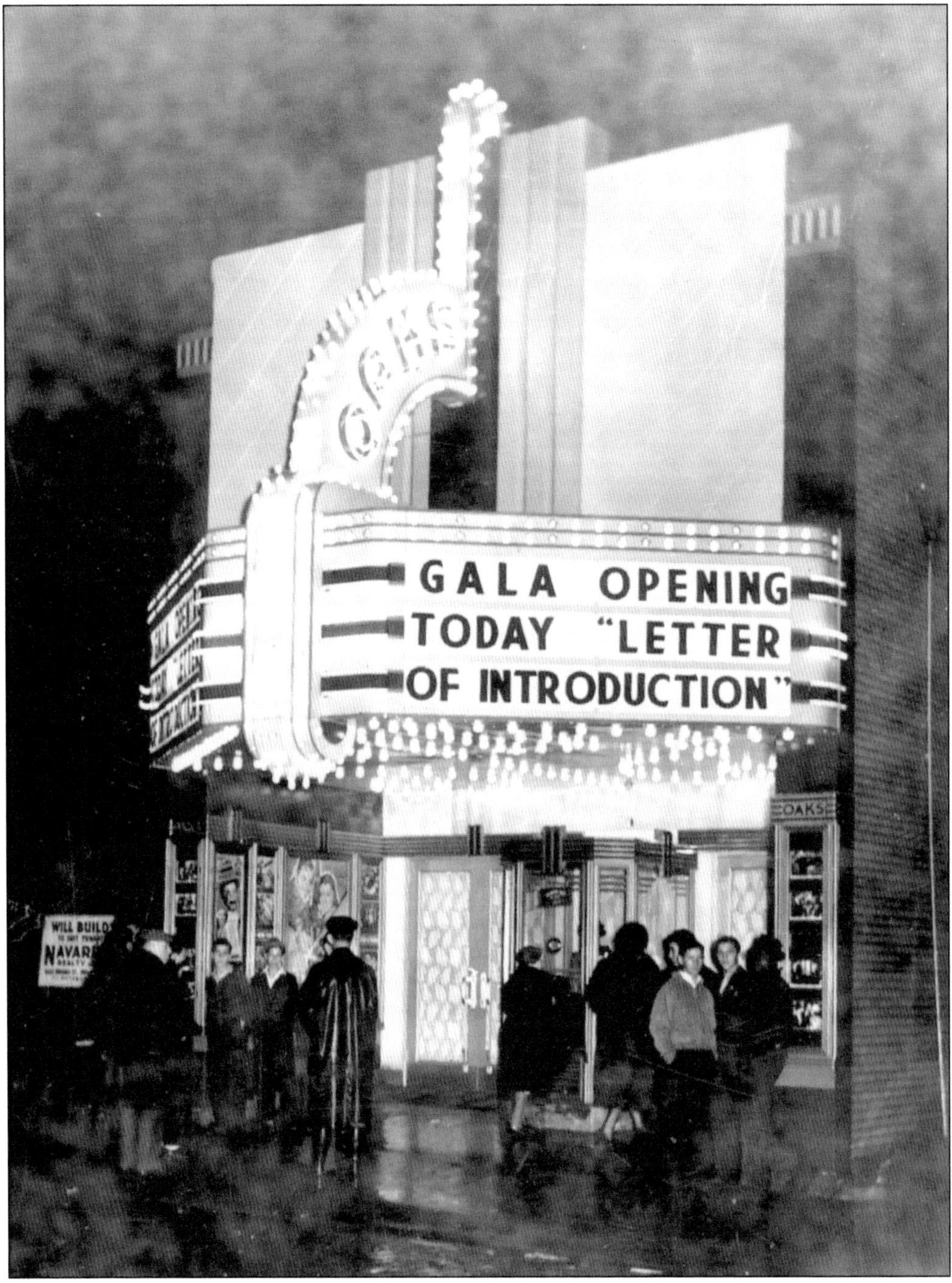

The Oaks Theater's gala opening in November 1938 featured Adolphe Menjou and Andrea Leeds in *Letter of Introduction* and drew a packed house for the inaugural showing. A raincoat-wearing policeman, shown talking with some young boys, provided crowd control. The Oaks, still operating on Allegheny River Boulevard between California and Washington Avenues, was owned and operated by Stephen M. Rodnok. He broke ground for the Oaks, which he referred to as his "new deluxe motion picture theater," in July 1938. Rodnok also owned the Lehigh Theater on Delaware Avenue in town.

Five

A Town Revitalized

Fortunately, Oakmont's economy began to recover in 1940. Unfortunately, the recovery resulted from increased industrial activity in preparation for the country's anticipated entry into the war that had been raging in Europe. The war was getting closer to home. The first group of local men were drafted in 1940 and called to active duty the following February.

As war fears grew more intense, armed guards were stationed on the Hulton Bridge and at the town's industrial plants to protect against sabotage. All Oakmont churches began conducting special prayer services, a practice that continued throughout the war years.

But not all of the news was war related in the early 1940s. The Oakmont Heights Golf Course, now Oakmont East, opened in 1941, and the Oakmont post office finally got its permanent home on Allegheny River Boulevard that year.

The town's first scrap drive was held in March 1942. The Scaife Company received a government armaments contract and built a 90,000-square-foot plant to handle the work. The new plant replaced Scaife Field, so the company agreed to grade property across Ann Street for a new field and install lights. The high school football team opened the 1942 season with its first-ever night game there but lost to Shaler 13-7. To help get people's minds off the war, the Oakmont Lions Club presented its first variety show at the high school in 1943.

The war's end brought a slowdown in industrial activity and the local economy declined once again. But Oakmont continued to grow. By 1949, when the town bought its first patrol car, Oakmont police had more than 7,250 residents to protect with more to come. In 1950, the area from Twelfth Street to the Pennsylvania Turnpike was annexed from Plum Borough. A year later, East and West Crystal Drives and Oakwood Terrace also were annexed.

New facilities opened in the latter 1950s, including the Presbyterian Home on Hulton Road, Memorial School on Fifth Street, and St. Anthony's School for Exceptional Children on Hulton Road. Kellogg American Incorporated, then part of the Scaife Company, opened a plant here in 1959.

Local women's organizations became more involved in borough affairs with remarkable success in the late 1950s. In 1955, members of the Dark Hollow Garden Club persuaded Maria B. Satler to donate to the borough the wooded area she owned at the top of Pennsylvania Avenue, which led to the creation of Dark Hollow Woods. Seven years later, through the efforts of the Oakmont Garden Club, adjoining acreage owned by the Bessemer and Lake Erie Railroad was deeded to the borough. The area now is officially called Dark Hollow Woods-Karl E. Satler Memorial Park and Nature Preserve.

In 1959, the Woman's Club and Junior Woman's Club rallied support for a $150,000 bond issue to purchase land for Riverside Park.

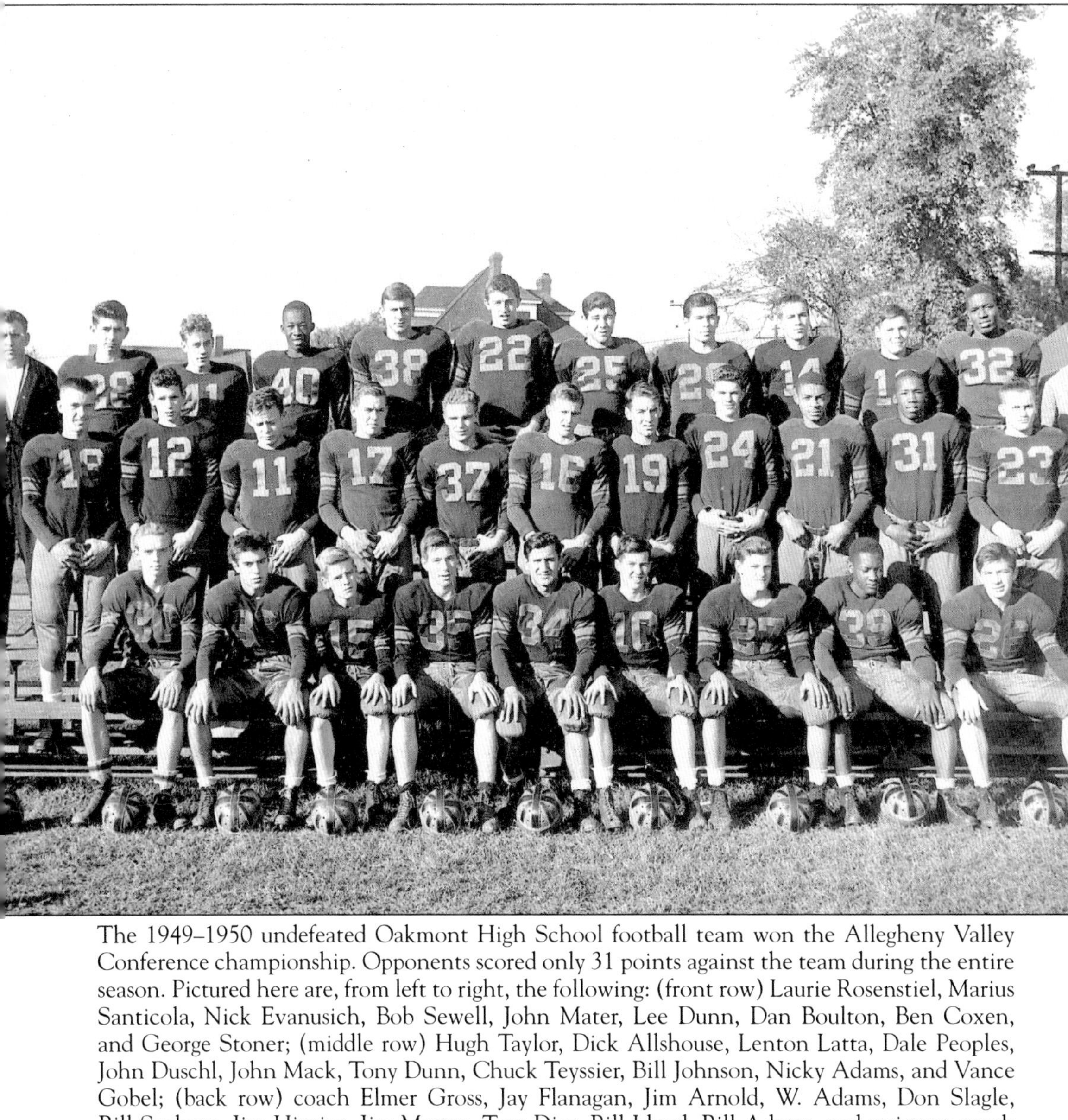

The 1949–1950 undefeated Oakmont High School football team won the Allegheny Valley Conference championship. Opponents scored only 31 points against the team during the entire season. Pictured here are, from left to right, the following: (front row) Laurie Rosenstiel, Marius Santicola, Nick Evanusich, Bob Sewell, John Mater, Lee Dunn, Dan Boulton, Ben Coxen, and George Stoner; (middle row) Hugh Taylor, Dick Allshouse, Lenton Latta, Dale Peoples, John Duschl, John Mack, Tony Dunn, Chuck Teyssier, Bill Johnson, Nicky Adams, and Vance Gobel; (back row) coach Elmer Gross, Jay Flanagan, Jim Arnold, W. Adams, Don Slagle, Bill Seaburn, Jim Higgins, Jim Mastro, Tom Diez, Bill Lloyd, Bill Adams, and assistant coach Dan McCann.

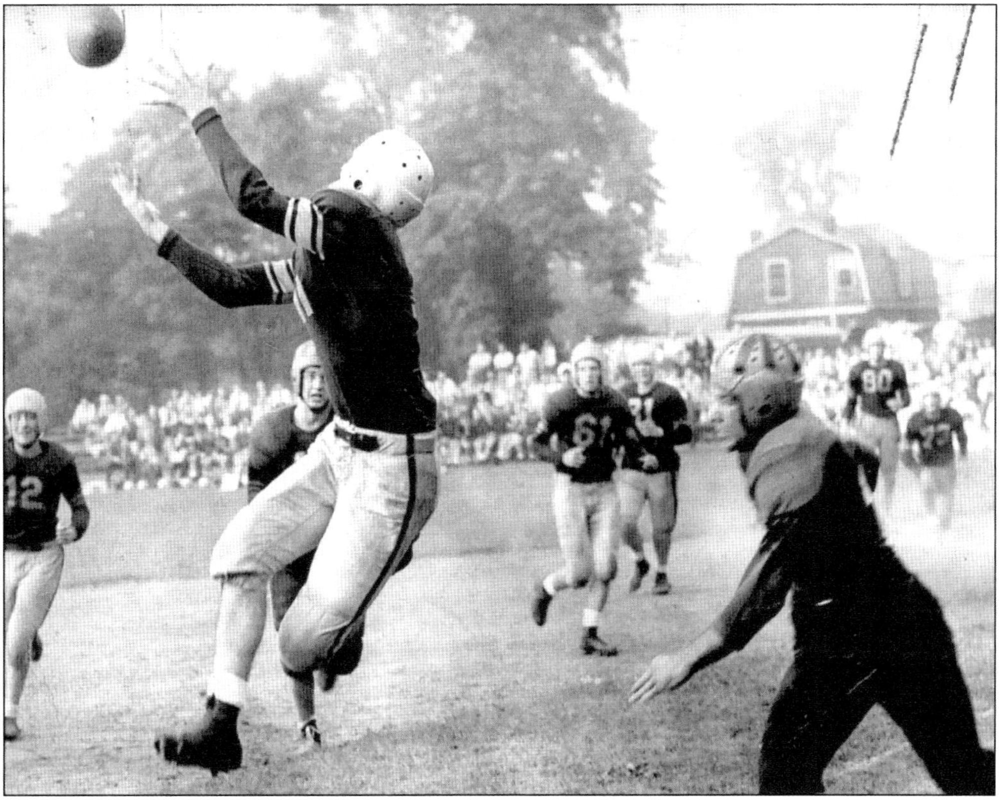

An Oakmont High School defender in a striped helmet prepares to make a hit on the visiting school's pass receiver in a 1950 game played at Scaife Field. The game had to have been played early in the 1950 season. The nearby trees still sported an abundance of leaves and the field was covered with grass, not mud, as was often the case later in the season.

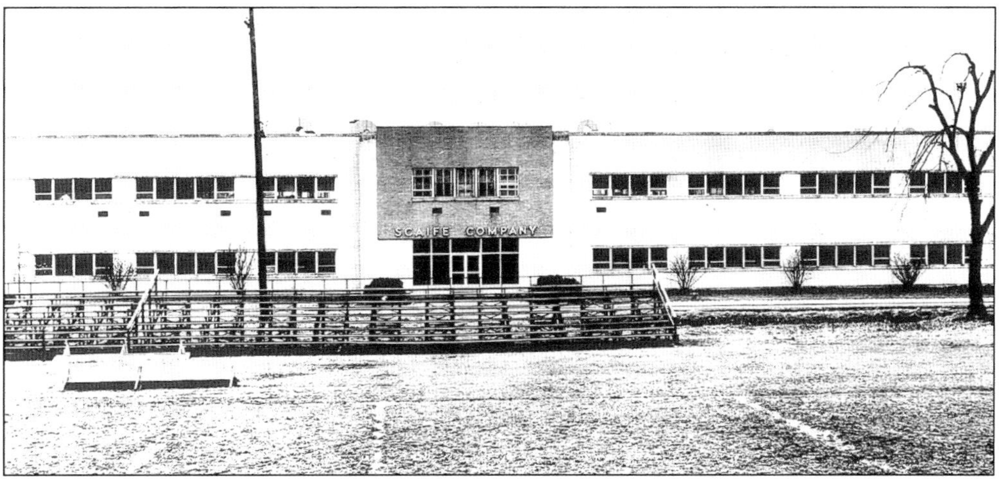

The Scaife Company headquarters was directly across Ann Street from Scaife Field, which the company owned. Oakmont High School played home games on Scaife Field, as did the town's many sports teams, until Riverside Park was built in the 1960s. The bleachers in this photograph overlook a muddy field lined, barely, for football. The Scaife building now is Beverly Healthcare-Oakmont, a nursing home.

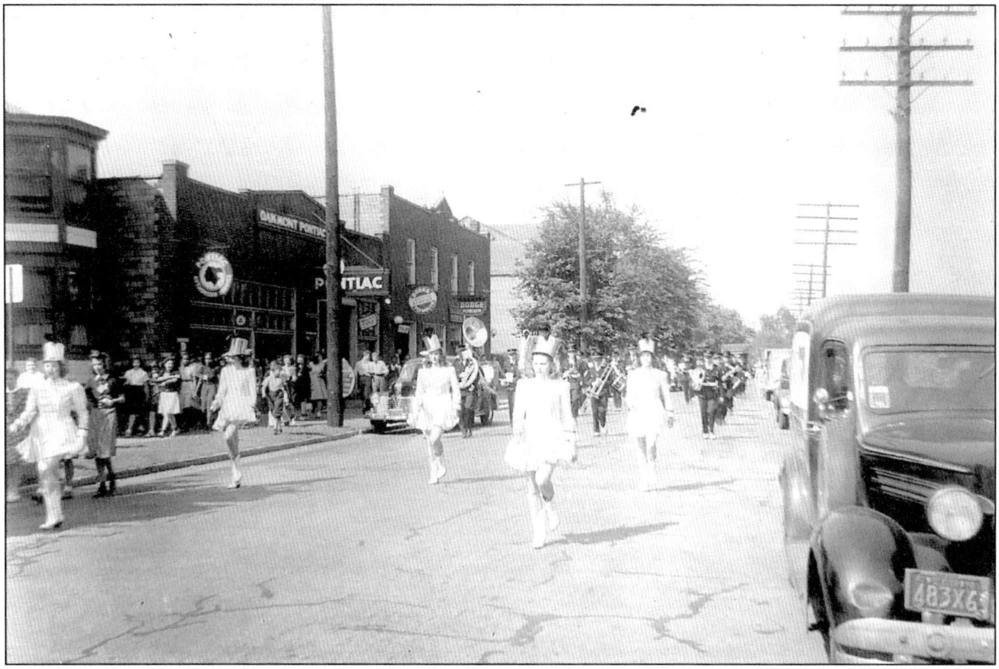

The Oakmont High School band marched from the school to Scaife Field on Ann Street, where home football games were played before Riverside Park was built. This photograph was taken in the autumn of 1941 (a 1941 license plate is seen on the delivery truck on the right), as the band approached Ann Street on Allegheny Avenue.

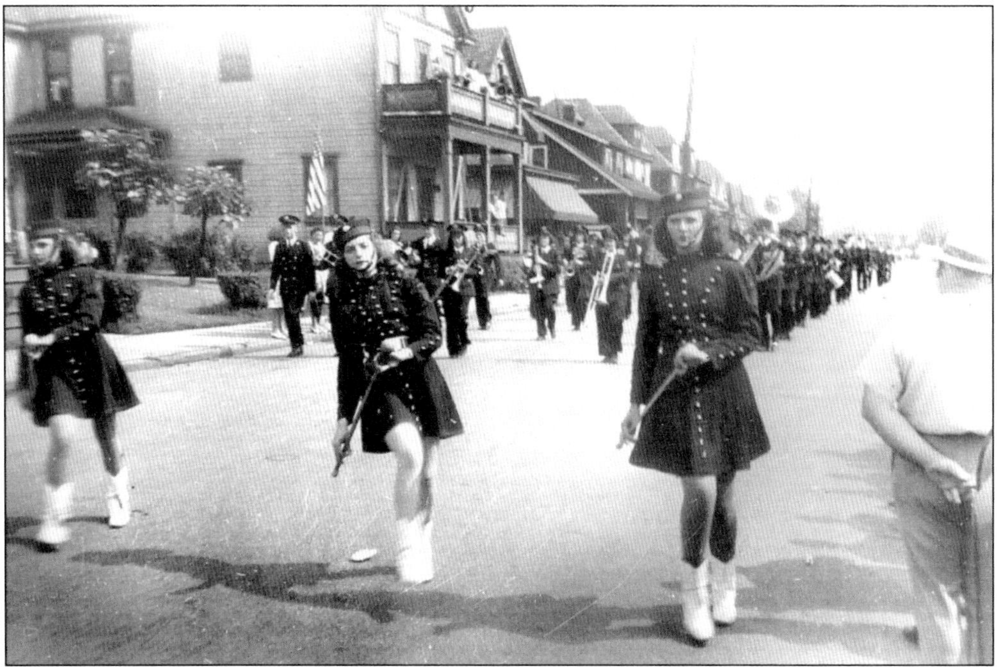

Three majorettes led the high school band in a parade in August 1946. Music always has been a strong component of schools here. Before the Oakmont and Verona school districts merged, both high schools were intensely competitive, not only in sports, but in music as well.

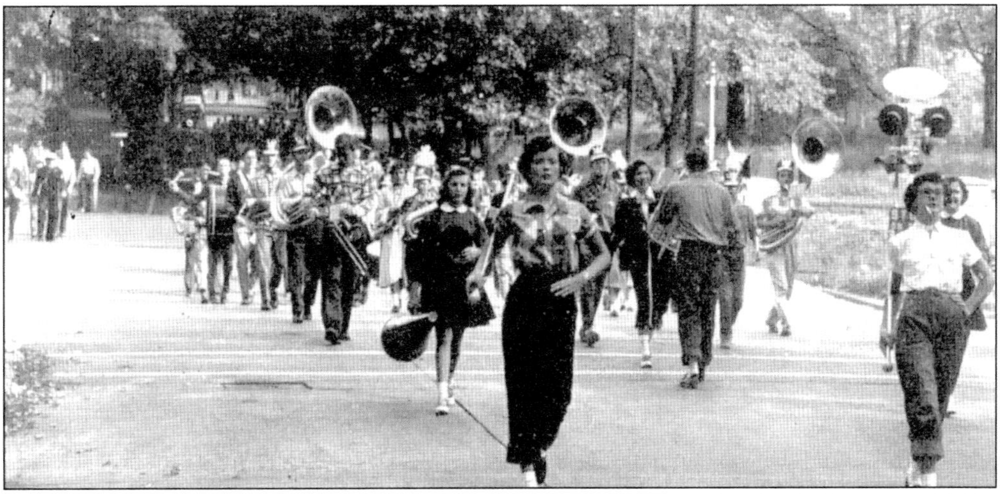

Students followed behind the band marching to pep rallies at Scaife Field in the 1950s. This is the 1953 Oakmont High School Band, led by majorettes and cheerleaders, marching along Allegheny Avenue near Pennsylvania Avenue on their way to a rally at the field on Ann Street.

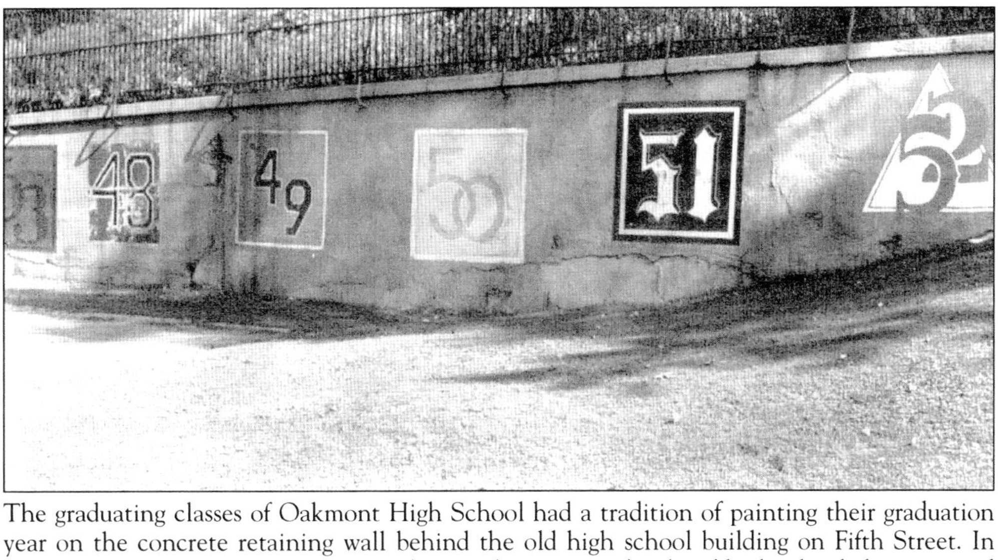

The graduating classes of Oakmont High School had a tradition of painting their graduation year on the concrete retaining wall behind the old high school building on Fifth Street. In 1961, when the building was converted to an elementary school and high school classes moved to the Tenth Street School, the tradition ended for a simple reason: there was no suitable retaining wall at Tenth Street.

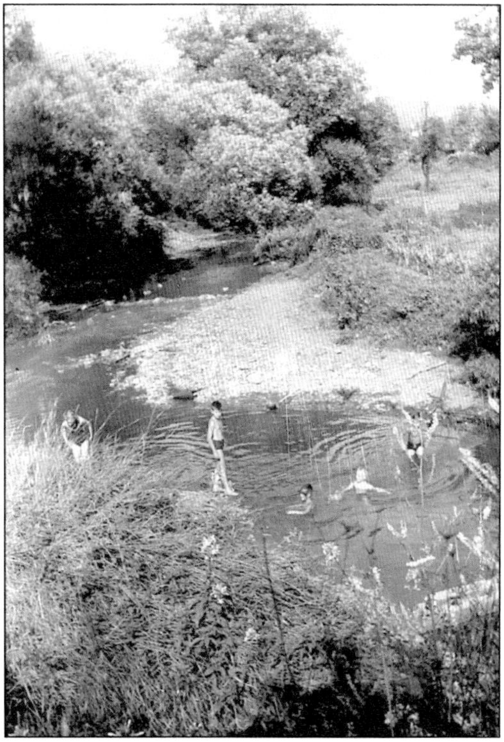

The Willows pool was not the only place for summertime fun in Oakmont. Local youngsters like these in this July 1940 photograph, who preferred to swim where there were no guards, no regulations, and no admission price, found their fun at a swimming hole on Plum Creek. Both boys and girls escaped from the heat in Plum Creek.

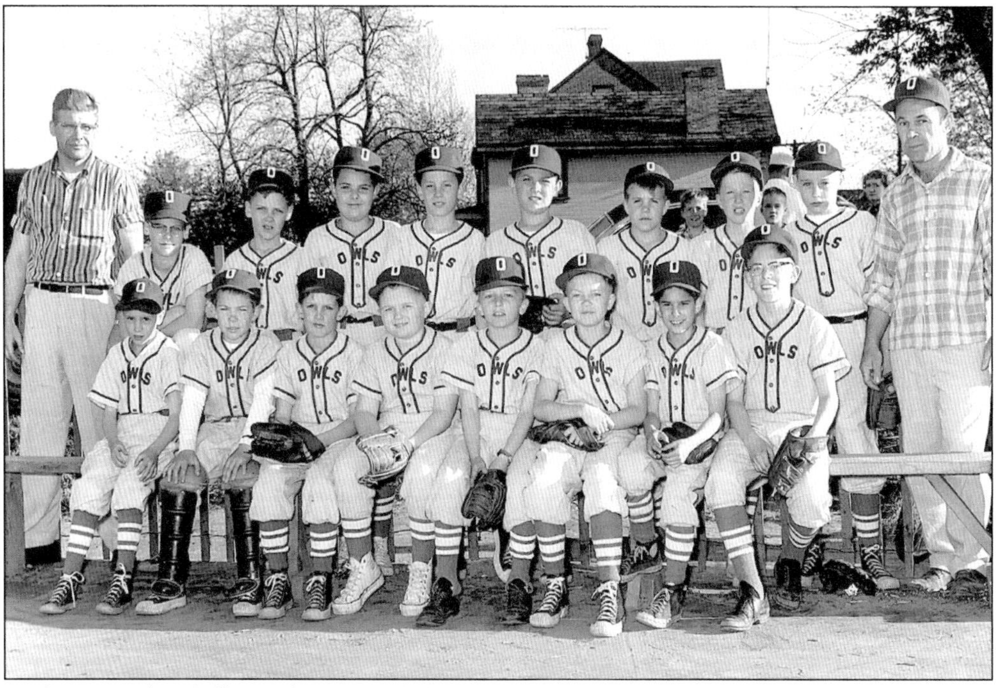

Little League baseball was the sport of choice for Oakmont's growing youth population in the 1950s. Like the other teams in town, the 1958 Owls, members of the Cub Baseball League, played their games at Scaife Field on Ann Street. Len Flowers (right) was the Owls' manager that year. He played a prominent role in sports and recreational activities in Oakmont for many years.

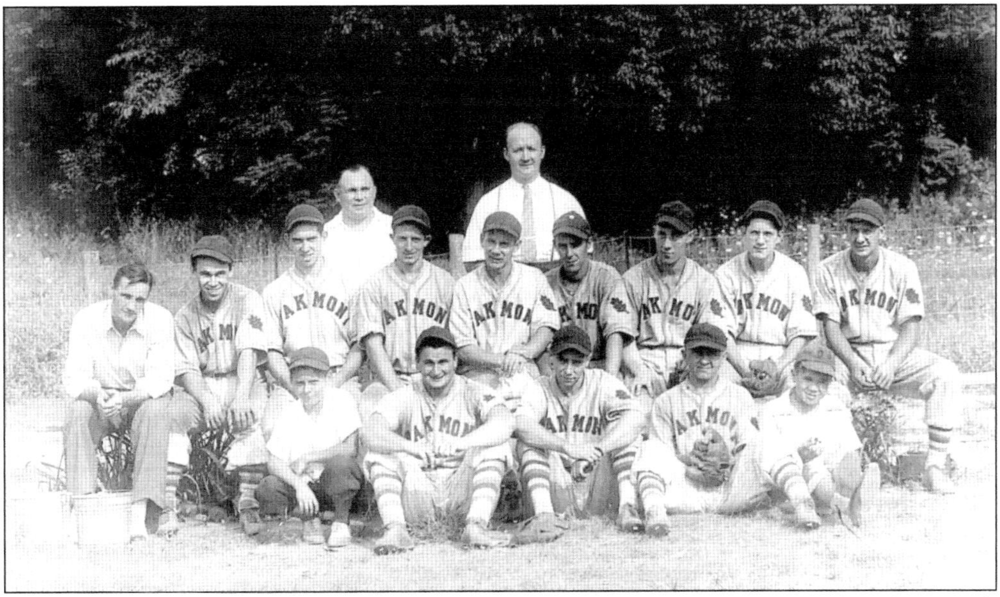

This team represented Oakmont in sandlot league play. In those simpler times (this photograph was taken in 1948), water buckets, shown in the left foreground, were all the players had to rely on for thirst-quenching refreshment during a game. The team played at Scaife Field on Ann Street, across from the Scaife Company plant, where all organized sports in Oakmont were played at the time.

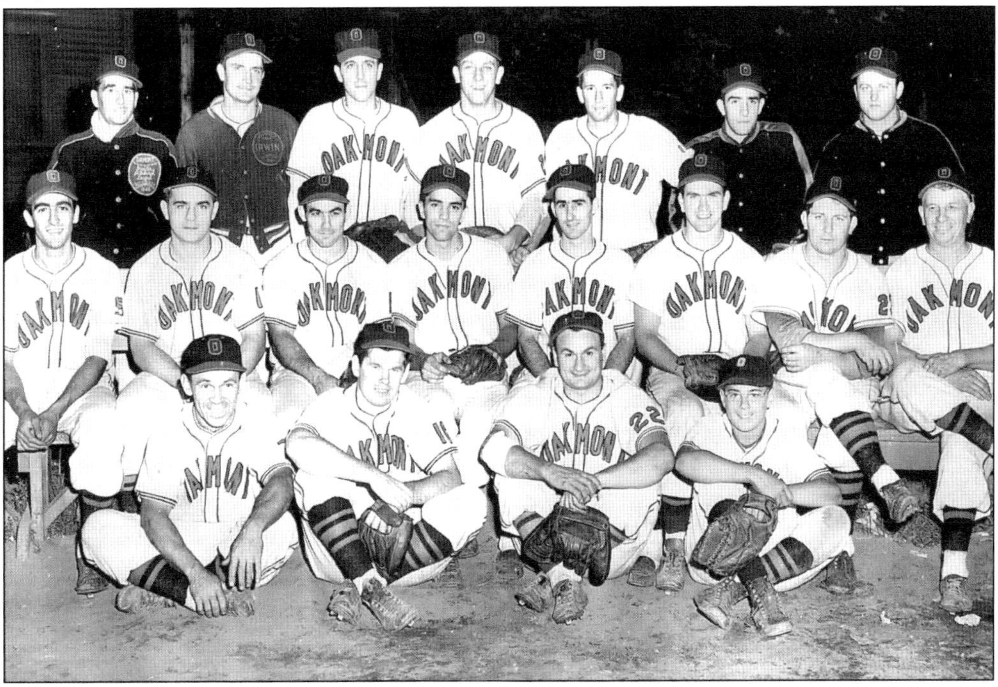

The man on the left in the third row is wearing a jacket identifying this Oakmont sandlot baseball team as the 1946 champions of the Greater Pittsburgh League. Not all of the players in this photograph, which was taken in the 1950s, were identified. Those who were include Len Flowers, Charles Mesiano, Bill Drinski, Howard Kleber, Joe Scalzo, Clyde Dreher, and Ray Linn.

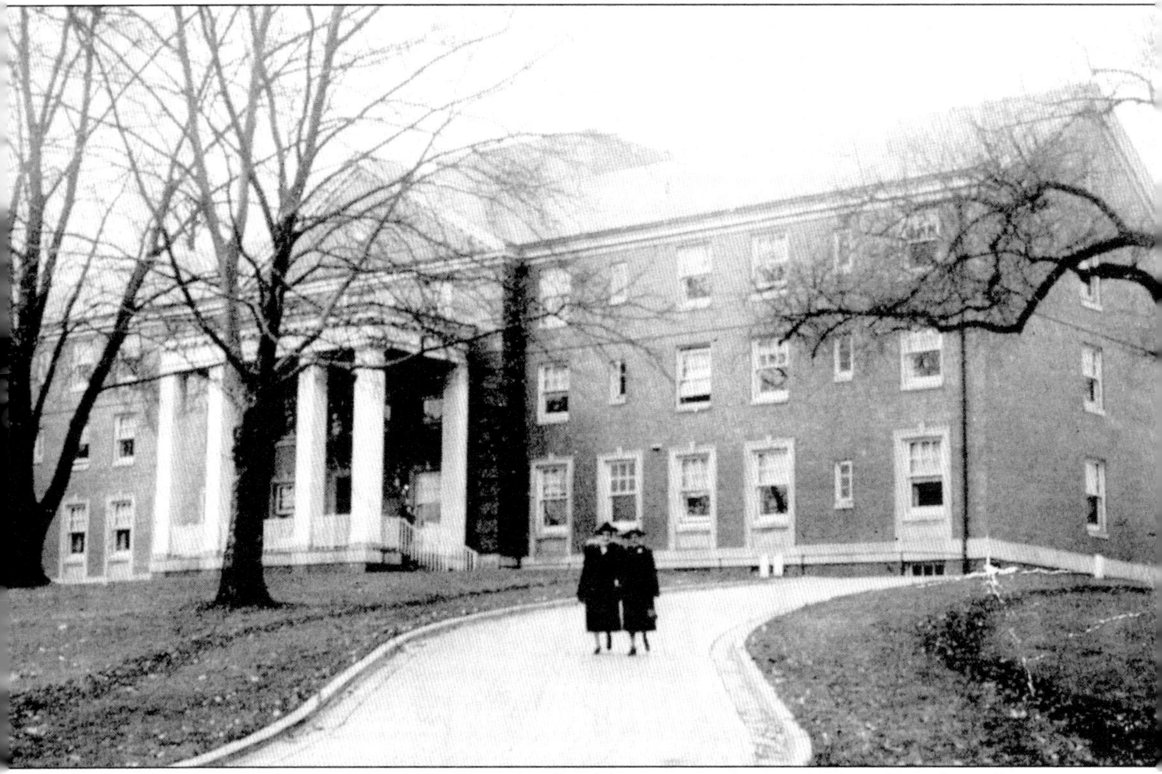

Now called Presbyterian Senior Care, this healthcare complex on Hulton Road was known as the Oakmont Presbyterian Home when it opened in May 1950. Established by the Presbyterian Church as a home for the aged, it has grown over the years to include a nursing home, the Presbyterian Medical Center of Oakmont (opened in 1986), and facilities dedicated to the care of those with special needs. Today, the original structure is a personal care facility called Westminster Place. Built on what was the Flannery estate, Presbyterian Senior Care borders the Oakmont Country Club.

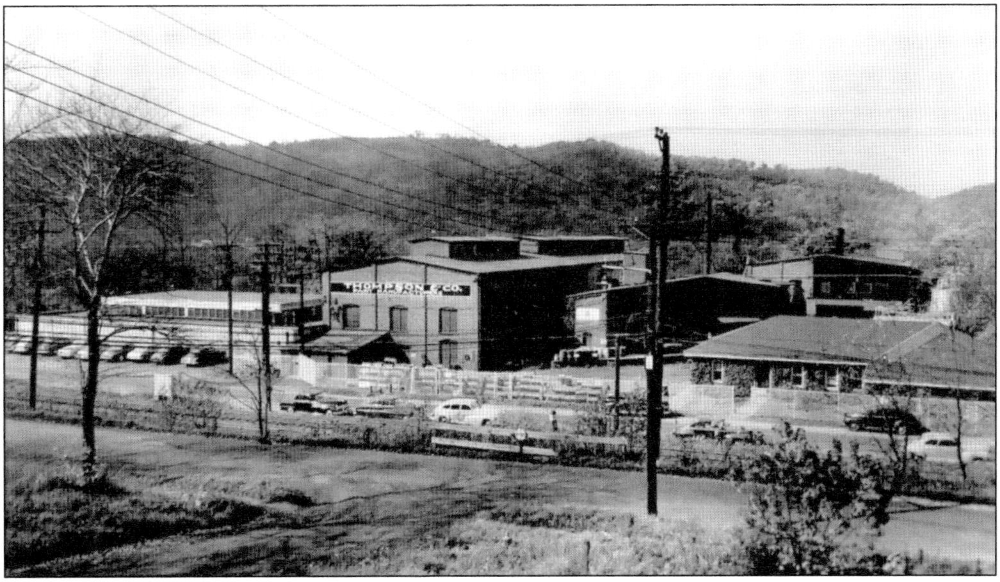

The Thompson Paint Company moved its plant to a nine-acre riverside site in Oakmont in 1927. The company consolidated its general offices and research laboratory at the local plant six years later. Thompson Paint manufactured industrial paints and chemical coatings at the plant, shown in this 1940s photograph, on Allegheny Avenue just north of the Hulton Bridge.

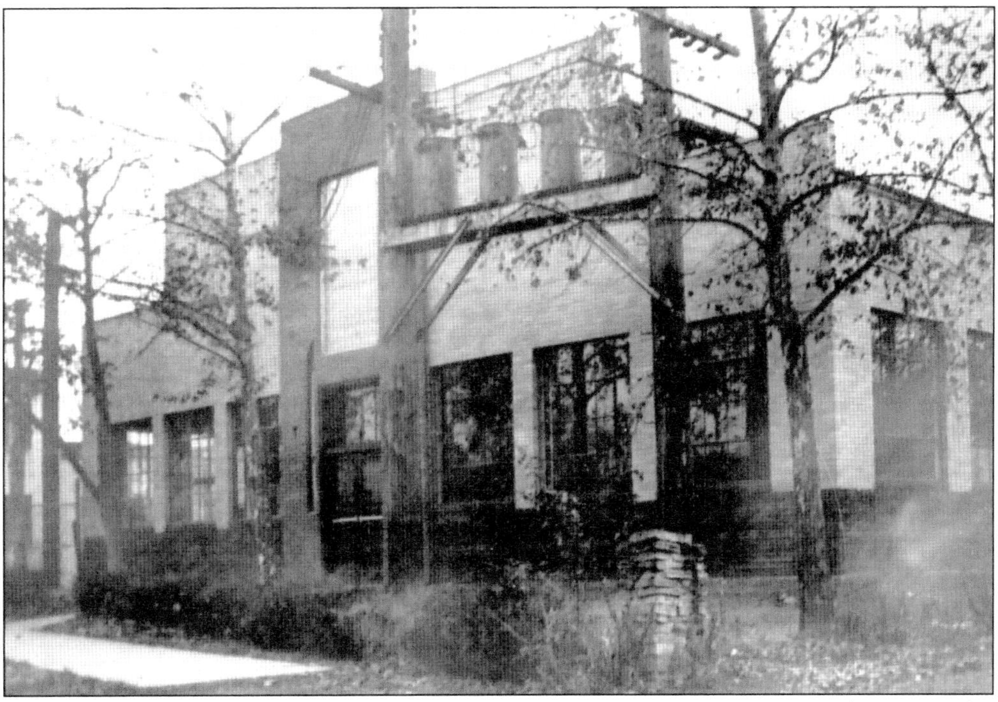
The Walters Manufacturing Company, which produced mill and mining supplies, opened a plant on Pennsylvania Avenue in June 1930. The company managed to maintain its Oakmont operation during the Great Depression and expanded its facility here in 1941, as it prepared to manufacture defense-related products to meet the growing demand brought on by country's entry into World War II.

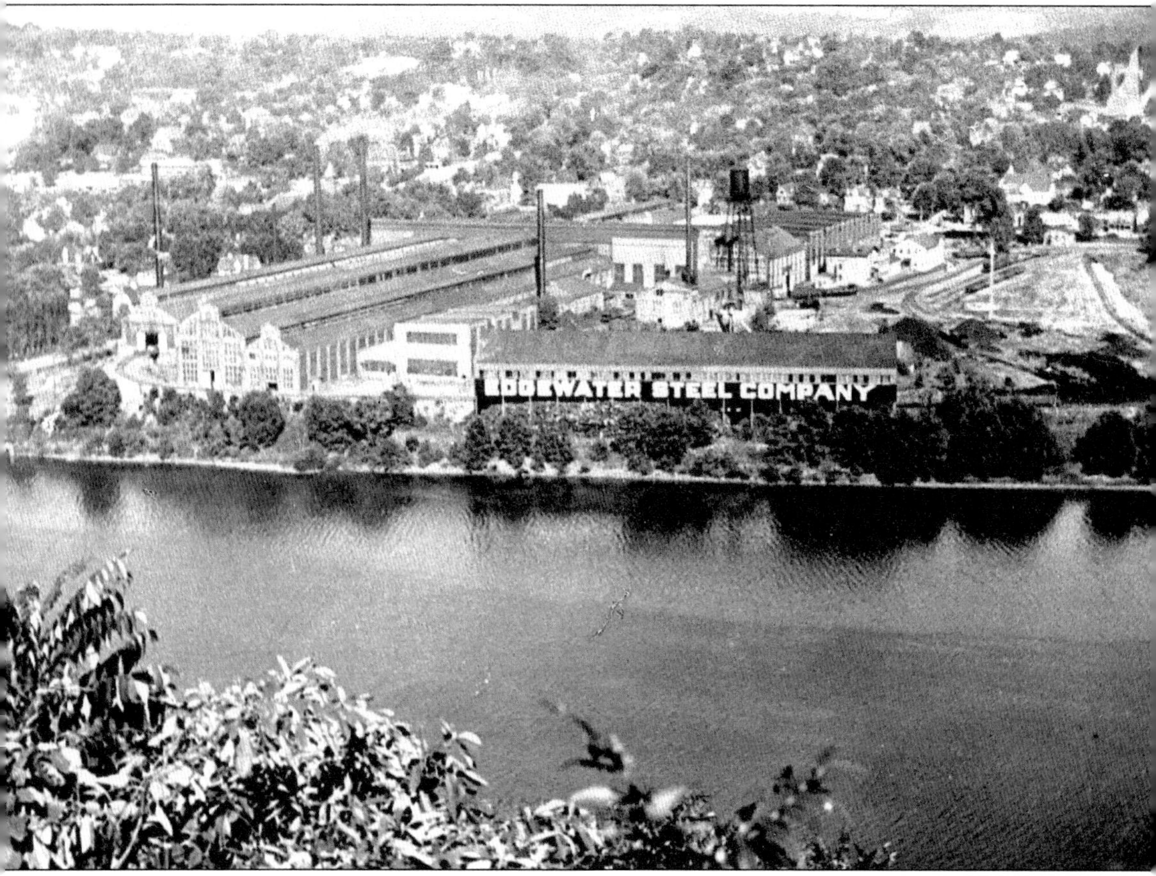

The Edgewater Steel Company, located on 35 acres on the Allegheny River, was Oakmont's largest industry and largest employer from its founding in 1916 until it closed in 2001. Edgewater's bankruptcy filing on August 6, 2001, was the third in the company's recent troubled history.

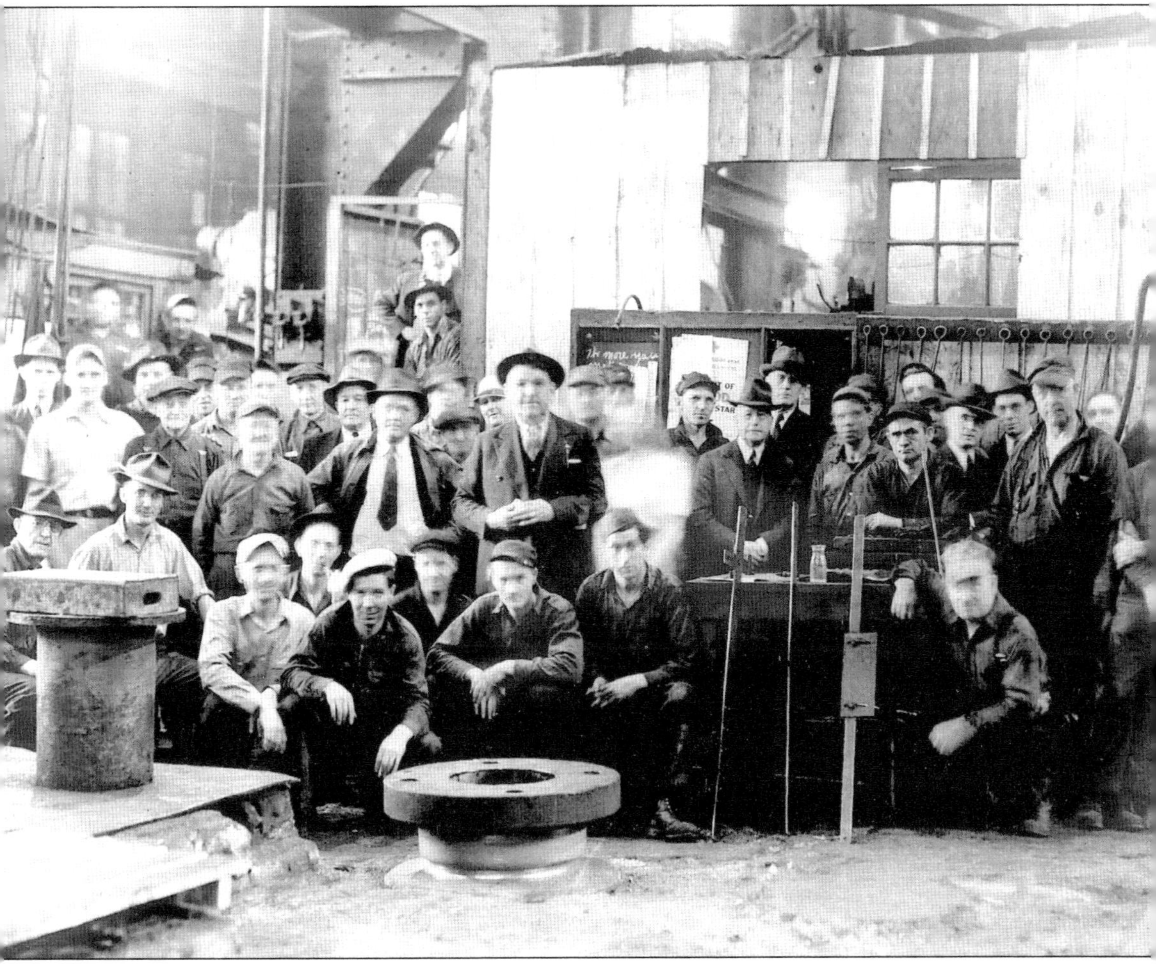

Edgewater Steel manufactured steel wheels, rings, forgings, and other industrial products in its Oakmont plant. In 1944, Edgewater Steel workers and supervisors were photographed when they gathered for an impromptu ceremony to mark the production of the plant's one-millionth wheel.

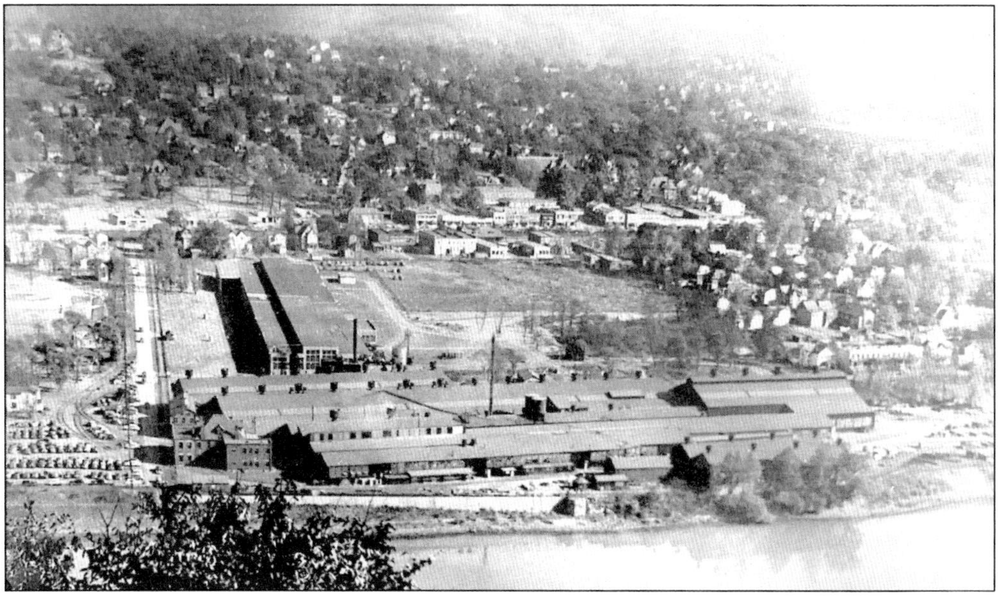

The Scaife Company manufactured water heaters, boilers, and other products in its plant on the Allegheny River between Ann Street and Delaware Avenue. Charles Scaife relocated his Pittsburgh plant to Oakmont in 1891 on land his wife inherited from her father, James Verner. Scaife Field, later donated to the borough, is seen on the left. The company ceased operations in 1964.

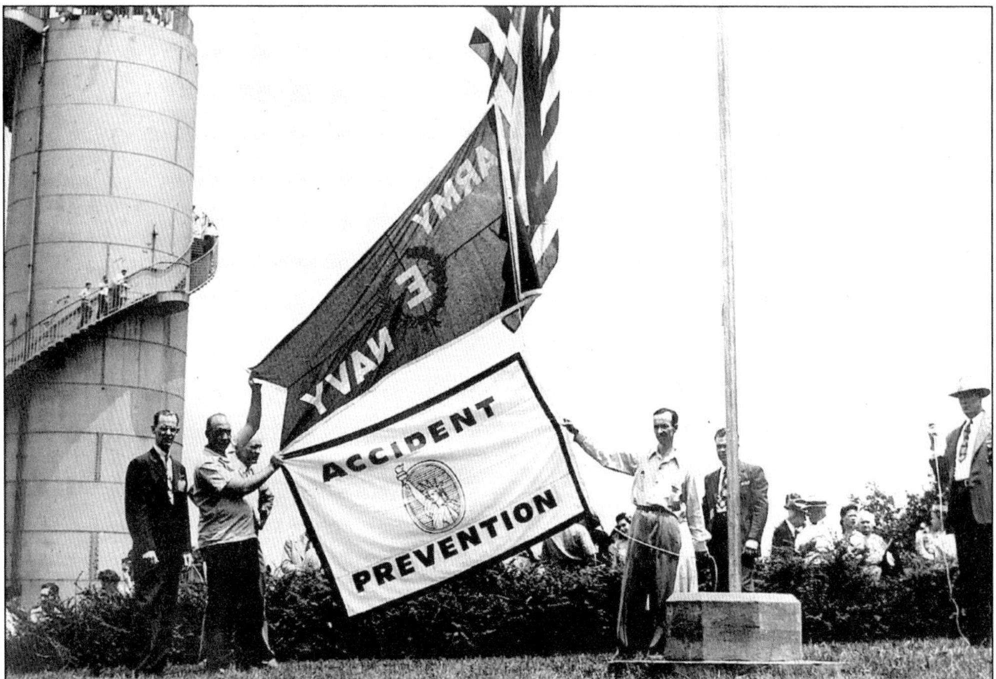

Manufacturing bomb casings for the army, the Scaife Company set production records during the 1940s. Here, Scaife employees raise the Army-Navy "E" flag the company was awarded for war production efforts, and an accident-prevention pennant was presented by an insurance company.

The Scaife Company had a natural gas well on its river front property that provided fuel for its plant's operations. The well was a very valuable resource for the company, especially during the World War II years, when the Oakmont plant was operating at full capacity.

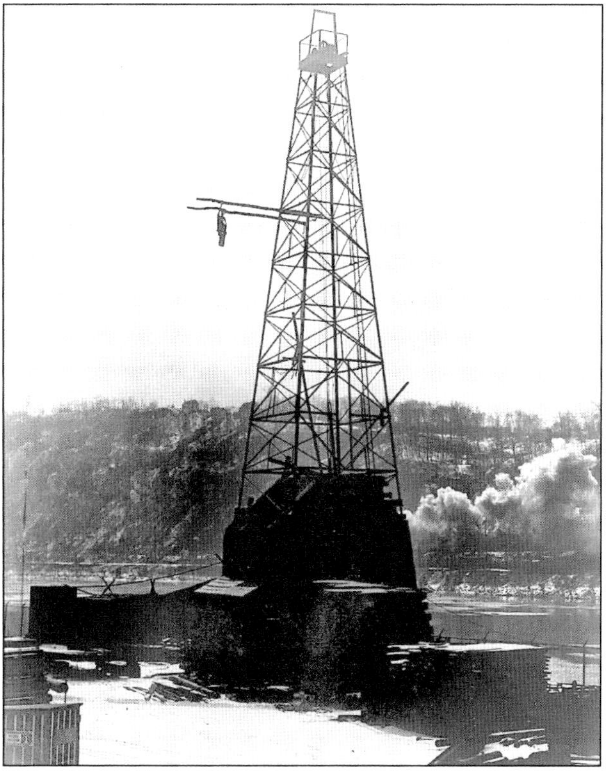

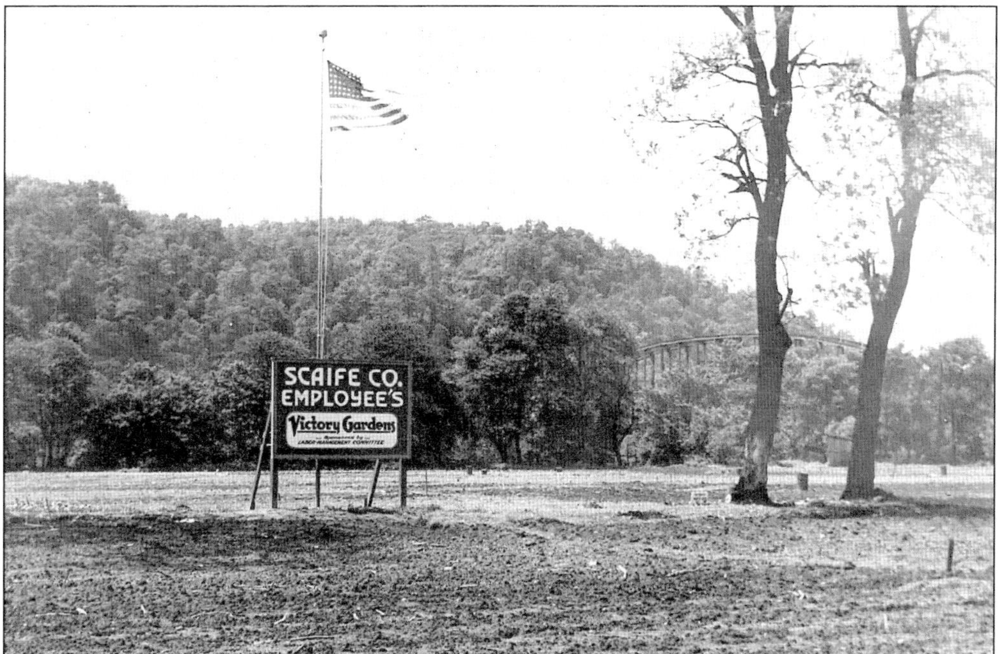

Victory gardens were very popular during World War II, and people across the country planted and tended small plots to grow their own vegetables. The Scaife Company sponsored a victory garden for employees near the Allegheny River in an area that now is the site of Riverside Park.

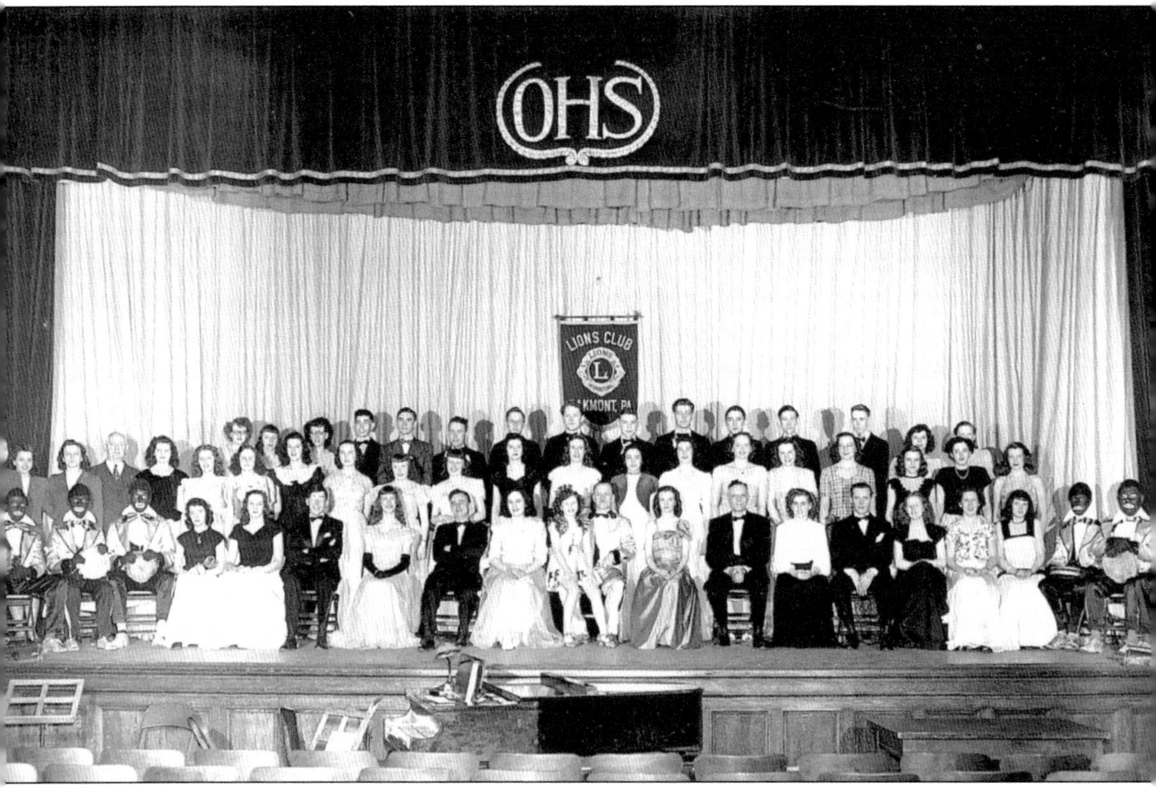

The annual Lions Club variety show is a longtime Oakmont tradition. The show, still put on annually, features local performing talent. This minstrel show, a popular entertainment at the time, was performed in the auditorium of Oakmont High School on Pennsylvania Avenue and Fifth Street when this photograph was taken in the 1940s. The shows continued in the building's beautiful auditorium after the high school was converted into an elementary facility in 1961 and renamed the Gilmore School. At one time, a Lions Show Queen was selected from among the girls in the high school's senior class and her crowning was one of the highlights of the show. Today, the Lions Club show is performed before sell-out crowds in the auditorium of the Tenth Street School.

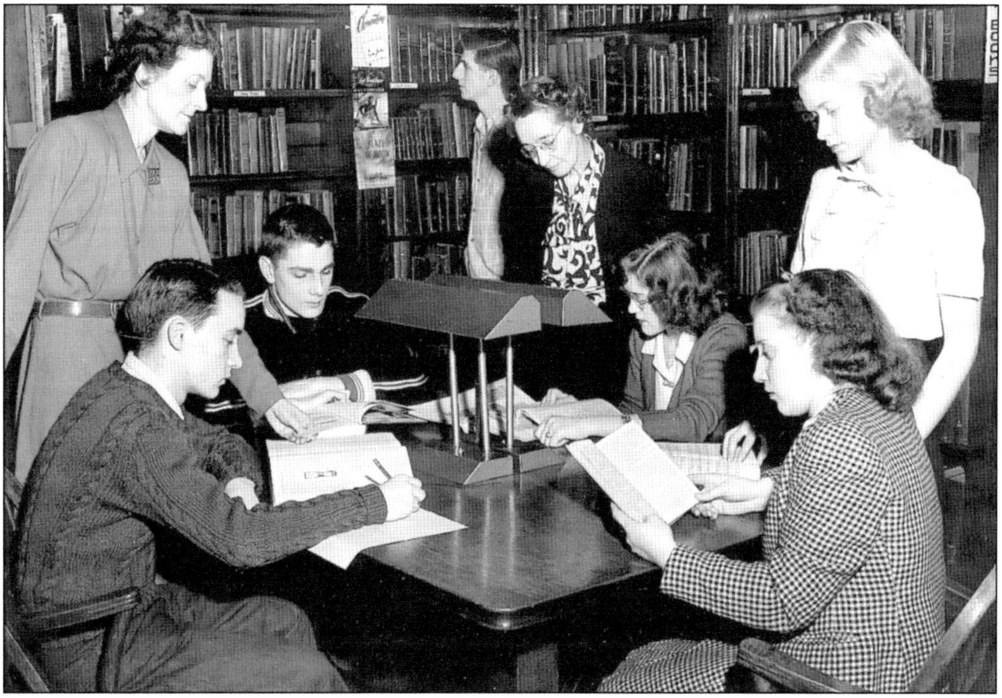

Until 1966, the Oakmont Carnegie Library, in addition to serving the public, was the main library for the borough's schools. Members of the 1947 high school class are shown researching term papers. They are, from left to right, Donald Meehan, Louis Grey, Raymond Bluestone (standing), Sarah Dunkle, and Nancy Braden. Shown standing are librarian Sara M. Boyle (left) and assistant librarians Asia Ecker (center) and Eleanor Molleston (right).

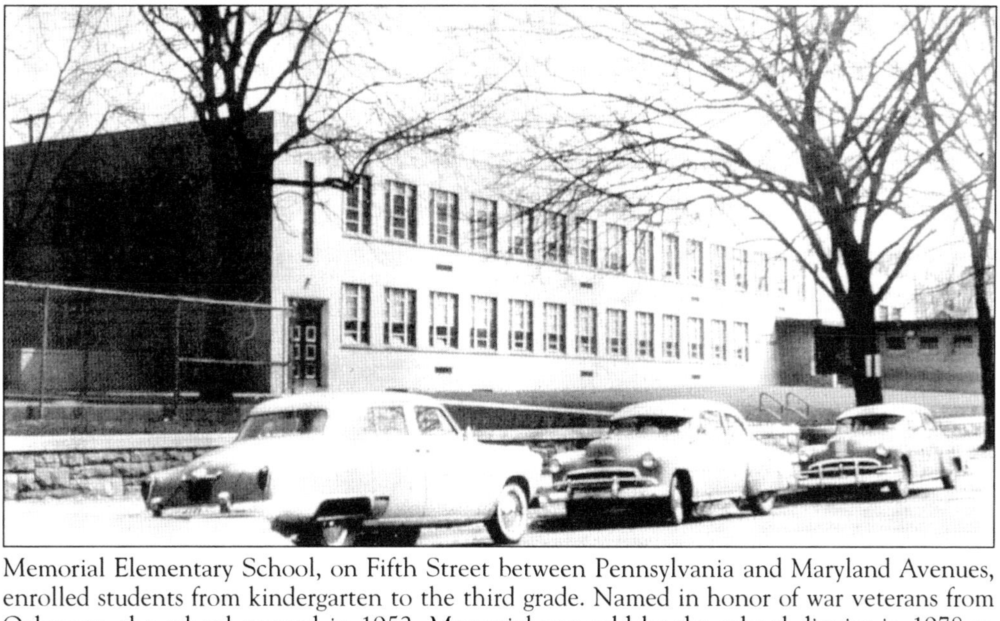

Memorial Elementary School, on Fifth Street between Pennsylvania and Maryland Avenues, enrolled students from kindergarten to the third grade. Named in honor of war veterans from Oakmont, the school opened in 1952. Memorial was sold by the school district in 1978 to the V-J Corporation, a local developer, and converted into a residential complex called Oakridge Condominiums.

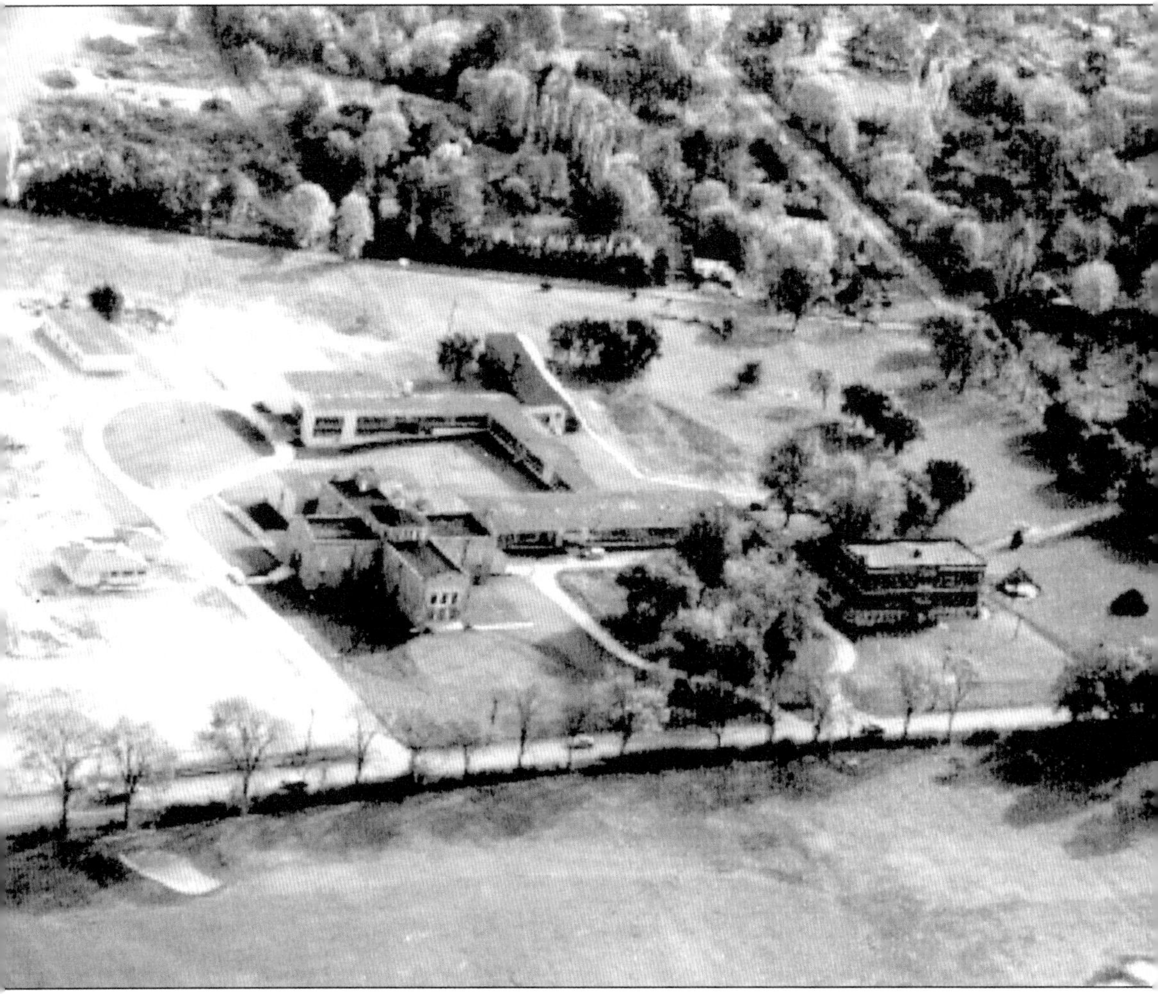

This aerial view of St. Anthony's School, on Hulton Road between Thirteenth and Fifteenth Streets, shows the original classroom building on the right and the large classroom building and chapel, which were built in 1959. Originally a home for dependent children, St. Anthony's was established by the Pittsburgh Catholic Diocese as a facility for children with disabilities. There were 45 students enrolled when the diocese opened the school, but that number increased significantly, necessitating the 1959 expansion. St. Anthony's initiated a vocational training program for older students and young adults in 1963. In the 1990s, the school's enrollment declined as students began to be mainstreamed into programs at parochial schools throughout the diocese. The complex then was closed and sold to developers. The property now is the location of a private home development called the Summit at Oakmont.

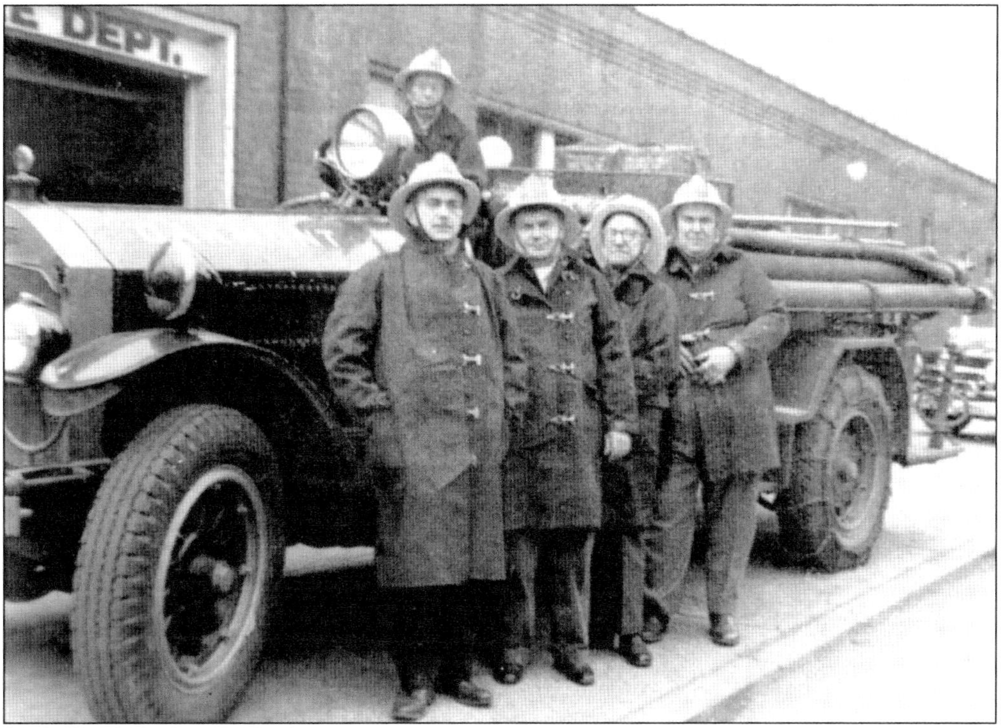

These firemen were longtime veterans when they posed with their truck outside the borough fire station, which then was located on Fifth Street near Virginia Avenue. Shown are Charles Helwig in the driver's seat and, standing left to right, Capt. Oliver Nicholas, Assistant Chief Paul Nicholas, George Weible, and William Bauer.

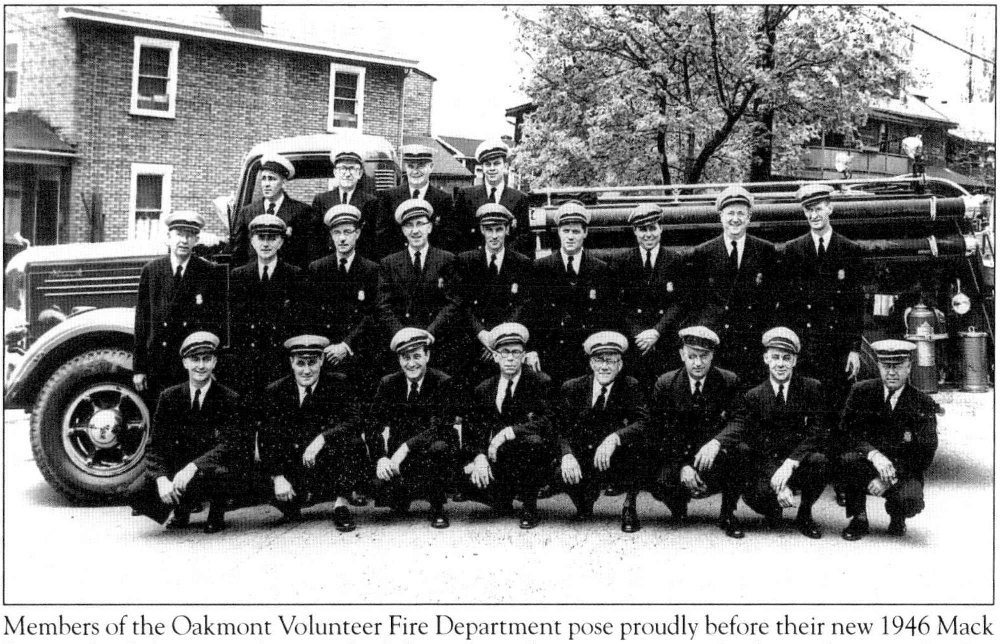

Members of the Oakmont Volunteer Fire Department pose proudly before their new 1946 Mack fire truck. Oakmont volunteer firefighters have been protecting the borough since the fire company was first organized in 1907.

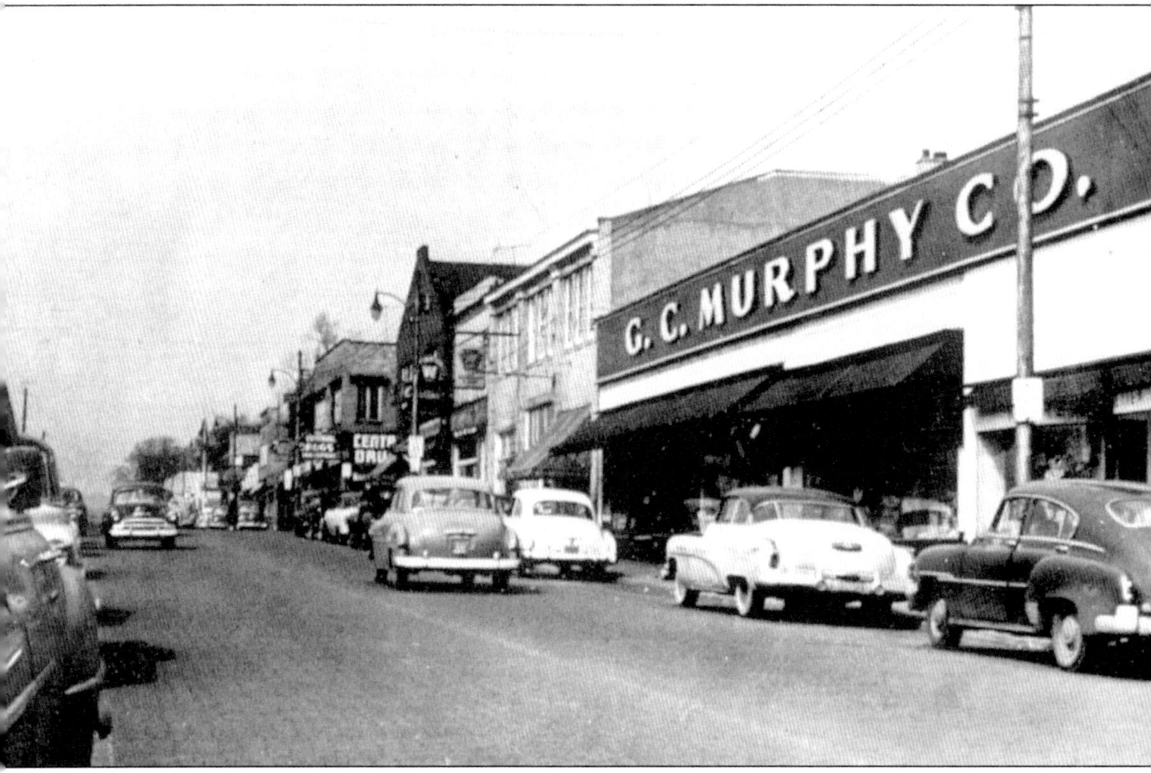

The G.C. Murphy Company variety store occupied the biggest storefront on Allegheny River Boulevard for many years. In fact, several of today's shops and stores are located in the area that Murphy's alone occupied from September 1945, when it replaced the Ben Franklin store at that location, until it closed in the 1980s. Located between Washington and Delaware Avenues, Murphy's was known as the five-and-ten because, like most variety stores of the time, much of the merchandise on its shelves sold for a nickel or a dime. The store sold everything from goldfish to work clothing. Many longtime residents remember the smell of popcorn and roasting cashew nuts that greeted them when they walked into the store. This photograph, taken in the 1940s, looks north on Allegheny River Boulevard.

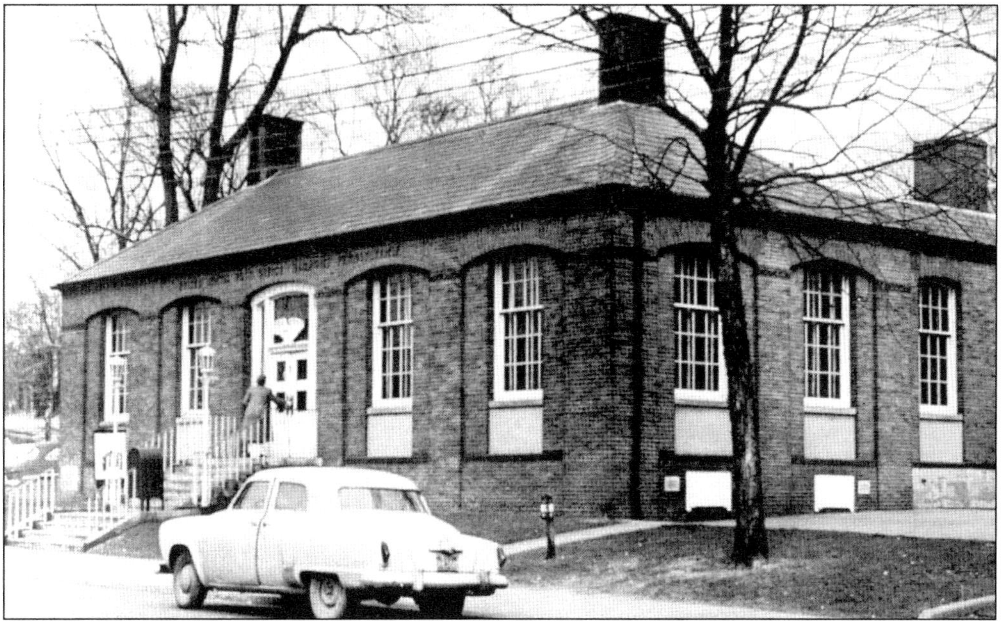

The Oakmont post office, which was built in 1941 and dedicated in August of that year, was the last post office built in the Pittsburgh area before the outbreak of World War II. It featured wall murals by artist Franc Etting. The site of the building on Allegheny River Boulevard at Maryland Avenue was bought in November 1939 for $14,000.

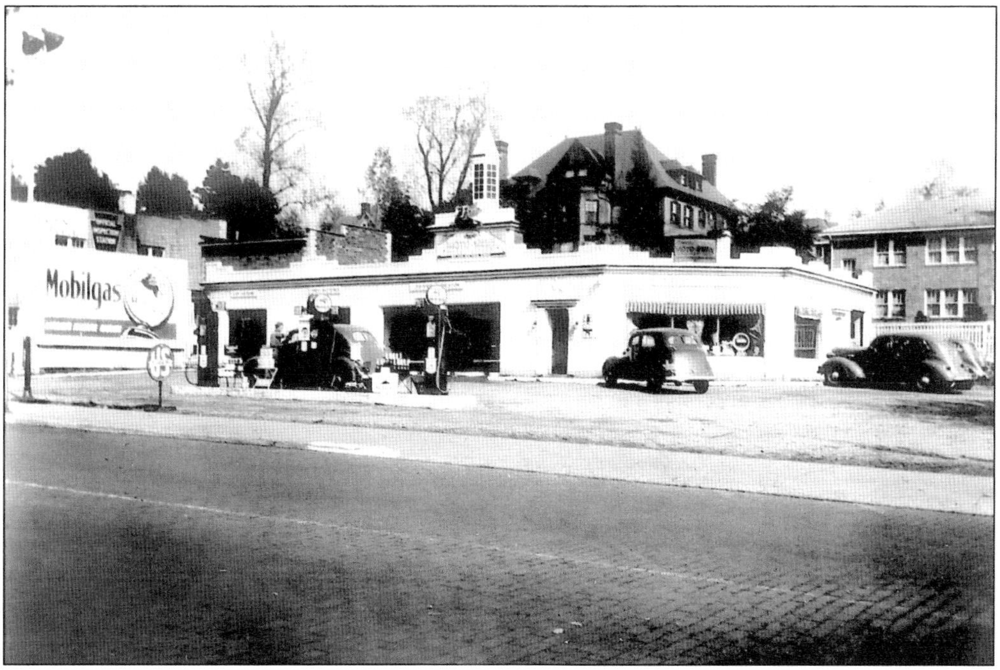

The Mobil service station at the intersection of Allegheny River Boulevard and Washington Avenue was one of several gasoline stations operating in town when this photograph was taken in the 1940s. Notice the attendant cleaning the windshield of the automobile getting gas at the pumps—standard practice before the days of self-service.

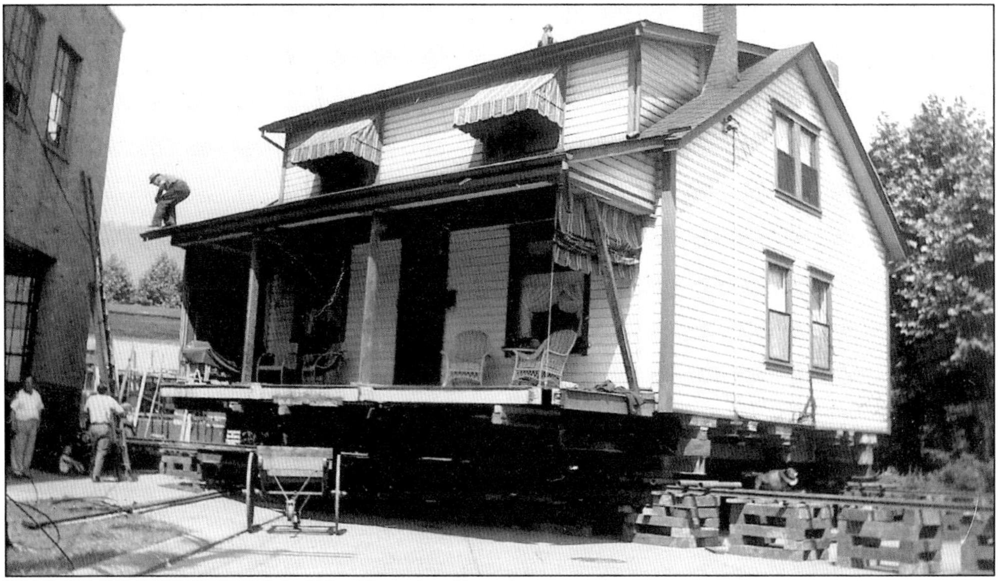

It took three days for workmen to move the Flowers family home from its location on Pennsylvania Avenue to nearby Second Street in 1942. So little of the interior of the house was disturbed during the move that the family continued to live there the whole time. Even chairs on the front porch remained in place during the house's journey across Pennsylvania Avenue to its new resting place.

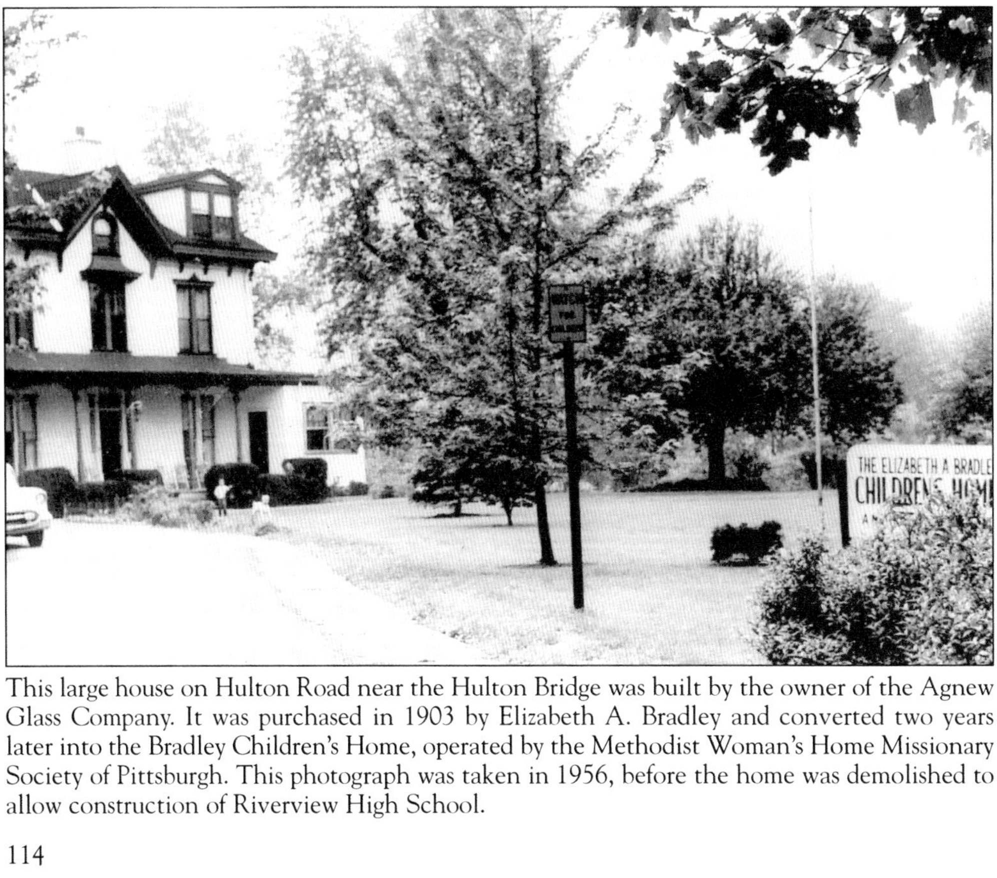

This large house on Hulton Road near the Hulton Bridge was built by the owner of the Agnew Glass Company. It was purchased in 1903 by Elizabeth A. Bradley and converted two years later into the Bradley Children's Home, operated by the Methodist Woman's Home Missionary Society of Pittsburgh. This photograph was taken in 1956, before the home was demolished to allow construction of Riverview High School.

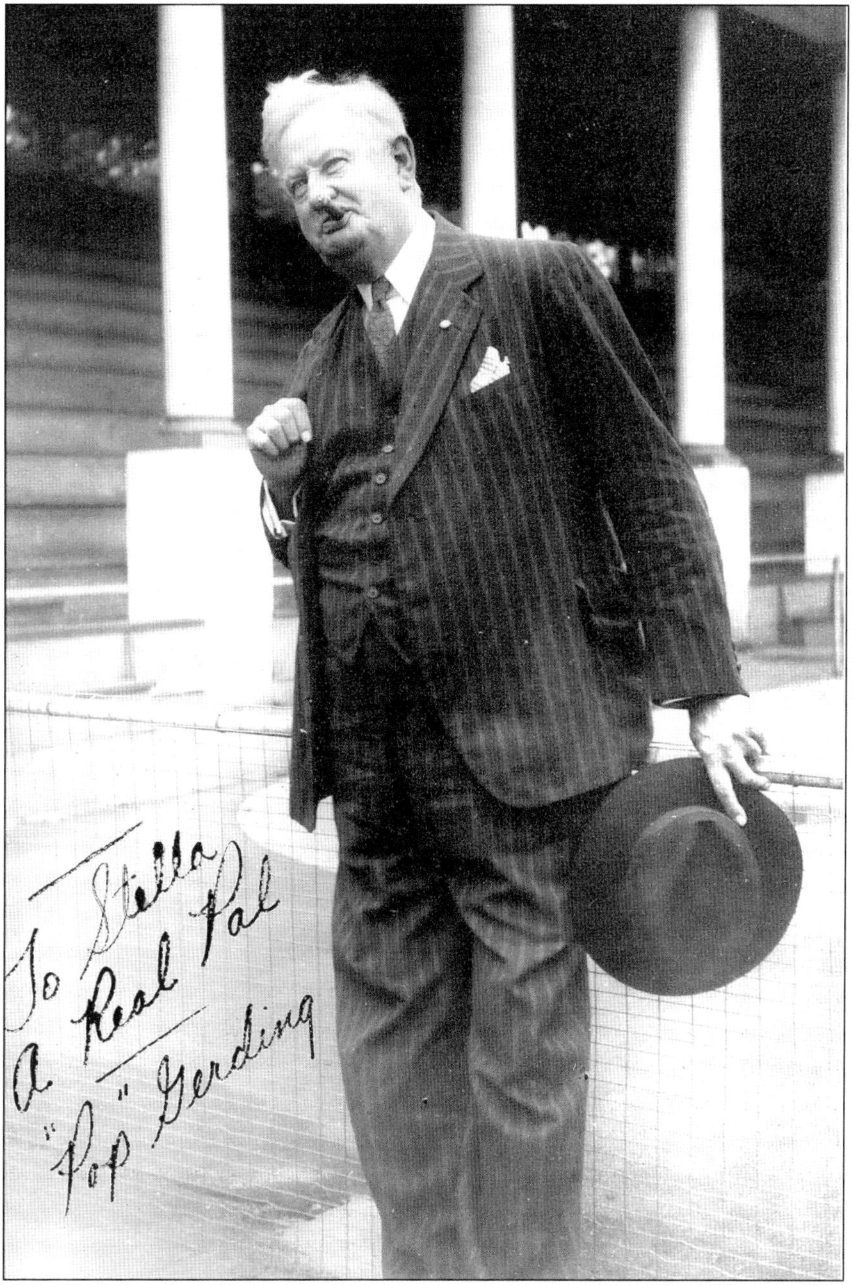

Charles C. Gerding II, known by almost everyone in town as "Pop," not only was the manager of the Willows pool in the 1940s, he also was, as a newspaper story reported at the time, the pool's "director of public relations and ambassador of good will." He was known for such publicity ploys as mailing passes to the Willows to movie stars, celebrities, sports figures, and political leaders around the world. He proudly displayed the acknowledgement letters he received from people prominent in the news of the day, including J. Edgar Hoover, Babe Ruth, Gen. Douglas MacArthur, and the duke and duchess of Windsor. In the winter, when the pool was closed, he wrote a weekly column for the *Advance Leader*. "Pop" Gerding was a tireless promoter for years despite his age. When this photograph was taken in 1947, he was 71 and blind.

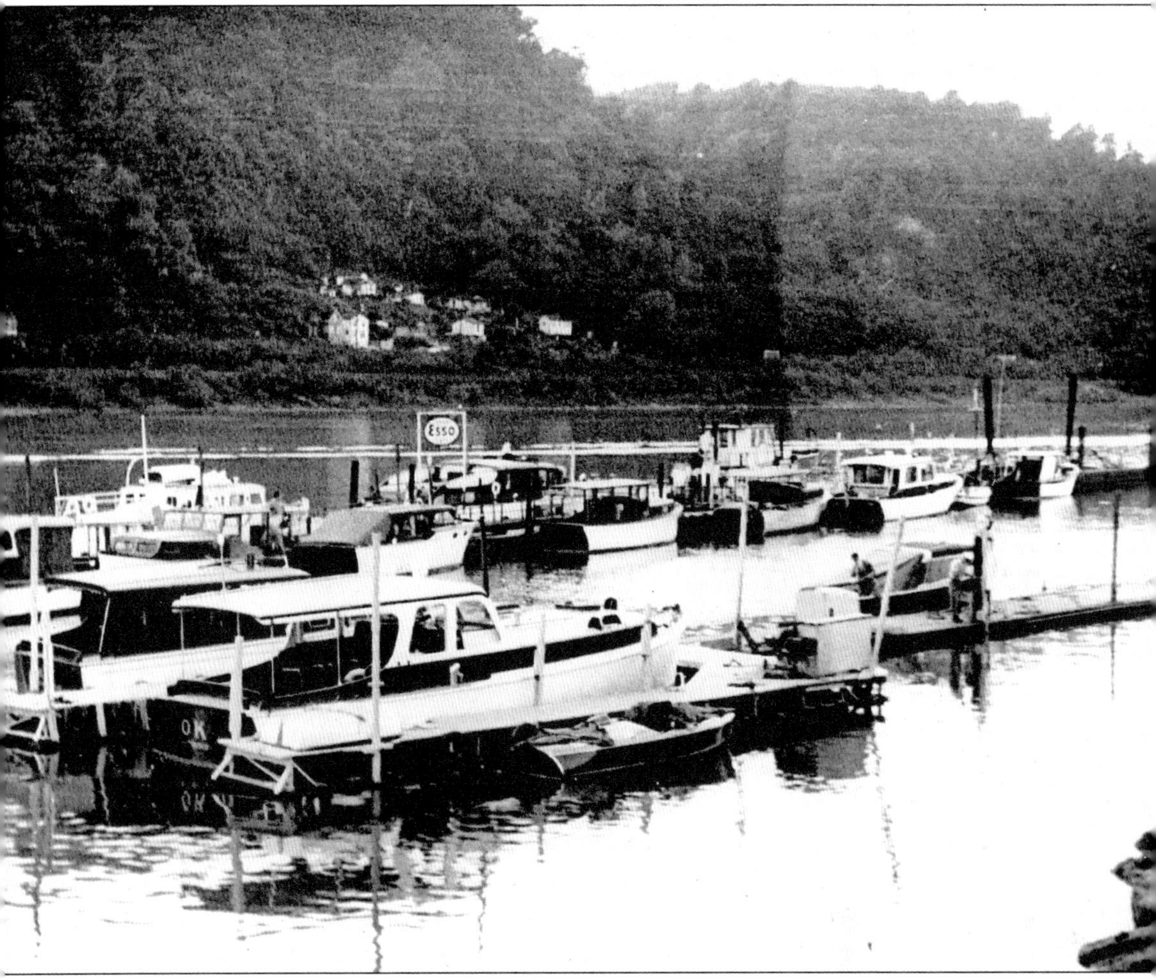

Cabin cruisers and powerful motorboats replaced canoes and rowboats in the fleet moored at the Oakmont Yacht Club in the 1950s. The club, with its clubhouse on the Allegheny River at the bottom of Washington Avenue, boasts of being the oldest inland yacht club in the United States.

Six

Maturity and Growth

Oakmont voters began the 1960s by approving, by a three-to-one margin, a $150,000 bond issue to finance the purchase of 13 acres of land along the Allegheny River and build Riverside Park. When completed, the park became a popular playground for the town's burgeoning population, which by 1960 had reached 7,504 men, women, and children. To ease the pressure being put on educational facilities in town by so many new school-aged children, school officials in 1961 expanded the Tenth Street School, which then was Oakmont's high school.

The borough's industrial base also was expanding. In 1962, Transamerica Freight Lines built a terminal in town. Two years later, the former Scaife Company buildings found new leases on life. Scaife's Ann Street headquarters was converted into the Oakmont Residence, a nursing home, now called Beverly Healthcare-Oakmont. The Andy Gard Company began manufacturing plastic hardware and toys in what had been the Scaife plant. The plant was destroyed in a spectacular fire in January 1967.

While new uses were found for the Scaife properties, another town landmark did not fare so well. The ending of passenger service by the Pennsylvania Railroad in 1964 meant the end of the Oakmont Railroad Station, which had been built in 1908. There were many in town who wanted to preserve the station and convert it to some public use. After years of debate and unsuccessful efforts by the Pittsburgh History and Landmarks Foundation to have it declared a historic landmark, the station was purchased by the borough in 1969 and demolished.

By the beginning of the 1970s, development in Oakmont had slowed, as did the town's rate of population growth. The borough's population recorded in the 1970 census was 7,550, only 46 more than the 1960 figure. What many Oakmonters considered the unthinkable happened in 1970, when declining attendance at the Willows pool prompted the owners to close the pool, which had been operating for 44 years. They sold the property to a Pittsburgh developer who built the Oakmont Landing apartment complex on the site.

Another event, considered equally as unthinkable as the Willows pool closing by many Oakmonters, occurred the following year when the Oakmont and Verona school districts merged to form the Riverview School District. In December 1976, five years after the merger was completed, high school students from both towns began attending classes together in the new Riverview High School, built where the Bradley Children's Home had operated for 70 years.

That marked the end of an era. It also marked the beginning of yet another chapter of the story of Oakmont.

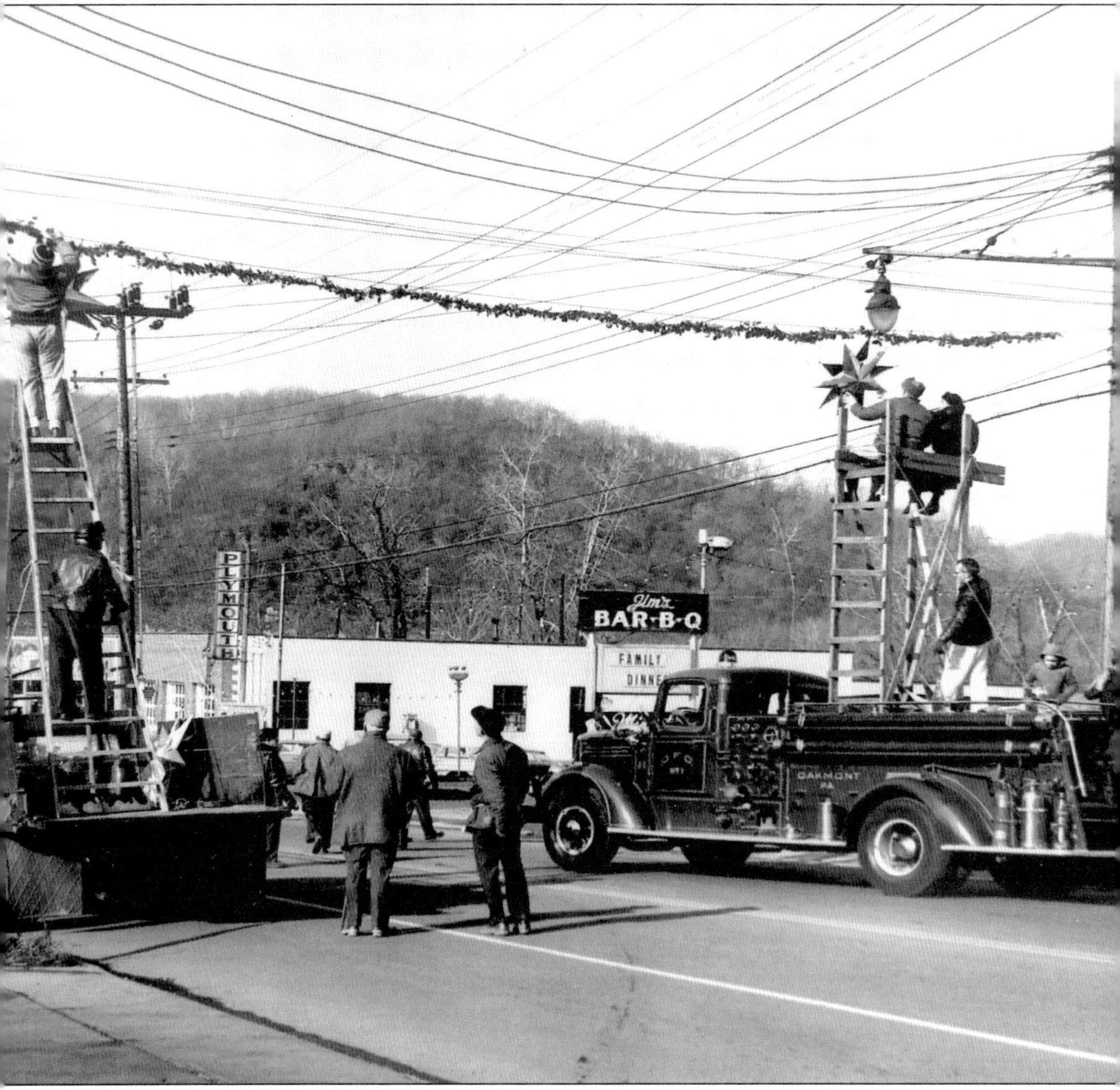

Oakmont gets ready for the Christmas holidays every November by hanging decorations on utility light poles along Allegheny River Boulevard. For many years, the decorating was done by members of the fire department. They rigged the fire trucks with ladders and platforms so they could string the decorations between poles on either side of the main street. The firemen, helped by members of the Oakmont Chamber of Commerce and volunteers, strung the decorations from Plum Street to Hulton Road. When this photograph was taken in the 1960s, firemen perched above their trucks were finishing up the job on Hulton Road. Traditionally, those doing the decorating began the day with a 7:00 a.m. breakfast at the Edgewater Restaurant and ended the afternoon with lunch at Hoffstot's provided by the chamber of commerce.

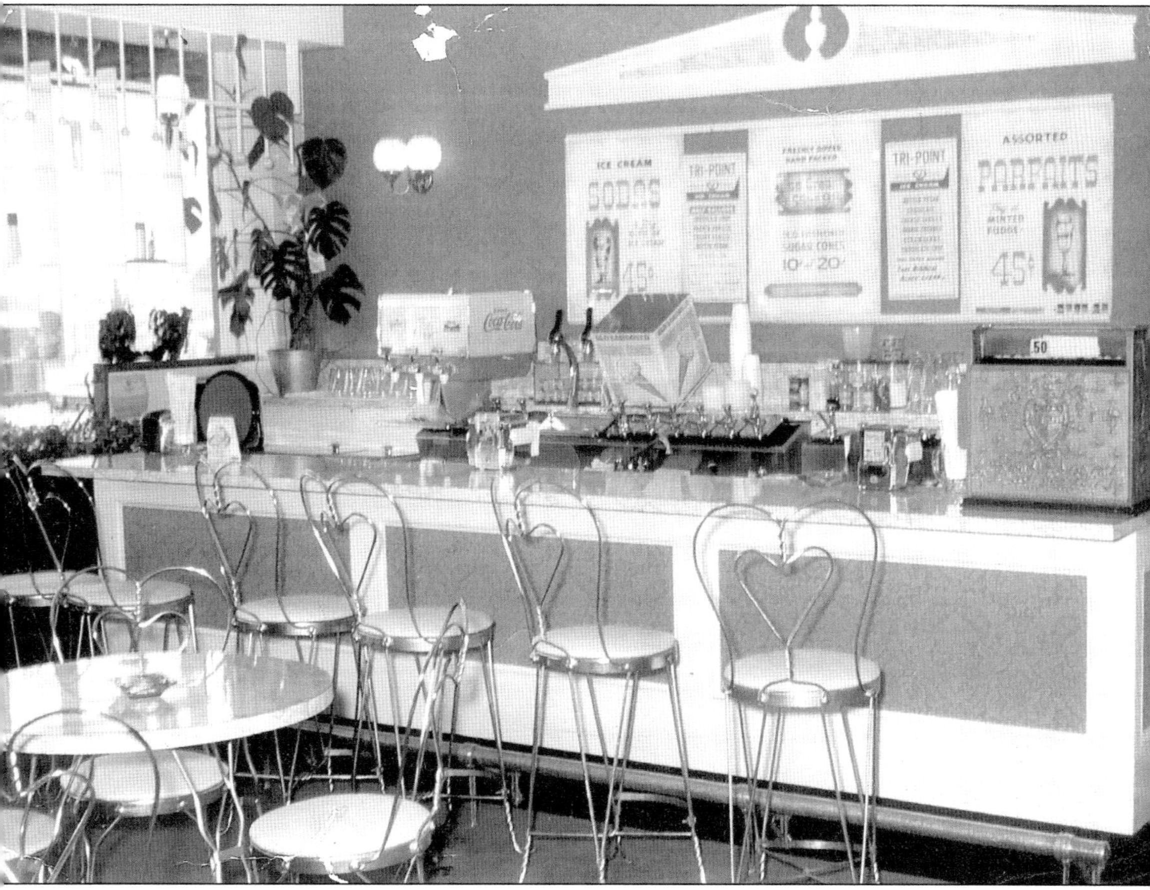

The Oakmont Pharmacy's soda fountain specialized in root beer floats and Cherry Cokes and was a popular gathering spot not only for the town's teenagers but for adults as well. Stopping for ice cream or a drink at Bud's, as it was known for owner Bud Vollbrecht, was often how Oakmonters ended a shopping trip or just a stroll along Allegheny River Boulevard in the 1960s.

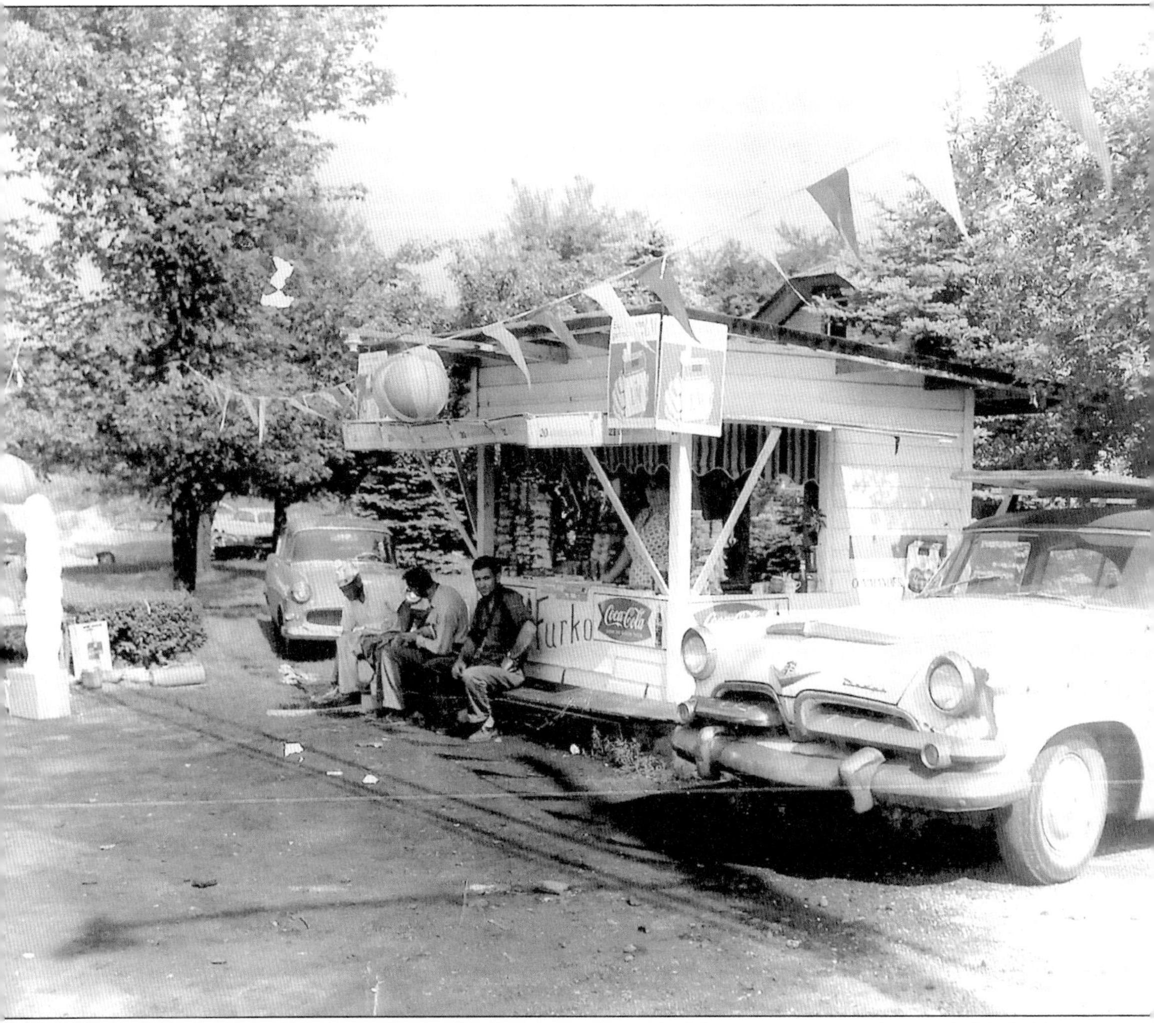

Furko's produce stand on Hulton Road was in an ideal location when the 1962 U.S. Open golf tournament was held just across the road at the Oakmont Country Club. Furko's had refreshments for sale to hot and thirsty spectators walking back to their cars, parked behind the stand, after watching Jack Nicklaus win that year's open.

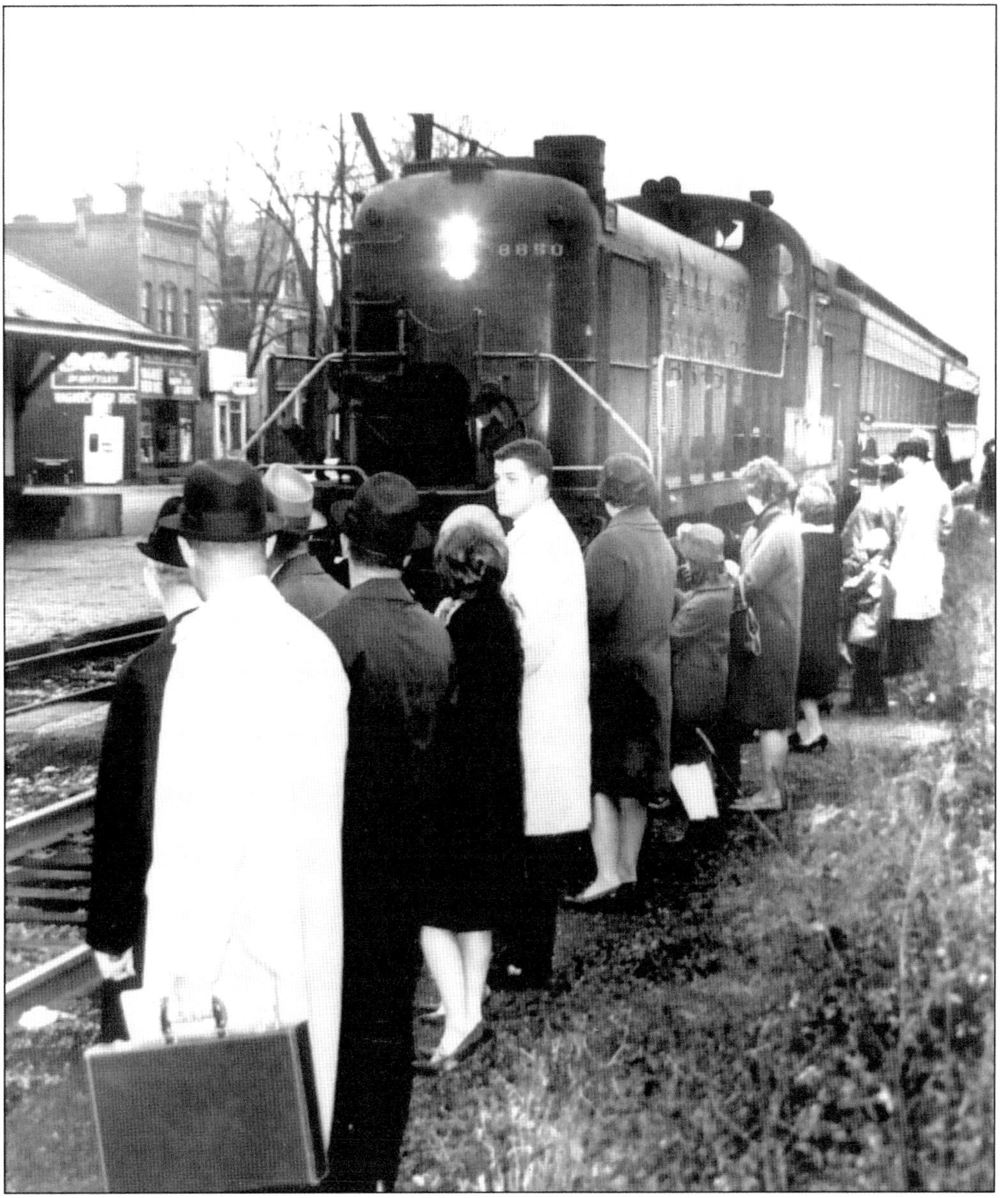

Oakmont passengers—hat-wearing businessmen and well-dressed women and children—waiting to board the Pittsburgh-bound commuter train had to stand in a grassy plot across from the station platform for some reason. This photograph shows one of the train's last runs in 1964, when the Pennsylvania Railroad ended local passenger service (although freight service was maintained). That ended an era dating back more than 100 years, to 1853, when passenger trains operated by the Allegheny Valley Railroad first traveled through what now is Oakmont. Passengers on that line then could travel by train all the way from Pittsburgh to Kittanning. In June 1970, six years after the passenger trains stopped running, the Oakmont train station, the roof of which can be seen on the left, was demolished.

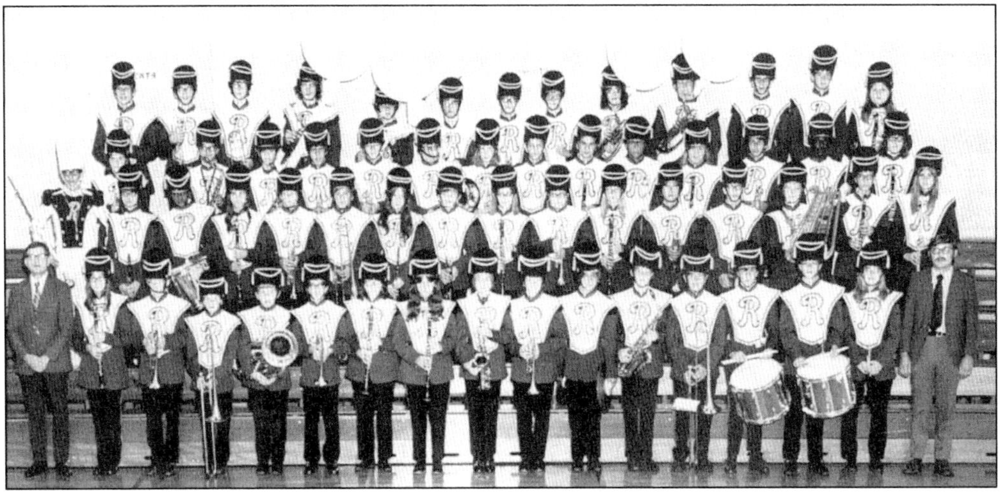

Resplendent in their brand-new uniforms, members of the equally brand-new Riverview High School marching band posed for this photograph in 1971, the year of the merger of the Oakmont and Verona school districts into the Riverview district. Joseph Debsky, on the left in the front row, and James Lozenski, on the right in the front row, shared directing duties.

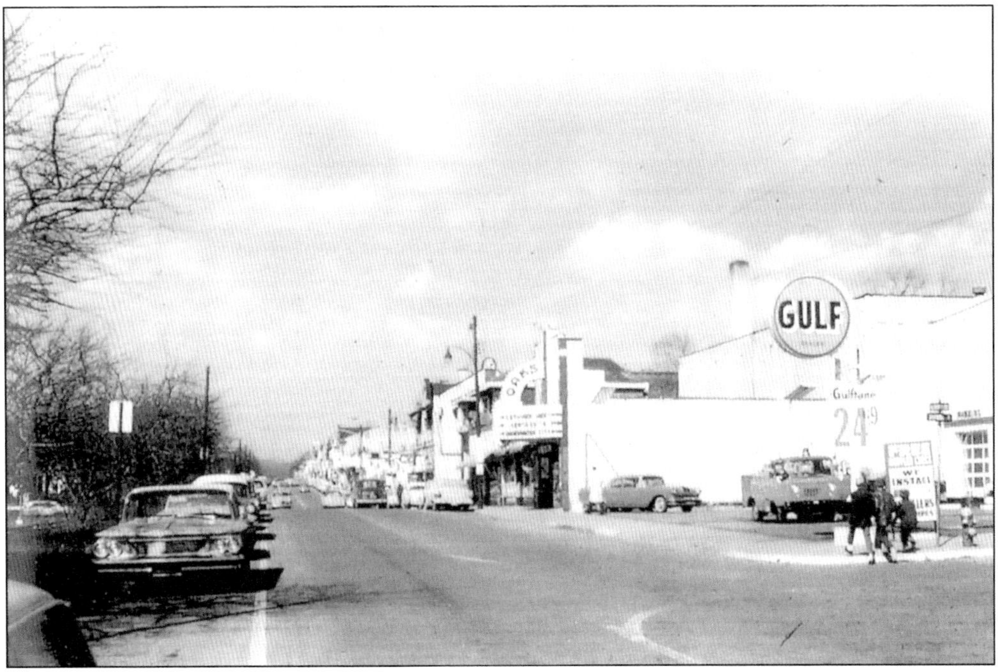

The Three Stooges Meet Hercules was the feature film at the Oaks Theater when this photograph was taken in 1962. The Gulf service station at the corner of Allegheny River Boulevard and California Avenue offered Gulftane gasoline for 24.9¢ a gallon, a price that attracted the fire department's red fire jeep in for a fill-up.

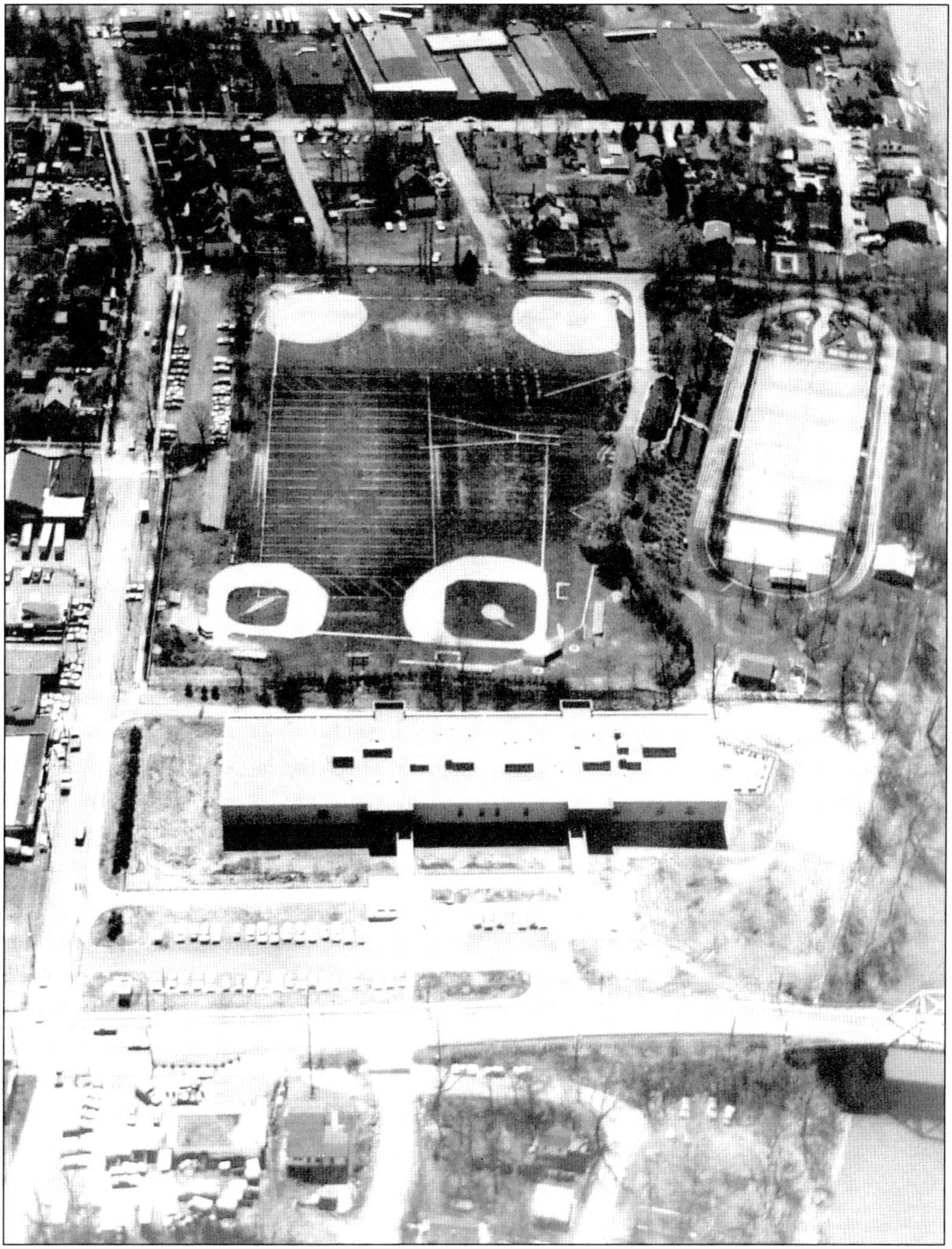

This aerial photograph of Riverview High School and Riverside Park was taken shortly after the school was completed in 1976. In the foreground is Hulton Road, which fronts the school. Third Street intersects with Hulton on the left. Riverside Park, completed in 1962, is shown with four baseball and softball diamonds as well as the football layout. The quarter-mile oval track, the children's playground, and the picnic shelters are shown to the right of the ball fields. The park serves as a public facility and home field for school district athletic teams. It is built on a 13-acre plot of land purchased by the borough from the Wilson Brothers Company, a successor firm to the Scaife Company, after voters approved a $150,000 bond issue in 1962.

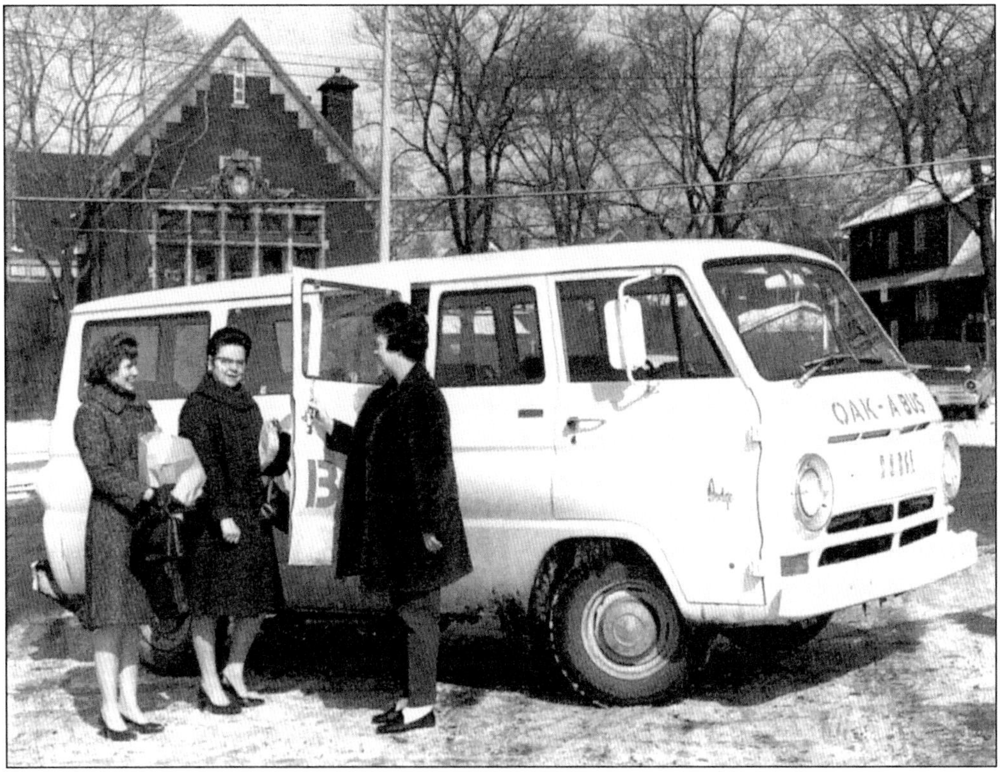

The Oak-A-Bus provided rides around town for Oakmont residents beginning in April 1967. The bus traveled a regular route through town, but residents also could arrange to be picked up or dropped off at their homes. The bus, a gift of the Oakmont Junior Woman's Club, was operated by the Action Committee, now the Riverview Community Action Corporation. Here, driver Marilyn Yonick (right) welcomes passengers Dorothy Giles (far left) and June Recklein.

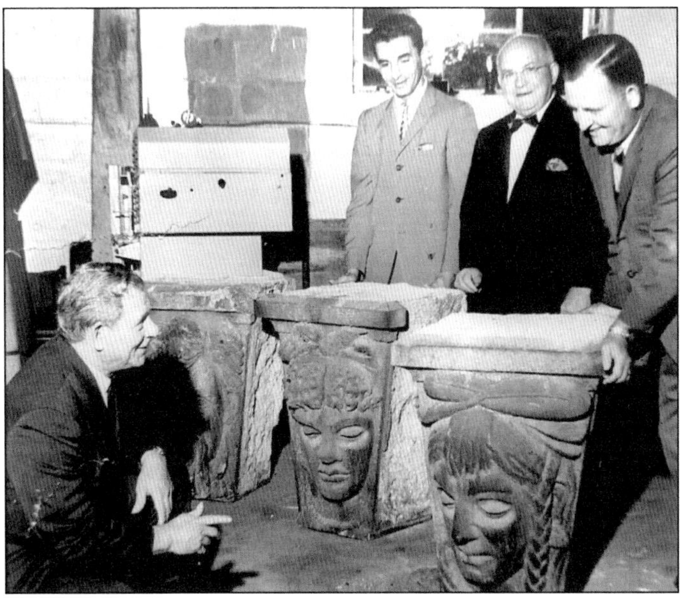

Granite figures carved by sculptor Frank Rinaldi, retrieved from the Old Post Office Building in Pittsburgh when it was demolished, were returned in 1966 to Oakmont, where Rinaldi had lived and worked. Resident Betty Raphael and the Oakmont Italian American Civic Club paid for the retrieval. Admiring the sculptures are, from left to right, Frank Cosnotti, Ed Calfe, Frank Catanzaro, and Mayor Ed Cooke.

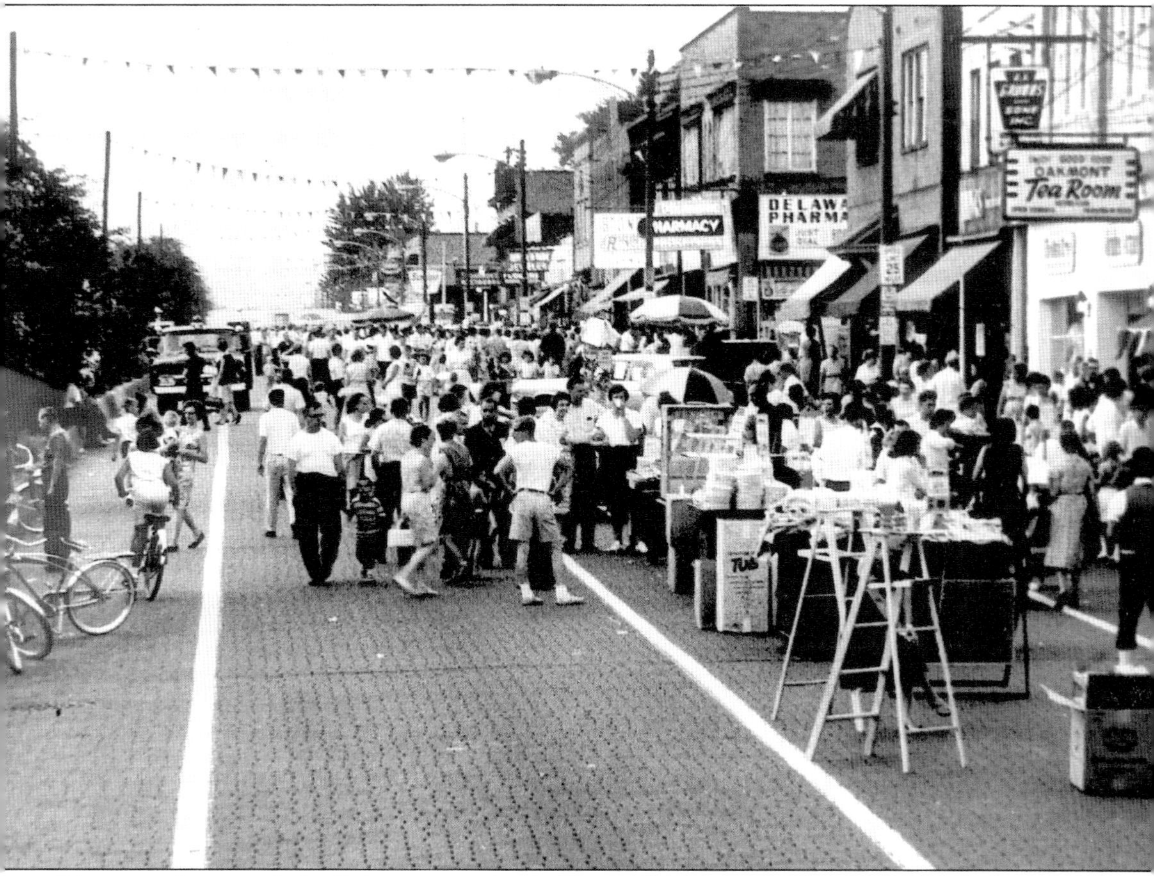

The annual street sale by Oakmont merchants along Allegheny River Boulevard is a longtime tradition in town. Held each summer, the sale attracts many hundreds and is as much a casual social gathering of friends and neighbors as it is an opportunity to shop for bargains at the tables set up by merchants outside their stores. Church groups, civic and fraternal organizations, and other groups also set up tables to sell refreshments to those attending the sale. There have been several changes since this street scene was photographed in the 1970s. The Oakmont Tea Room, the Delaware and Stone's pharmacies, the jewelry store, and the Sinclair service station at the boulevard and Maryland Avenue, among several others, have since been replaced by other businesses.

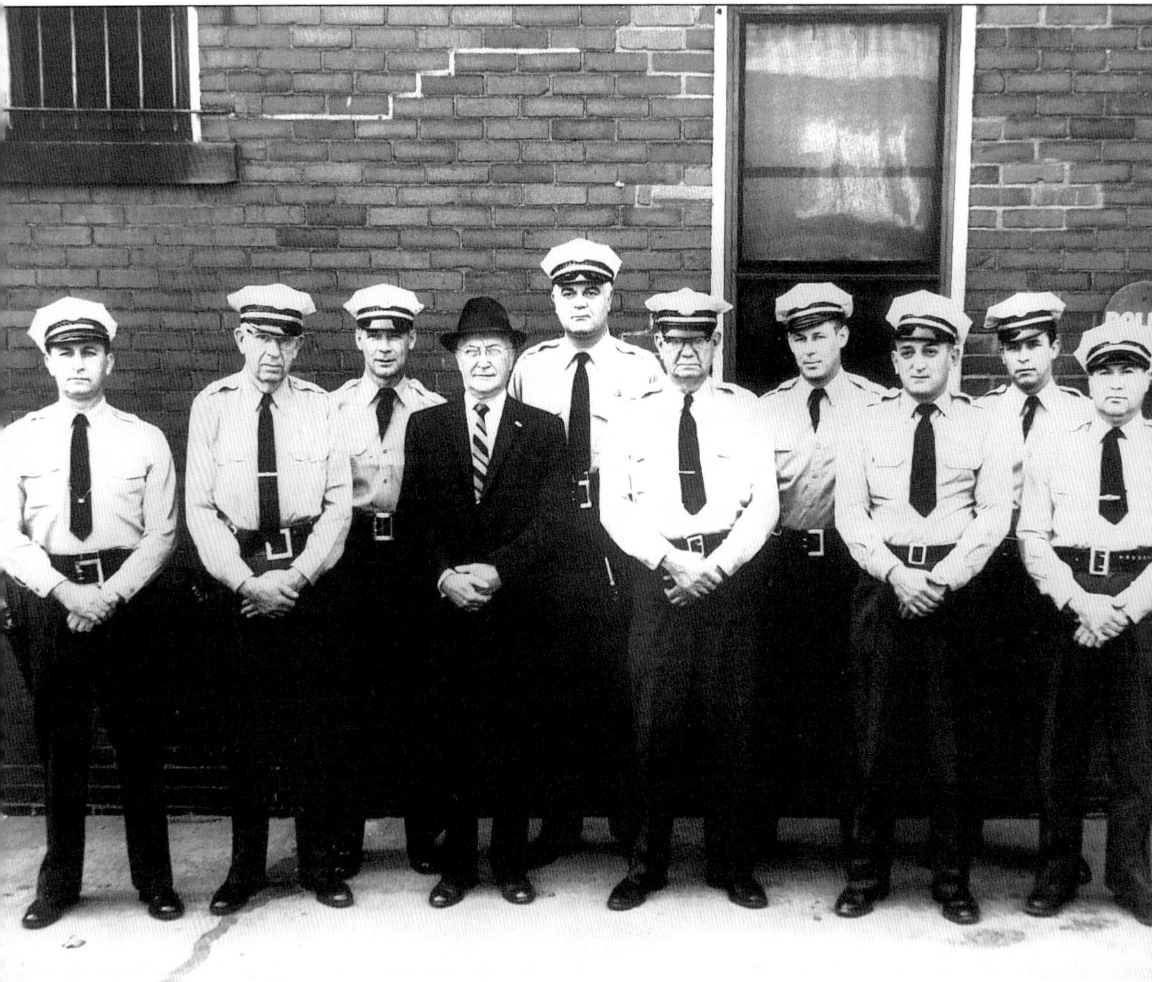

Oakmont's police force was nine members strong in 1960. Posing here in front of the old police station on Fifth Street with Mayor Raymond B. Saylor are, from left to right, Roy Mast, Chief Charles Helwig, Bob Campbell, "Slim" Macaluso, Ed Helwig, H. Seanor, John Miceli, Floyd Pyle, and Robert Beatty.

Jim's Bar-B-Q and Jim's Miniature Golf, next to the restaurant, were Oakmont landmarks in the 1960s. Jim's operations were located in the 300 block of Hulton Road, not far from the Hulton Bridge.

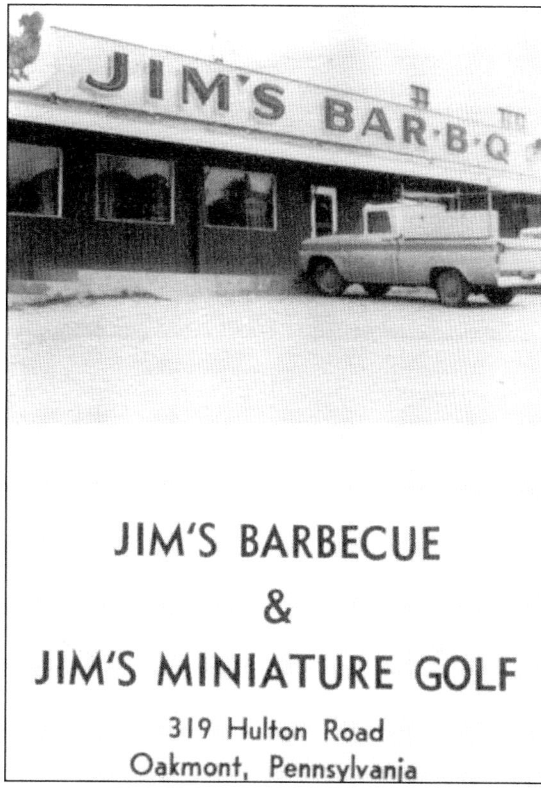

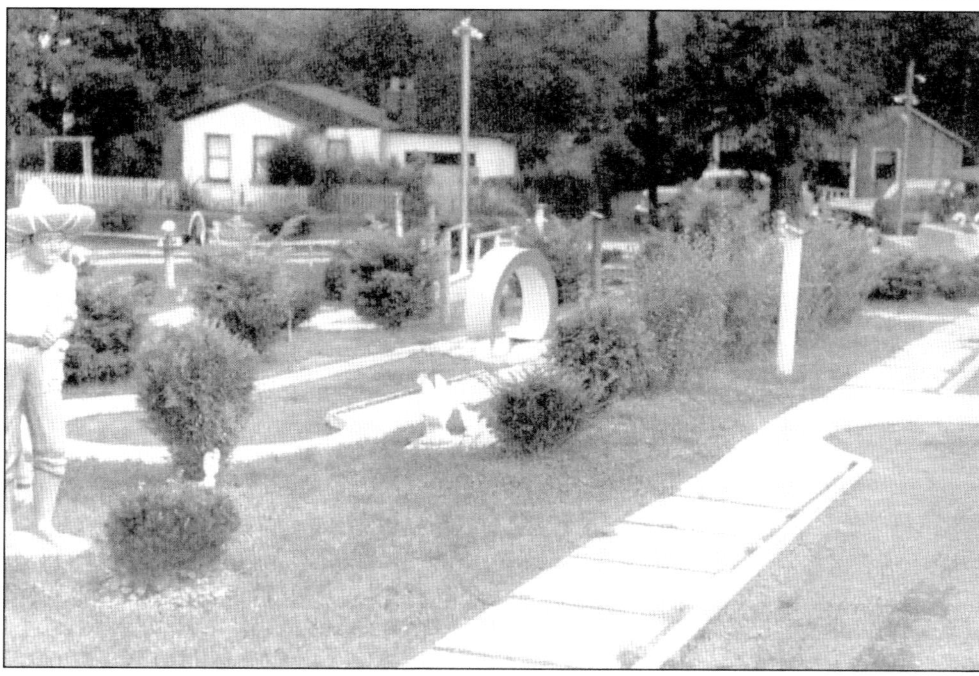

This photograph of the miniature-golf course is rather rare. The course is empty. Usually during the warm weather months, it was filled with players—youngsters and adults—who enjoyed the course's not-too-challenging layout.

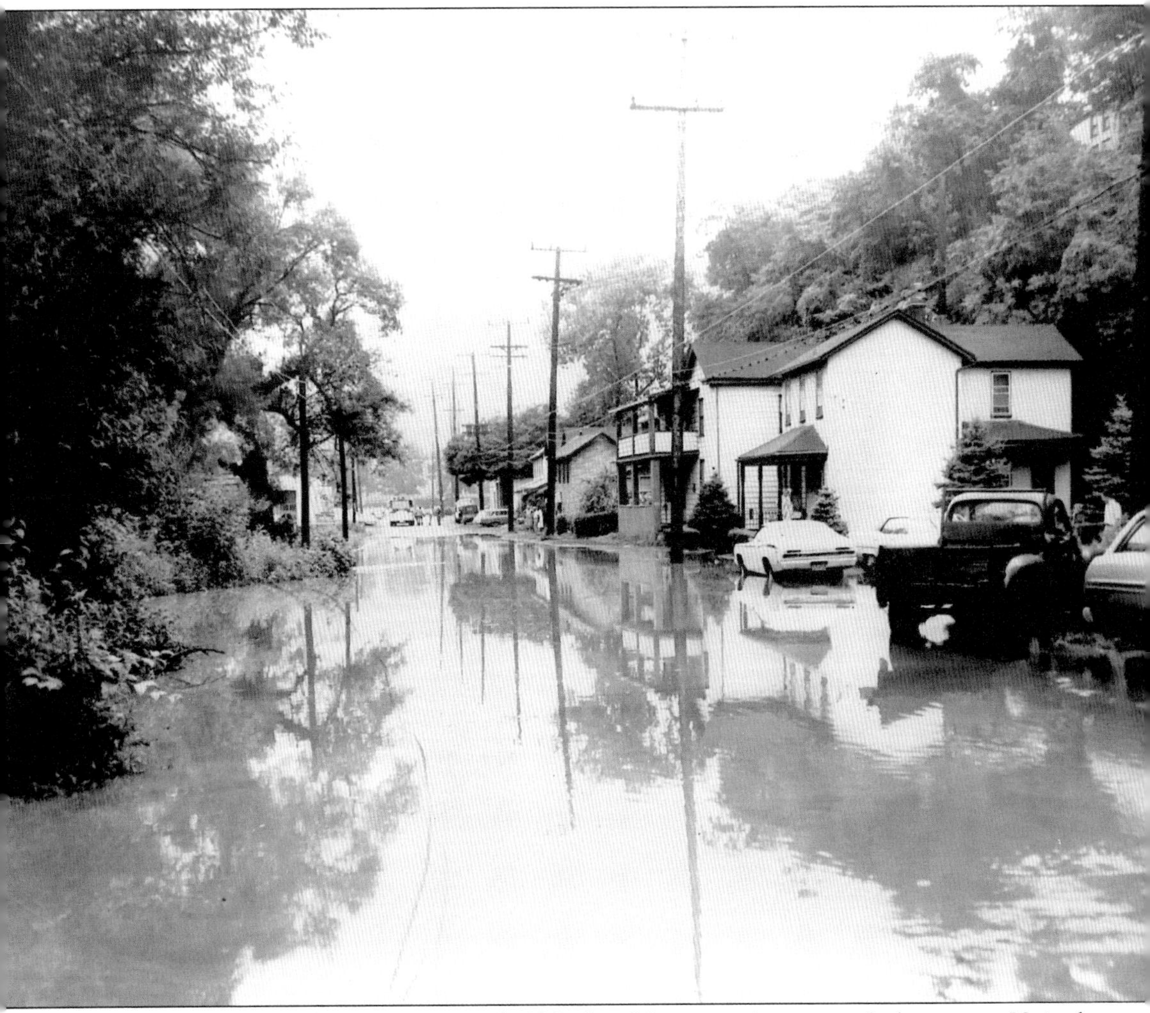

It brought back the bitter memories of 1936 when Hurricane Agnes struck the eastern United States with torrential rains in June 1972. Locally, there was flooding along both the Allegheny River and Plum Creek, although not nearly to the extent as the disastrous St. Patrick's Day flood. Shown here is Plum Street after Plum Creek overflowed its banks, stranding residents for a time and causing considerable damage to homes.